TRAVESTY OF JUSTICE

The Politics of Crack Cocaine and the Dilemma
of the Congressional Black Caucus

ARTEMESIA STANBERRY

DAVID R. MONTAGUE

SECOND EDITION

Kendall Hun
publishing compan

Contents

Acknowledgments

Writing a book is a very long and arduous process. We are very fortunate to have a network of support. With respect to this second edition, we wish to thank our families, friends, and all those who have supported and helped guide this project. We also appreciate the continued partnership with our publisher, the Kendall Hunt Publishing Company.

Finally, while we acknowledge those who helped with the research, we take full responsibility for any mistakes that may be found in this manuscript.

About the Authors

Dr. Artemesia Stanberry received her doctorate in political science from Howard University. She has several years of congressional experience. While obtaining her master's degree from The George Washington University, she began her congressional experience, which spanned from 1996 to 2004. She has had the opportunity of working for five members of congress, two of whom were members of the Congressional Black Caucus (CBC). This experience gave her access to key members of the CBC that will be utilized in this research. In addition, she served two terms as president of the Congressional Black Associates, a congressional staff organization dedicated to community service, education, and networking for congressional staff and organizations on and off Capitol Hill. She also served two terms as Second Vice President of the Congressional Legislative Staff Association, the largest Capitol Hill staff organization devoted to planning intellectual, social, and networking opportunities for congressional staff. She is currently an associate professor at North Carolina Central University where she teaches American Government, Black Politics, and special topics courses on race and the criminal justice system. Prior to teaching at North Carolina Central University, she spent three years teaching at Prairie View A &M University. She resides in Durham, North Carolina with her dog Buddy.

David R. Montague is an associate professor of criminal justice at the University of Arkansas at Little Rock and director of the UALR Senior Justice Center, which mentors college students while addressing elder crime. Dr. Montague earned a BA in Political Science at Morehouse College, an MA in Crime in Commerce at The George Washington University, and a Ph.D. in Political Science at Howard University. Since joining UALR in 2004, he has served as the graduate coordinator for the UALR Master of Science Program in criminal justice and is the recipient of both the 2009 UALR College of Professional Studies Faculty Excellence Award in Teaching and the 2014 Faculty Excellence Award in Service. Dr. Montague completed federal investigations for 14 years in law enforcement and intelligence capacities working for the United States Drug Enforcement Administration (DEA) as a federal drug diversion investigator, the United States JFK Assassination Records Review Board (ARRB) as the Senior Investigator, and as a consultant on national security matters with US Investigations Services, Inc. In 1990, Dr. Montague periodically taught administrative asset forfeiture at the FBI Academy in Quantico, VA, and in 2007, he completed the Federal Bureau of Investigation Citizens' Academy for business and community leaders. Also in 2007, he completed the Faculty/Staff internship program in Austria and Slovenia sponsored by UALR and Karl- Franzen Universitat Graz, including a lecture on pre-scription drug crime to the law faculty of Uni-Graz. Dr. Montague serves as Chair of the Pulaski County Juvenile Crime Prevention Coalition is Chair of the Arkansas Depart-ment of Correction's Inmate Leadership Council Community Reentry Program Board of Directors at the Pine Bluff Prison Facility, the Board of Directors for the Repara-tory Theater of Arkansas, President of the UALR Chapter of the Honor Society of Phi Kappa Phi, and is a founding member of the UALR Chancellor's Committee on Race. He teaches the only Inside-Out prison course in Arkansas, which is endorsed by the International Inside-Out Center of Temple University and brings UALR students and inmates together weekly within prison. In addition to his extensive work within the prisons, Dr. Montague also volunteers as a reserve deputy sheriff in Pulaski County, Arkansas, in which he completes enforcement activities to support the community. He has published numerous articles and reports and is the coauthor of the book Travesty of Justice: The politics of crack cocaine and the dilemma of the Congressional Black Caucus. Dr. Montague is currently working on a new book dealing with his role as part of the Congressional reinvestigation of JFK assassination records during the 1990s. Since completion of a project to research health care fraud against senior citizens via the U.S. Administration on Aging and partnership with the Arkansas SMP and the Tri-County Rural Health Network, his most recent project was to complete research on disproportionate minority contact via the Arkansas Division of Youth Services to shed light on three counties within Arkansas. In 2013, Dr. Montague presented research on prisoner reentry at the 33rd International Congress on Law and Mental Health held at Amsterdam and has been invited to organize a panel on reentry for the same conference in 2015 at Sigmund Freud University in Vienna, Austria. In October of 2010, he ended his term as president of the Southwest Association of Criminal Justice, the associa-tion of criminal justice educators for this region of the U. S. falling under the umbrella of the Academy of Criminal Justice Sciences and currently serves as Regional Trustee for the Southwest Region on the ACJS Board of Directors. He recently graduated as a member of Class 15 of the University of Arkansas Division of Agriculture Cooperative Extension Service LeadAR Program, which was a 2-year training for emerging Arkan-sas leaders. This leadership program required completion of seminars as a delegation across Arkansas, the State of Nebraska, Washington, DC, and several cities in China. Dr. Montague resides with his family in Little Rock, Arkansas.

Preface

Unbelievably, the need for a second edition of Travesty of Justice has arrived rather quickly; primarily due to the reality of numerous events connected with the topic of mandatory minimum laws dealing with crack cocaine and powder cocaine. This topic has garnered enormous segments of media attention in print stories, lengthy opinion editorials, television debates, and even debate among government officials in all three branches of our federal government. We as a society have seen in just the past 3–4 years, actions by the courts, legislation from elected officials, and promulgation of regulations by appointed officials. These actions have also stirred a firestorm outrage by some current and former drug officials who are against ameliorative changes in these policies and, more shockingly, congressional officials who have turned a new leaf in order to correct this travesty which has lasted decades.

Therefore, this second edition of the book was a decision partly based on the changes we mention earlier but also based on the obvious continued interest by the public on this topic as demonstrated by various events involving the first edition of the book. One such event was a discussion (as the authors) on a half-hour live program called The Talk Back Radio Show with Professor Val Atkinson. This event was held in Raleigh, North Carolina, and reached the municipal area there. The authors also completed an interview for KUAR Radio (Little Rock, Arkansas) "UALR Difference of Degree" radio spot. This is an NPR affiliate and was broadcast statewide for about 2 months as a 30-s spot on work by faculty impacting societal issues. A rare hour-long-lived interview about the first edition was held with the authors for a nationally broadcasted program called On With Dr. Wilmer Leon Radio Show (Sirius XM Radio Channel 128) in Washington, DC. In addition, a scholarly event to allow community leaders and faculty to discuss the first edition and implications on race and crime generally was held on the campus of North Carolina Central University, in Durham, North Carolina. Entitled Race, Justice, and the Law in the 21st Century this panel discussion was sponsored jointly by the University of Arkansas at Little Rock's Institute on Race and Ethnicity and the North Carolina Central University Department of Political Science.

The authors were able to bring the reality of debate on drug policy and the dimension of race and ethnicity to students during a "Lunch and Learn" session at the North Carolina Central University. The first edition of the book was discussed and the students were able to apply their understanding of how the sentencing realities of when the disparity was created, compare to today (Circa 2012). The beauty of this event was that the professors for these students saw real application of concepts from their classes by their students and toward the end of the event, offered praise for their students being willing to think "outside the box." The authors appreciate the access to students during their classes as part of the *Dr. Jeffrey M. Elliot Memorial Lecture Series* in the North Carolina Central University Department of Political Science.

The first edition of the book was also featured during the "Travesty of Justice Book Signing for The Links, Inc., Little Rock, AR Chapter" in 2012, which was held at a prominent book store in Little Rock, Arkansas. This event brought in members of the community and allowed a seminar style discussion. The importance of this format was that the audience were able to interact in discussing the historical aspects of what was happening in our society during the evolution of the disparity. A great deal of discussion surrounded the death of basketball player Len Bias. The authors signed copies of the book after the discussion until they sold out; extra orders had to be made as well as signature plates completed for when those copies would arrive. Our thanks for the dedication to community service by the *Little Rock Chapter of The Links, Inc.*, and the use of *Pyramid Art and Custom Framing* for the event.

One of the participants in the book signing at Pyramid Art and Custom Framing was an employee of the Little Rock, Arkansas School District; specifically she was an organizer for some of the summer programming the District participated in. Based on what she gleaned from the book signing, she determined that it would be advantageous for children involved with some of the summer programming to have access to it. Therefore, the first edition was used for a summer workshop project in 2012 by a school in the District. This entailed the school district purchasing several copies and incorporating the material into the curriculum for the summer workshop in a manner that was age appropriate. We applaud the leadership of those running that program in recognizing the importance of bringing knowledge of historical realities impacting our community.

Another observation the authors made from the first edition was that the authors were contacted by numerous students and community stakeholders with respect to questions on "how" to write and publish on a topic that for so many years many in the public were unwilling to discuss. The fact that several librarians and community leaders referred students to us in order to ask these questions was at the minimum, humbling, yet gratifying in the knowledge that some people felt empowered to share knowledge on other important topics. Our gratitude goes out to the people who referred students to us, for we know these folks have enormous options of authors they could recommend to people.

Another surprise to the authors was the number of inmates who purchased copies of the first edition and asked for them to be autographed. In understanding the gravity of this statement, it is important to recognize that most incarcerated people have rather limited financial resources and usually must care-enough about something to ask someone to obtain it from the outside for them. One of the authors, who teaches a class in prison and also volunteers running three rehabilitative programs in different prisons, literally saw copies of the first edition in the inmate cells/barracks. Imagine if you will, carrying students on a prison tour and seeing one of them sitting on their bed reading your book, knowing it was not easy for that person to obtain it; again, a humbling feeling. More so, several inmates who read the first edition approached one of the authors during rehabilitative programming to discuss sections of the book; many of them purchased it based on being incarcerated on drug charges.

The publisher of the first edition, Kendall Hunt, was able to move a lot of copies via amazon.com, and the timing of the release of our first edition was perfect in that The New Jim Crow: Mass Incarceration in the Age of Colorblindness (The New Press; January 16, 2012) was released around the same time. This book, written by activist and law professor Michelle Alexander, became a huge hit globally, and our luck was that if people purchased her book, they also saw our first edition of Travesty of Justice suggested as well, among other books dealing with incarceration. Certainly, this dimension of visibility we had not planned and appreciate not only the amazing work of Professor Alexander, but we appreciate the technology which allowed the public to see how her book, among other books, and our first edition, are connected; something beneficial for those seeking to truly understand the complexities of the topic. Based on this reality, the book sold out on amazon.com, which the authors found amazing. Granted, the publisher did not supply huge runs of the first edition, so that the selling power of it could be recognized. However, the fact that no matter the size of the first edition run, it was on a topic many ignored for decades and demonstrates the serious level of interest at present.

In 2013, the reunion committee for Merrill High School in Arkansas invited one of the authors to attend their class meeting to be held in Dallas, Texas; they alternate locations by holding one reunion in Arkansas 1 year and the reunion is in another state the next year. This was the reunion meeting for the classes 1951–1954 and the significance is that all of these alumni graduated High School during Segregation. Therefore, the invitation was to serve as keynote speaker at the reunion, explain the first edition, and connect the racial elements of the book to the reality of race relations generally; something these alumni easily related to. The event was a success and several legal professionals made suggestions during and after, which have been incorporated into the second edition.

Finally, in discussions with the publisher and based on the numerous changes in the laws dealing with mandatory minimums, the authors felt compelled to grab onto the timeliness of the series of waves changing the landscape of (and culture of) how society views mandatory minimum laws. More importantly, how society and policymakers view their role to be honest about mistakes of the past as ameliorative change sweeps our nation. Therefore, the authors have responded by answering the call of so many to delve into this topic even more; this time, as a second edition.

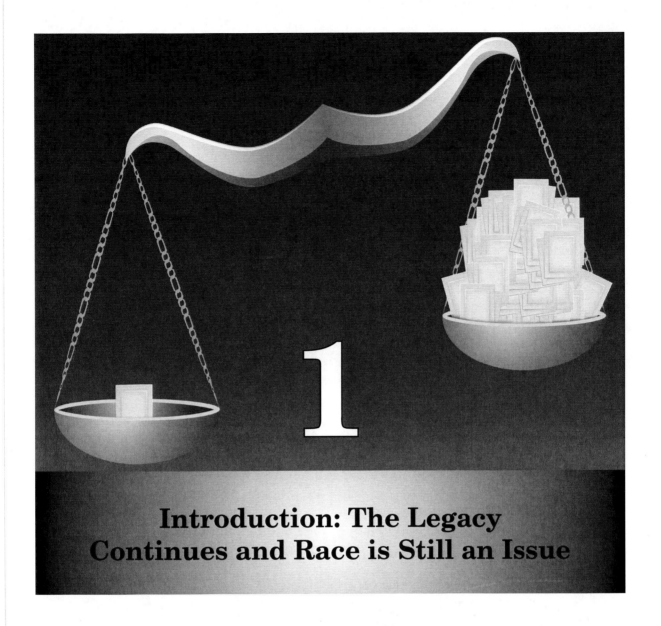

Introduction: The Legacy Continues and Race is Still an Issue

Chapter 1 Synopsis: This chapter provides an overview of this book and emphasizes the impact mandatory minimum laws for cocaine have had on the African American community. It also provides an overview of how the politics of race and crime can compromise the decision making of African American legislators and the Democratic Party. This chapter also provides a brief history of the role race has played in crafting drug policies in the United States. In terms of the overall manuscript, this thesis essentially asks the question "What should be the role of black elected functionaries?"

I think I am in agreement with most judges in the Federal system that mandatory minimum sentences for Federal crimes are imprudent, unwise and often unjust mechanisms for sentencing. . . . I simply cannot see how Congress can be satisfied with the results of mandatory minimums for possession of crack . . .

(Supreme Court Justice Anthony Kennedy, March 1994).

We do not intend nor want this manuscript to be a treatise against the Congressional Black Caucus (CBC). We do, however, want the public to understand the dilemma of the CBC when challenged with rising drug-related crime rates in some communities and rising get-tough-on-crime rhetoric from their colleagues in Congress that focused less on a comprehensive approach to fighting crime and more on incarceration, the latter being an approach that the CBC collectively would not hold in accordance with its mission. We actually demonstrate this dilemma when Congressman Rangel, an influential member of Congress and CBC member, is managing the floor debate when another tough measure is being considered. An amendment was proposed that would establish a mandatory minimum sentence for the mere possession of crack cocaine, making it the only federal mandatory minimum penalty for a first offense of simple possession of a controlled substance, and he chastised his colleague for proposing such an amendment. He said that while the amendment:

. . . is consistent with our get-tough or look-tough policy, and I really think this is an ideal amendment to vote for just prior to an election, but I know the gentleman believes that we have a get-tough Attorney General with a get-tough Justice Department that has really supported everything right down the line that has been presented to increase penalties. . . . But, Mr. Chairman, the gentleman has read the Attorney General's report on this provision, and they clearly indicate that they are in opposition to it, that this would permit some of the traffickers to manipulate drug statutes so as to minimize the penalties that are imposed in this.[1]

In spite of his concern with this amendment, he did not call for a vote on the measure that ended up passing via voice vote with no one being on record for passing what Rangel referred to as an unnecessary measure. The end result was another measure to treat crack far differently than any other drug. This is the dilemma of many Black politicians, the desire to address the rise in drug use and crime while also having to see their Democratic colleagues maintain control of Congress and/or win back the White House. The backdrop of Speaker of the House Tip O'Neill wanting a tough crime bill on the floor in record time so that the Republicans would not "outcrime" them is important, as we show in the book. When we listen to people talk about mandatory minimums, we either hear that the measures were passed because of the high crime rates or we hear that it was under the Clinton era when these laws passed, and that the CBC has consistently fought against them. As some of the interviews included in the book demonstrate, some CBC members were unaware of how and when the 100:1 disparity between crack and powder came about.

It is important to note that after Congressman Rangel was approached by the American Civil Liberties Union (ACLU) in the early 1990s, after the incarceration numbers increased and after the realization that many young African Americans were serving longer prison sentences, some members of the CBC began to speak out against the 100:1 disparity that passed.[2] We think we continue articulating the same challenges the CBC faced under a Democratic speaker and a Congress seeking tough law enforcement with a Democratic president during the 1990s seeking much of the same. Many African American critics of President Clinton, including participants at Tavis Smiley's annual State of the Black Union forum, which attracted well-known African American scholars, politicians, and activists when it was held from approximately 2000–2010, blame President Clinton for building more jails and encouraging Congress to pass more drug laws to keep more people in jail. President Clinton was asked about the crack cocaine disparity in a series of interviews by journalist and author *Dewayne Wickham* that can be found in Wickham's book entitled *Bill Clinton and Black America*. In an interview that took place on August 15, 2001, Clinton responded to the question about the disparity between crack and powder cocaine by saying: "On the disparity between crack and powder cocaine, I just don't agree with that. We urged the Congress to reduce it. They said- well there's more violence associated with crack than with powder cocaine. So we said okay, then don't eliminate it, just reduce it. It doesn't have to be ten to one. Cut it down to two to one. And I remember Senator Hatch saying that Congress would cut the disparity by raising the penalties on powder cocaine. It was very frustrating to me.

I don't blame people in the African-American community for being disappointed that I didn't do a better job of closing that gap. I had the Congress to deal with. By the time we got to this issue, the Republicans were in the majority and we just couldn't do it." (Wickham 2002, p 161). During the 1990s, another part of the policymaking community, activists and civil rights and civil liberties organizations, became more vocal on this issue.[3]

Understanding the Complexity of Drug Issues in the 1980s and 1990s

African Americans have endured many struggles and have made great achievements in spite of of said struggles. While civil rights legislation and the War on Poverty have done much to help poor communities and communities of color, drug laws and the War on Drugs have done much to take away those gains. Whether it is housing, student aid, or voting rights, African American communities have experienced tremendous setbacks over the past couple of decades.[4] As part of the War on Drugs, mandatory minimum laws for cocaine were passed. These laws created a disparity in the treatment of blacks and whites with regard to the possession of cocaine. While it wasn't a Jim Crow era law that explicitly laid out the doctrine that African Americans will be treated one way and Whites will be treated another, the impact of the law has had the same effect as a Jim Crow law (see Michelle Alexander's The New Jim Crow: Mass Incarceration in the Age of Colorblindness for how the War on Drugs has perpetuated a modern day caste system). Ironically, while African Americans had sought protections from the federal government, it is the federal government that has, in fact, contributed to hardship when it comes to seeking equality and fairness in the criminal justice system.

It is these laws, the impact these laws have had on the African American community, the use of racial politics, the role of the CBC, and the role of Democratic politicians in the support of these laws that will be the focus of this book. The underlying theme of this book is that African Americans have long been subjected to a compromise between political battles and compromises among white politicians seeking policy outcomes that may not be in the best interests of the African American community as a whole. Whether it was the compromises that led to the sanctioning of slavery in the United States Constitution to the Hayes-Tilden compromise that led the newly freed slaves vulnerable to a racist southern dynasty, black people have been used by politicians as a dispensable commodity. When mandatory minimum laws for crack and powder cocaine were passed in 1986, African Americans again saw themselves as a dispensable commodity for politicians interested in obtaining and keeping seats in the United States Congress. When Democratic President Bill Clinton, in the days after the Million Man March took place, refused to veto legislation that kept the "unjust mechanism" of mandatory sentencing for crack and powder cocaine in place, African Americans again saw themselves being treated as a dispensable commodity to a politician who wanted to remain in office. And as the 20th anniversary of the crack/powder cocaine mandatory minimum law approached in 2006, African Americans saw themselves as a dispensable commodity to politicians who recognized that a wrong had been committed, but still refused to pass legislation that would eliminate the 100:1 disparity for fear of being soft on crime, and thus risk losing a seat in Congress. African Americans have been loyal to both Republican and Democratic politicians at various times in their history with the two-party system, yet they have been subjected to crude compromises and have been victims of the political expediency and the politics of race and crime. African American political leaders in Congress cannot escape from the accusation that they, too, have treated their own constituencies as a dispensable commodity. Because African American politicians tied their fate to the Democratic party, many would thus support these sentencing measures and/or avoid criticizing the party because they wanted the party to have power in Congress. The rank and file African American person in the community was caught between a rock and a hard place—White politicians who cared little about their fate and the Black politicians who, playing a dangerous political game, allowed the mission of the CBC to take a backseat to partisan politics.

In the post–Civil Rights era, political parties continued to define themselves on the issue of race. Democrats positioned themselves as the party that supported the interests of African Americans, whereas Republicans positioned themselves as the party of the silent majority who were fed up with protests, riots, welfare, and affirmative action programs. Democrats, under the leadership of President Lyndon B. Johnson, and moderate Republicans were successful in pushing through voting rights and civil rights for African Americans during the 1960s. By the 1970s, the Democratic Party was seen as the party that champions the civil rights of African Americans. Barry Goldwater, a candidate for the Republican Party during the 1960s, implemented a southern strategy in an attempt to win the votes of whites who believed that the civil rights movement had gone too far. By the 1970s, former President Richard Nixon also attempted to attract southern white voters. "In the 1960s and 1970s, Richard Nixon used the 'law and order' theme to energize a white backlash in opposition to African American political mobilization."[5]

In 1980, Ronald Reagan ran a successful campaign with the vote of what has become known as Reagan Democrats. His use of race and crime contributed to his success in winning over these voters. The 1980s also saw an explosion of drug-related crimes. This resulted in major anti-crime legislation passing in the U.S. Congress since the mid-1970s.[6] Democrats, in seeking to be seen as tough on crime legislators, crafted tough, anti-crime legislation during the 1980s. Thus Republicans and Democrats were using the issue of crime to win over voters concerned about rampant crime. Traditionally, Democrats have emphasized treatment and rehabilitation, as well as preventive measures over simple incarceration, whereas Republicans have emphasized making it easier for law enforcement agencies to catch and punish criminals.[7] In fact, when Congress put in place the Federal Sentencing Guidelines,[8] which were designed to address the issues of the disparities in sentencing for similar offenses, the goal was to move, at least the federal criminal justice system, from one that supports the goal of rehabilitation to one that supports the goals of retribution, education, deterrence, and incapacitation.[9]

During the entire decade of the 1980s and the early 1990s, the House of Representatives was controlled by Democrats.[10] The president proposed legislation and Congress enacted legislation. Rather than continue an emphasis on treatment and rehabilitation, Democrats introduced, supported, and overwhelmingly voted in favor of policies that were punitive in nature. The enactment of these laws had more to do with winning elections on both the congressional and presidential level and less to do with fighting crime. According to Democratic pollster Stan Greenberg, who was the Democratic Party's expert on campaign and election strategy, during the 1980s white middle-class voters believed that Democrats were soft on crime and welfare. To these middle-class voters, Democrats were considered to be the party of minorities. In an effort to change this image, many Democrats, on both the congressional and state level, began to change their rhetoric on crime. The perception among the general public, partly driven by the media coverage of crime in inner cities, was that drugs and violence were a way of life in the Black community and Whites, who feared the rise in crime, demanded that their politicians address this issue by supporting a tough crime policy not by blaming society for the conditions in black neighborhoods.[11] Although the data indicated that "drugs were as prevalent in white neighborhoods as in black, and that when economic factors were taken into account, blacks were no more violent than whites,"[12] the statements and articles placed into the Congressional Record by members of Congress on the floor of the House of Representatives focused on drugs in the inner city. We will focus on these statements and articles in Chapter 4. Subsequently, the legislation passed resulted in overtly punitive penalties for those living in inner cities. While race was not specifically mentioned by most who delivered statements on the House and Senate floor about the need to treat crack cocaine more harshly than powder cocaine, the fact that African Americans quickly began to fill the prisons was an indicator that these were the individuals that law enforcement officers believed were at the root of the drug problem. In writing about how race has played a significant contributing factor in the enhancement of penalties for crime, Floyd Weatherspoon writes:

Early in our nation's history, legislatures were motivated by racial discrimination to differentiate between crimes committed by whites and crimes committed by blacks.

For example, "An Act Against Stealing Hogs" provided a penalty of 25 lashes on a bare back or a 10 pound fine for white offenders, while nonwhites (slave and free) would receive 39 lashes, with no chance of paying a fine to avoid the whipping. In 1697, Pennsylvania passed a death sentence legislation for black men who raped white women and castrated them for attempted rape. White men who committed the same offense wound be fined, whipped, or imprisoned for one year.[13]

Weatherspoon also discusses what he refers to as "unconscious racism" among whites. This racism has developed over the course of the founding of this nation. Also, many whites will argue that the increased incarceration rate among African Americans since the passage of the Anti-Drug Penalty Act had nothing to do with racism and that the policy is actually race neutral. However, African Americans have long faced the stereotype that they are criminally prone and violent. The media portrayal of gang violence that put a black face via the television in the living rooms of white Americans exacerbated this fear. This unconscious racism, Weatherspoon argues, resulted in the criminal penalties we saw during the 1980s. He writes:

Given the racially segregated nature of the American economy and social life, the media has played an important role in the construction of a national image of black male youth as "the criminal" in two respects which served to enhance crack cocaine violators; 1) generating public panic regarding crack cocaine; and 2) associating black males with crack cocaine. Ergo, the decision maker who is unaware of this selection perception that had produced this stereotype will believe that his actions are not motivated by racial prejudice.[14]

Even as the ink was drying on the new anti-drug legislation, the House Select Committee on Narcotics Abuse and Control (HSCNAC) issued a 1986 major city survey on drug arrests. The survey showed that even though marijuana remained the number one illegal drug of abuse, "heroin traffic and use remain an extreme threat that could increase at any time if foreign production expands."[15] Further, according to the report, "the most arrests in the thirty-nine cities studied for 1986 were cocaine sale or possession, with 51,462 arrests (including cocaine and its derivative, "crack"). Second was marijuana, with 34,191. Third was heroin, with 16,543. There were 12,158 arrests for all other illegal or illegally obtained drugs combined, including lysergic acid diethylamide (LSD), phencyclidine (PCP) . . . and other prescription and non-prescription drugs."[16] While there was not a racial breakdown in this report, as has been mentioned, it is the substantial increase in the incarceration of African Americans that bore the brunt of the legislation, media reports, and perceptions among law enforcement officers that African Americans were key to the drug problem. Thus the words of H.R. Haldeman, President Richard Nixon's top aide, is important to remember. In 1969 he wrote, "Nixon emphasized that you have to face the fact that the whole [drug] problem is really the blacks. The key is to devise a system that recognizes this while not appearing to."[17]

Few Democratic politicians during the 1980s and 1990s were willing to focus on the need for preventive measures. Indeed, by 1994 when a Democratic president and a Democratically controlled Congress passed a major crime bill, in order to win the vote of Republican lawmakers, the final passage of the bill had fewer preventive measures than intended by the committee of jurisdiction and only addressed mandatory minimum penalties for crack cocaine in a minor way. This put members of the CBC in a quandary. As Democrats, they felt the necessity to support their party; as African Americans, they felt loyalty to their African American constituents. Further, they did have a legitimate need to fight crime, but the group has as its mission to support progressive legislation, which, in the area of crime, would include supporting rehabilitation, preventive measures, and structural changes in the economy as opposed to long prison terms.

Drug-related crimes were indeed causing havoc in inner city communities during the 1980s. CBC members such as Congressman Major Owens (D-NY) introduced legislation targeting the trafficking of cocaine in 1986.[18] Congressman Rangel, who chaired the House Select Committee on Narcotics Abuse and Control (HSCNAC) during the 1980s, held hearings about the dangers of crack cocaine. There was a rash of car break-ins because those addicted to crack were stealing radios for drugs. While there was a legitimate need to address the issue of drug-related crimes, members of the CBC, like most African Americans, were aware of the historical racism that exists in the criminal justice system. Thus, the challenge of the CBC was to address the issue of crime, while also addressing the root causes of crime. During the 1980s, and to some extent during the 1990s, the root causes of crime were not the top priorities among their Democratic colleagues; rather, both Republicans and Democrats supported legislation that emphasized punishment.

Mandatory Minimums Impact on African Americans

Mandatory minimum penalties for crack cocaine have had a detrimental and disproportionate impact on the African American community. While the legislation did not specifically target African Americans, it did specifically target a form of a drug believed to be used and/or distributed by and in African American neighborhoods. Even when one considers the fact the drug policy was also based on class, considering that crack cocaine was believed to be cheaper and therefore more prevalent in poorer communities, the fact that over 80 percent of those in federal prisons for crack violations are African American puts the question of inequities to the issue of race not class. Since the 1980s, tough sentencing laws have put a number of individuals in prison. Although African Americans make up approximately 12 percent of the population, they account for over 50 percent of inmates in federal and state prisons.[19] There has been a greater focus since the 1980s on federalizing crimes. These sentences tend to be longer and often affect first-time, nonviolent drug offenders. Mandatory minimums for crack cocaine have resulted in a disproportionate number of African Americans serving long prison terms for drug crimes. Indeed, at the federal level, the emphasis on drug cases has grown significantly in 50 years. In 1947, the criminal caseload at the federal level was 5 percent, 6 percent in 1957, 7 percent in 1967, 18 percent in 1977, 28 percent in 1987 and 36 percent by 1997.[20] "Not surprisingly, the federal prison population has exploded. From 1954 to 1976, it fluctuated between 20,000 and 24,000. By 1986, it had grown to 36,000. Today it exceeds 190,000 prisoners, up 527 percent in 20 years. More than half of this population is made up of drug offenders, most of whom are serving sentences created in the weeks after Len Bias died."[21] Eric Sterling, architect of the mandatory minimum law passed in 1986, has made the argument that as the United States abolished the separate but equal system, she began to focus on controlling the African American community via the use of prisons. We will attempt to explore this argument in this book. Looking at the aforementioned data, President Nixon's statement that we must make the drug issue a black issue, may not be far from the truth.

There are no shortages of data that clearly demonstrates the disproportionate impact mandatory minimum laws have had on the African American community. Since federal mandatory minimum laws are classified as felonies, they impact the right to vote. Because the laws require a minimum of five years in prison without the possibility of parole, they remove a family member, including a mother or a father, from the home for a substantial period of time. Mandatory minimum laws also remove young men and women from the community. These young people could possibly become better citizens with the proper amount of educational investment. The psychological impact of having a large segment of communities entering the prison system also aggravates the problems facing African Americans. In addition, during the 1990s Congress passed legislation that (1) prohibits those with drug convictions from receiving welfare benefits unless they meet certain conditions established by states, (2) prohibits the receiving of federal student loans unless certain conditions are met,[22] and (3) prohibits eligibility to reside in public housing. In most cases, it is only drug convictions that receive the treatment mentioned above. With the enactment of mandatory minimums for crack cocaine, it has been African Americans that have made up the bulk of the individual impacted by these policies.

Len Bias, Political Opportunism, and Patriotism

Since this work focuses on mandatory minimum laws for crack cocaine, it is important to provide a brief overview as to why crack cocaine made it onto the congressional agenda during the 1980s. With the election of President Ronald Reagan came a shift in crime policy. Reagan espoused that big government programs were not the solution to crime policy. Since the sole person responsible for committing a crime was the individual, the solution was to punish the individual.[23] During the early 1980s, Reagan established that fighting the use and abuse of drugs would be a key focus of his administration. In 1982, Congress passed a law authorizing $125 million to establish new drug task forces to be "staffed by more than a thousand new FBI and DEA agents and federal prosecutors."[24].

In 1983 the Reagan Justice Department issued a briefing paper that undermined the notion that increased incarceration would lead to a substantial reduction in crime. Thus, as early as 1983, the Reagan administration understood that their strategy of "punishing offenders convicted of a certain offense with the same prison sentence"[25] was not sound policy. In the final year of the Reagan administration, his Assistant Attorney General, William Bradford Williams, issued a memorandum to key leaders of the Justice Department stating that they needed to continue to polarize the issue of prisons and crime and if individuals began to talk about alternatives to incarceration, then they must mention those leaders by name and accuse them of being soft on crime.[26]

For its part, the Democratically controlled Congress did not want to be seen as being soft on crime. The death of star basketball player Len Bias seemed to be a turning point for Congress. Len Bias was a superstar basketball player at the University of Maryland. He was headed to play in the NBA for the Boston Celtics, a team located in the state of then-House Speaker Tip O'Neill. According to Eric Sterling, Speaker Tip O'Neill instructed every congressional committee to draft a tough drug law. It was an election year and Democrats were determined to be as tough on this issue as Republicans were. O'Neill wanted a Democratic anti-crime bill to be written and passed by Congress for political reasons as much as for reasons to fight the spread of drugs.[27]

It cannot be underestimated how the death of Len Bias contributed to the harsh mandatory minimum penalties. Congress introduced a series of bills addressing crack cocaine and other illegal drugs after Bias' death. Prior to that time, Congress introduced legislation that focused on crack cocaine, but the legislation was generally non-binding sense of Congressional resolutions stating that the public and Congress should be aware of the dangers of crack cocaine. After the death of Bias, Congress introduced the Mandatory Crack and Drug Penalties Act, the Drug Free Workplace Act of 1986, and the Narcotics Penalties and Enforcement Act. The legislation that ultimately became law was HR 5484, the Anti-Drug Abuse Act of 1986. This legislation contained a mandatory minimum sentence for crack and powder cocaine. It created vast disparities between the treatment of the two forms of the same drug. HR 5484 was a comprehensive drug bill, but it is the crack penalties that is of most concern to this work. There was evidence in the discussions of the bills that preceded HR 5484 that Congress intended to treat crack more harshly than powder. Congress claimed that the intent was to go after serious offenders and traffickers. The definition of "serious traffickers" changed as members made changes to the legislation. For example, a 1986 committee report issued by the House Judiciary Subcommittee on crime labeled a major trafficker as "the manufacturers or heads of organizations who are responsible for creating and delivering very large quantities" and serious traffickers as "the managers of the retail traffic, the person who is filling the bags of heroin, packaging cocaine into vials . . . and doing so in substantial street quantities."[28] According to the USSC,

> Of particular relevance to this report, there is no authoritative legislative history that explains Congress's rationale for selecting the 100–1 drug quantity ratio for powder cocaine and crack cocaine offenses. The legislative history shows that Congress considered a variety of powder cocaine/crack cocaine drug quantity ratios before adopting the 100-to-1 ratio. The original version of the House bill that was ultimately enacted into law, House Bill 5484, contained a drug quantity ratio of 50–1. A number of other bills introduced during this period contained drug quantity ratios of 20–1, including one (Senate 2849) introduced by Senate Majority Leader Bob Dole on behalf of the Reagan Administration that proposed five year mandatory minimum penalties for cases involving 500 grams of powder cocaine or 25 grams of crack cocaine.[29]

The floor and committee statements by members of Congress seemed to confirm that the decision to make penalties for crack as stiff as possible was driven by media reports about the dangers of crack. In his book, Floyd Weatherspoon provides a transcript of a judge's criticism of the media for portraying negative images of African American males, which can be found in Appendix 1. The description provides an understanding of the role of the media in conjuring up the image of the dangerous Black man.

By the time HR 5484 (a bill essentially inspired by Tip O'Neill) was voted on in the House of Representatives, it overwhelmingly passed by a vote of 392–16 on September 11, 1986. In commenting on the bill, Congressman Brian J. Donnell (D-MA), who voted for the bill stated that "It's mob mentality in there . . . . It's the biggest, it's just become the single biggest issue in the country."[30] On the same tone, Congressman Barney Frank (D-MA), who was one of 15 Democrats who opposed the bill, said the following: "I fear this bill is the legislative equivalent of crack. It yields a short-term high, but does long-term damage to the system and it's expensive to boot."[31] Patricia Schroeder (D-CO), who did not record a vote on this issue, likened this process to political football with "political piling on right before the election."[32] The bill went to the Senate. Because of the many floor amendments added to the House bill, many in the Senate were not satisfied with what was initially a consensus bill among the House and Senate. Most of the dissatisfaction surrounded a death penalty amendment offered by Congressman Gekas (R-PA). This amendment, which passed by a vote of 296–112, allows the death penalty to be imposed on certain drug traffickers who "knowingly cause the death of any other individual."[33] The passage of this amendment prompted Parren Mitchell (D-MD and CBC member), who voted against the final passage of the overall bill, to remark "This is one of the most tragic days of my life when in our hatred of drugs, we trample the Constitution."[34]

In a *Washington Post* editorial published approximately 20 years after the death of Len Bias, Eric Sterling and Julie Stewart, founder of Families Against Mandatory Minimums, stated that by enacting mandatory minimums it was the intent of Congress to encourage the Department of Justice to focus on high-level traffickers and to reassure voters that members of Congress were as interested in fighting crime as were law enforcement. Instead, Congress passed tough mandatory minimum penalties that targeted low-level offenders. What resulted from initial good intent was, as stated by Sterling and Stewart, legislation that provided for long mandatory prison sentences for the following quantities of drugs: "five grams (the weight of five packets of artificial sweetener), 50 grams (the weight of a candy bar), 500 grams (the weight of two cups of sugar) or 5,000 grams (the weight of a lunchbox of cocaine). Large-scale traffickers organize shipments of drugs . . . filling tractor-trailers, airplanes and fishing boats."[35]

Within a week after this legislation was overwhelmingly passed by a Democratically controlled House of Representatives, President Reagan delivered a televised message from the White House to the American people about the dangers of drugs. As reported by the *Congressional Quarterly*, "The battlefield where official Washington's 'war on drugs' has been raging since the June 19 cocaine death of basketball star Len Bias shifted to the White House and Senate the week of September 15."[36] In his address to the nation, President Reagan and his wife, Nancy "Just Say No to Drugs" Reagan, talked about how drugs were threatening the values of the American people and that there must be a crusade against drugs because it mocks our heritage. Reagan said that "despite our best efforts, illegal cocaine is coming into our country at alarming levels, and 4 to 5 million people regularly use it. Five hundred thousand Americans are hooked on heroin. One in 12 persons smokes marijuana regularly. Regular drug use is even higher among the age group 18–25—most likely just entering the workforce. Today there's a new epidemic—smokable cocaine—otherwise known as 'crack.' It is an explosively destructive and often illegal substance which is crushing its users. It is an uncontrollable fire."[37] Both the President and his wife discussed how illegal drug use is a national problem and how it affects every American. They concluded their address to the nation by invoking the image of Lincoln. "Right down the end of this hall is the Lincoln bedroom. But in the Civil War, that room was the one President Lincoln used as his office. Memory fills that room, and more than anything, that memory drives us to see vividly what Lincoln sought to save. Above all, it is that Americans must stand for something. And that our heritage let us stand with a strength of character made steelier by each layer of challenge passed upon the nation."[38] With the speech, President Reagan stepped up the war on drugs.

President Reagan invoked images of patriotism, religion, freedom, and protecting the union against those (drug dealers and users) who are seeking to destroy it. These images coincided with the images the public was seeing from the media of angry, young black males acting violently in their use and distribution of drugs.[39] It was the perfect campaign speech. It was what Tip O'Neill feared. The reader should know that in 1982, Democrats lost control of the Senate; the Speaker did not want the House to follow suit in 1986. Being viewed as soft on crime was not something that Democrats wanted, thus the death of Len Bias from a cocaine overdose was exploited by the Speaker. It is within this context that CBC members had to essentially choose between their loyalty to the Democratic party and their loyalty to African Americans. This choice also included the reality that at least in some areas, drug crimes were rising; the CBC also had an interest in fighting crime in these communities. It is also within this context that Democrats sacrificed their most loyal constituencies. The drug laws not only focused on incarceration, but they would also attack public housing residents, welfare recipients, and even families with foster care legislation. African Americans are often portrayed in this country as relying on welfare, public housing, and not adequately caring for their kids.[40] Given that this is the case, it comes as no surprise that under the auspices of fighting drugs, these programs were attacked. That the Democratic party went along with this legislation and the CBC was unable or unwilling to hold Democrats accountable is what contributes to the travesty of justice surrounding the drug war in general and crack cocaine in particularly.

Keyterms

Mandatory minimum 1	Patriotism 8
Len Bias 8	HR 5484 9
Political Opportunism 8	

Endnotes

1 Rep. Rangel (NY), *Congressional Record*, September 16, 1988, p. 24275.

2 We referenced a report by the United States Sentencing Commission about the percentage of drug offenders incarcerated and the disproportionate impact drug laws passed in the 1980s had on African Americans. The report is entitled the "Federal Prison Population: Present and Future Trends." Hearings before the Subcommittee on Intellectual Property and Judicial Administration of the Committee on the Judiciary in the House of Representatives, One Hundred and Third Congress, First Session, May 12 and July 29, 1993, p. 28.

3 Wickham, D. 2002. *Bill Clinton and Black America*. New York: The Random House Publishing Group.

4 See *Invisible Punishment: The Collateral Consequences of Mass Imprisonment,* edited by Marc Mauer and Meda Chesney-Lind. W.W. Norton and Company, 2002 . . . Also, the National Urban League publishes an annual report entitled "The State of Black America." In its 2005 version entitled "The State of Black America: Prescription for Change," the group asserts that economic progress in the African American community is stagnant, and in some cases, declining. Further, the publication proclaims that "2005 showed the equality gap between whites and blacks in the criminal justice system as worsening from 73 percent to 68 percent. Blacks are three times more likely to become prisoners once arrested and a black person's average jail sentence is six months longer than whites for the same crime—39 months versus 33 months." "State of Black America," Executive Summary, www.nul.org/thestateofblackamerica.html.

5 Marion, O. 2000. Congress, Race, and Anti-Crime Policy, in *Black and Multicultural Politics in America*, ed. Y. M. Alex-Assensoh and L. J. Hanks, 226. New York: New York University Press.

6 Ibid., p. 240.

7 Ibid., p. 227.

8 Federal Sentencing Guidelines passed as part of the Sentencing Reform Act of 1984. In 2005, the Supreme Court, in *Booker vs United States*, ruled part of the federal sentencing guidelines unconstitutional and stated that guidelines were to be advisory as opposed to mandatory.

9 Seghetti, Lisa, and Alison Smith, *Federal Sentencing Guidelines: Background, Legal Analysis, and Policy Options,* CRS Report for Congress, April 4, 2005, p. 11.

10 Republicans won the majority in the Senate in 1982, but lost the majority in 1986. 2005 In *The Legislative Branch, Institutional of American Democracy*, eds P. J., Quirk and B. Sarah, Oxford: Oxford University Press.

11 Peter, B. 1991. *Minority Party: Why Democrats Face Defeat in 1992 and Beyond*, 103. Washington, DC: Regnery Gateway.

12 Ibid., p. 103.

13 Weatherspoon, F. D. 1998. *African American Males and the Law: Cases and Materials*, 4. Lanham, MD: University Press of America.

14 Ibid., p. 7

15 "1986 Major City Survey on Drug Arrests and Seizures: Report of the Select Committee of Narcotics Abuse and Control," 1987. One Hundredth Congress, First Session, 1. Washington, DC: United States Government Printing Office.

16 Ibid.

17 St. Clair, A. and St. Clair, J. 1998. *WHITEOUT*, 73. London: Verson.

18 From www.thomas.gov. The following legislation was introduced by CBC member Congressman Major Owens on July 17, 1986: H.R. 5195-Anti-Cocaine Amendments Act of 1986 - Amends the Controlled Substances Act and the Controlled Substances Import and Export Act to impose criminal penalties for dealing in: (1) five grams or more of cocaine, its salts, optical and geometric isomers, and salts of isomers, or a substance chemically identical thereto; and (2) 100 or more grams of other schedule I or II narcotic drugs. (Current law imposes such increased penalties on a kilogram or more of some schedule I or II narcotic drugs.)

19 See Smiley, Tavis, *The Covenant with Black America* (Chicago, IL: Third World Press), pp. 53–54.

20 American Bar Association, *The Federalization of Criminal 2006 Law*, p. 23.

21 Sterling, E. and Stewart, J. 2006. Undo the Legacy of Len Bias's Death. *Washington Post* June 24, 2006, A21.

22 It wasn't until 2006 that Congress finally voted to revise this law, thus allowing those with convictions before enrolling in college to receive aid. Congressman Mark Souder who originally introduced the legislation barring students with drug convictions from receiving loans claims that the Clinton Administration misread his provision; instead Souder meant that students convicted of a drug offense while currently enrolled in college will lose their student loan eligibility. For further explanation, refer to Congressman Mark Souder's congressional website at http://souder.house.gov (click on issues and legislation, and then on the drug-free loans link. Accessed on May 15, 2008.

23 Mauer, M. 1999. *Race to incarcerate, 60.* New York: New York Press.

24 Ibid., p. 61.

25 Ibid., p. 64.

26 Ibid., p. 63.

27 Personal interview with Eric Sterling, June 25, 2002. Sterling was Hughes' legal counsel. It was Hughes' committee that drafted the Anti-Drug Abuse Act of 1986 that was signed into law. He has taken an active role in the movement to reform the nation's drug laws and regrets his involvement in the crafting of the legislation in question. He vehemently opposed mandatory minimum laws for crack, powder, and other drugs. Also, Sterling wrote an article for the *Villanova Law Review* entitled "The Sentencing Boomerang: Drug Prohibition and Reform," November 1995, in which he discusses the speed in which the legislation passed and the usurpation of the normal committee process.

28 United States Sentencing Commission. 2002. *Report to Congress: Cocaine and Federal Sentencing Policy, 7.* Washington, DC.

29 Ibid., pp. 7–8.

30 Rovner, J. 1986. House Passes $6 billion Anti-Drug Package. *Congressional Quarterly*, September 13, p. 2125.

31 Ibid.

32 Ibid.

33 Ibid., p. 2126.

34 Ibid.

35 Sterling, E., and Stewart, J. 2006. Undo This Legacy of Len Bias's Death. *Washington Post*, June 24, A21.

36 "Reagan, Senate Republicans Join Drug War," *Congressional Quarterly*, September 20, 1986, p. 2191

37 "President and Mrs. Reagan on Drug Abuse and Prevention," *Congressional Quarterly*, September 20, 1986, p. 2227.

38 Ibid.

39 On this issue of the use of crack resulting in violent behavior, the American Civil Liberties Union has issued a report that dispelled those myths. It cites a study in 1988 about the homicides committed in New York City. According to the report . . . "of the 414 homicide cases that year, there were only 3 homicides associated with behavior caused by using crack and in 2 of those cases the crack user was the victim." "Cracks in the System: Twenty Years of the Unjust Federal Crack Cocaine Law," The American Civil Liberties Union, October 2006.

40 David Zucchino's book, *Myth of the Welfare Queen: A Pulizer Prize-Winning Journalist's Portrait of Women on the Line*, published a year after the Welfare Reform Act was signed into law, offers a compelling portrait of the lives of Black women trying to survive that defies the stereotypes. He writes in the opening of his book.... "I sought to discover whether anyone among a class of women so despised by mainstream America attempted to improve their circumstances and to raise their children for lives beyond poverty. I wanted to know whether such women were worthy more of contempt or compassion, or something in between. If there were any Cadillac-driving, champagne-sipping, penthouse-living welfare queens in North Philadelphia, I didn't find them." See also Ronald Waters' *White Nationalism Black Interests: Conservative Public Policy and the Black Community*, which discusses the creation of policy based on the negative images of the Black community, such as the one described by Zucchino.

ACTIVITY 1
How could a vote be so important?

September 11, 1986

Instructions:

In the space above, explain HR 5484 by covering details about the vote within Congress. Please consider politics, the social climate of 1986, race, and anything else you think is important in your response.

A Chapter 1 Exercise

[Please tear out your completed response so you can turn it in to the instructor]

ACTIVITY 2

In the boxes, please describe what the chapter covers as "Len Bias, Political Opportunism, and Patriotism" . . .

A Chapter 1 Exercise

Len Bias:

Political Opportunism:

Patriotism:

[Please tear out your completed response so you can turn it in to the instructor]

ACTIVITY 3

Applying a book concept to a real-life issue...

Complexity of Drug Issues
in the 1980s and 1990s

Mandatory Minimums Impact
on African Americans

Instructions:

Part 1: Within the *Complexity of Drug Issues in the 1980s and 1990s* box, please explain the realities of that time period according to the chapter. Feel free to do outside research using the Internet.

Part 2: Within the *Mandatory Minimums Impact on African Americans* box above, please describe in detail what the book covers as "impact." The chapter provides a clear understanding of this.

A Chapter 1 Exercise

[Please tear out your completed response so you can turn it in to the instructor]

The Congressional Black Caucus: Race Men and Women?

Chapter 2 Synopsis: This chapter provides a discussion of the CBC. It includes an overview of who are the members of the CBC, the history of the group, its mission, its voting behavior, and the challenges of race in the two-party system. This chapter also explores the changing makeup of the CBC's congressional districts. Prior to 1992, CBC members came from mostly urban and predominantly African American districts. This is no longer the case as a result of the 1992 elections that led to a large increase in the CBC membership. Attempting to maintain a unified voice when a caucus is made up of rural and urban members and members with a diverse constituency becomes a challenge. This challenge also contributes to the CBC's decision making on tough on crime legislation, such as mandatory minimum laws for cocaine. The chapter will include tables detailing the demographic makeup of the CBC during pertinent years in which Congress passed crack cocaine legislation (i.e., 1986, 1988).

The Congressional Black Caucus: No Permanent Friends, No Permanent Enemies, Just Permanent Interests

This chapter focuses on the mission and purpose of the Congressional Black Caucus. It attempts to examine why the CBC considers itself to be the voice of African Americans nationwide and how changes in its membership (i.e., diversity and growth) challenge its mission to serve as a collective voice for African Americans. This chapter also examines how the CBC's relationship with Democratic colleagues in Congress and with presidents of the United States has affected its overall unity on issues impacting the African American community. From its inception, the CBC has struggled with an "identity crises."[1] "Should CBC members act as a collective body, play a non-partisan role, representing both inside and outside of Congress the interests of the national black population, or should they engage in the fragmented world of pluralistic congressional politics, in which compromise and accommodation of black interests are necessary forms of conduct?"[2] There is evidence that the CBC at first viewed its mission not only theoretically but acted in accordance to the idea that it was to be non-partisan and to represent the national African American community. However, the CBC is a caucus within Congress, and reasons involving reelection, the benefits of seniority, the need to support the Democratic Party all factored in to move the CBC from a collective body articulating and working on behalf of African Americans and the disadvantage to a body where members act as individual legislators first.

Further, in understanding why the CBC has become more individualistic it should be noted that the African American community does not fully unite around issues, there is a class and demographic bias that exists. With the growth and diversity of the CBC, it becomes more difficult to speak as a collective voice. This chapter will, in part, focus on institutional demands as well. Those African American constituents who have a higher socioeconomic background than those living at or below the poverty line may not want their representatives to expend political capital on criminal justice issues. This chapter will also include data from the Joint Center for Political and Economic studies on attitudes of African Americans on increased expenditures for prisons and law enforcement.

The CBC and African Americans in Congress

The Congressional Black Caucus was originally formed in 1971 as a collective of African Americans in Congress with the purpose of articulating and affecting policies on behalf of African Americans. The early formation of the CBC, however, began in 1969 as the Democratic Select Committee, "a loose-knit group under the leadership of Charles Diggs."[3] Congressman Stokes, a founding member of the CBC, said: "When we started the Caucus in [1969] . . . we had no idea that it would have the kind of impact on black America that it's had. All we were trying to demonstrate was that nine blacks, given the responsibility to be in the U.S. Congress, could come together to try to work on behalf of black people as best we knew how."[4] Congressman Clay, in 1970, felt the need to bring formal organization to the Democratic Select Committee, which would lead to the formation of the CBC in 1971. The group settled on the name of the Congressional Black Caucus because they wanted to ensure that there was no doubt that the interests they were representing was that of African Americans.[5] The CBC, in 1971, established the formal election of a chairman, vice chairman, secretary and treasurer, in addition to subcommittees to work in areas of interest and specific concerns to African Americans.[6] The CBC added a whip position in 1991, which serves the function of persuading members to vote with the CBC on a given issue.[7]

Congressman Stokes also declared that "the Congressional Black Caucus is not a maverick organization. Instead, we are a coalition of U.S. congresspersons deeply concerned about the issues, needs, and aspirations of minority Americans. We, therefore, are interested in developing, introducing, and passing progressive legislation which will meet the needs of neglected citizens."[8] This and similar statements as well as the motto of the CBC demonstrates that the CBC is an organization formed exclusively to serve the interests of African Americans nationwide. These declarations by CBC members were essentially an indicator that the role of African American members of Congress is to advocate on behalf of African Americans beyond their district boundaries. On this point, two founding members used a strategy of mobilizing voters across congressional districts. The strategies were known as the Mitchell Initiative and the Fauntroy Initiative, which are discussed later in this chapter.

Phases of the CBC

The CBC, from its very beginning, has had difficulty achieving unity, in spite of its claim to speak as a united voice for African Americans. That the CBC is comprised of legislators with different ideas on how to become a collective voice, while addressing the needs of their individual constituents, the demands of their political party (Democrats), and the desire of individual members to obtain key committee seats and leadership posts, creates difficulty in speaking as one voice. Indeed, from its early stages, the CBC has attempted to adjust to the role of advocates on behalf of African Americans and as Congressmen and Congresswomen. The Caucus is now more than 40 years old, and it continues to try to define itself, with some members wanting to distance themselves from focusing specifically on race issues and some members wanting to maintain this focus. And as seen with the 2008 presidential primaries, there is a generational, gender, and even loyalty gap (meaning that several of those members who worked with Bill Clinton strongly supported his wife, Senator Hillary Clinton, instead of a viable African American candidate running for the office of the Presidency) that may be difficult to mend.

An example of the early challenges to the unity of the CBC is Margaret Barnett's analyses of the CBC. She identifies three distinct phases of the CBC: the *collective phase, ethnic phase,* and a *synthetic phase.* During the collective phase, which lasted from mid-1971 to mid-1972, the CBC saw itself as a single unified group representing a political construct known as the African American community.[9] The ethnic phase, which occurred in mid-1972 and lasted until 1974, asserted that each CBC member acted as individual legislators within Congress. This phase undermined the CBC's mission to act as a unified voice, because the number of African Americans in Congress was still very low, and their power, to the extent that it existed, would be enhanced by its leverage. The CBC's strength in negotiations would be its potential voting bloc. Further, as Barnett points out:

> . . . when Black elected representatives define their role in the narrowest, most individualistic terms, they obscure the reasons for institutionalizing a racially based political caucus and thus undermine their own legitimacy.[10]

After a series of retreats and internal discussions, the CBC moved into the synthetic phase, which created a leadership style that combined both the collective and ethnic phases. Out of retreats and self-evaluation sessions during the mid-1970s came a strategy to secure committee chairs and assignments on key committees by its members.[11]

The three phases of the CBC that occurred in the early years of its foundation demonstrated that the CBC would have challenges to its unity and in defining its role. These phases also occurred in the immediate post-civil rights movement where their fellow legislators were more willing to address issues important to CBC members. A decade after its founding, the CBC would experience an additional challenge: supporting a progressive agenda while Congress, the Presidency, and the country shifted to a more conservative stance on many issues.

Early Programmatic Strategies Embraced by the CBC

In order for a relatively small caucus in Congress to influence the larger body, strategies were developed to leverage the power of the CBC. Congressman Clay stated that Congressman Mitchell's and Congressman Fauntroy's plan were "the most significant strategies . . . and were at the core of whatever caused white members of Congress to redefine their relationship with us. These two mechanisms directly enhanced our influence within the deliberative body."[12] There was a third strategy as well. The CBC believed it would obtain more influence by spreading its membership across congressional committees. Each of the three strategies is expounded upon below.

THE MITCHELL STRATEGY

Congressman Parren Mitchell of Maryland created a "Brain Trust" that allowed the CBC to rely on a group of experts "to provide and interpret data from a black perspective."[13]

These experts provided data in several fields ranging from education to telecommunications. After the data were gathered, the CBC used the information to "inform and educate black constituents residing in districts represented by white congressman about the legislative agenda and its effect on the black community. The centers of influence in each district were responsible for disseminating this information and for applying pressure on elected officials to support the CBC agenda."[14] According to Barnett, Mitchell's Brainstormers "became an important technique for gaining the support and assistance of elements of the black middle class on legislative matters."[15]

THE FAUNTROY STRATEGY

The Fauntroy strategy came from the creation of a bill that would provide for home rule for the District of Columbia, which was represented by Congressman Walter Fauntroy, one of the founders of the CBC. After the Joint Center for Political Studies provided a series of studies showing that African Americans made up 25 percent or more of the population of 58 congressional districts and that in the majority of these districts, the African American voting age population was two or three times the margin of victory of the candidate who won during the 1972 congressional elections, Congressman Fauntroy employed a strategy that targeted members of Congress in these districts.[16] The strategy involved "a coordinated lobbying and peer-group approach to southern congressmen from targeted districts."[17] It is important to note that this strategy came under criticism because (1) there was opposition to the idea of the Caucus and its supporters collectively lobbying in the districts of their colleagues and (2), the long-term implementation of the strategy assumed a unity among the CBC that still did not exist.[18] However, during the 96th (1979–1980) and the 97th (1981–1982) Congress, the CBC used a modified version of the Fauntroy strategy called the CBC Action Alert Communications Network.

The Action Alerts were an effort to persuade non-African American members of Congress who represented a certain percentage (15 percent) of African Americans to support legislation that the CBC deemed to be important. While the strategy was not always successful, it was a signal that CBC members were watching the vote of their colleagues and expecting them to vote in a certain way. In initiating this strategy, the CBC worked closely with the Black Leadership Forum and the National Black Leadership Roundtable. "The Black Leadership Roundtable was a coalition of the chief executive officers of the 16 national black civil rights and political organizations, including the NAACP, the Urban League, the National Council of Negro Women, the Joint Center for Political Studies, and the Congressional Black Caucus."[19] "The National Black Leadership Roundtable is composed of officials representing 150 national black social, religious, professional, and civil rights organizations. Its primary objective is to ensure 'the effective representation of, and accountability to, black Americans by members of Congress.'"[20] Charles Jones concludes his article on the CBC Action-Alert Communications Network by stating that ultimately, the CBC's success in obtaining support of its policy preferences by non-CBC members will be determined by the country's political mood. When the public elects leaders that are more liberal in their ideology, the CBC will be more successful in achieving its policy goals.

THE COMMITTEE STRATEGY

The third strategy implemented after the series of retreats focused on a previous effort of obtaining more favorable committee assignments for CBC members.[21] The CBC collectively negotiated with the House Democratic leadership to provide key committee assignments for its members. It was a recognition that the CBC could be more influential if its members were spread across each committee in Congress. While this strategy could be viewed as a means to keep its members united (the payoff being that the CBC would lobby on behalf of members for good committee seats), subsequent Congresses would take away the CBC's influence in committee selections as many CBC members would personally lobby for committee assignments through the senior member of their respective state delegation.[22]

Types of Representation

No study on the CBC would be complete without addressing the issue of representational style: substantive representation versus descriptive representation, as well as delegate versus trustee. Substantive representation occurs when "representatives substantively represent their constituents through the realization of their political needs."[23] Descriptive (or symbolic representation) occurs when a member belongs to a social or demographic group that makes up his or her district. "Descriptive representation devoid of any substance impact is 'symbolic.'"[24] A representative acts as a trustee when he or she assesses the needs of his or her district and acts accordingly and a delegate when he or she directly reflects the vocal desires of the constituents. These representational issues will be further discussed later in this chapter. Because the CBC is a caucus within Congress that represents a unique constituency (in that they are perceived to represent the interests of African Americans as a group) and is tied to a particular political party, the types of representation it provides as a group and as individual members will collide, which, again, makes it difficult for the group to maintain unity and to provide the type of representation for African Americans as outlined in its mission statement.

The CBC as an Interest Group

The CBC, as a body, exists to work toward introducing and supporting legislation that will benefit African Americans as a whole. As Barnett writes, " . . . The Congressional Black Caucus focuses on issues of concern to the black community and consists solely of black members of the House of Representatives. Therefore, from its formation, the CBC has reflected its dual locus both in the Congress and in the black community."[25] Congressman William Lacy Clay, Sr., a founding member of the CBC, argues that African American members of Congress have been successful in protecting the interests of African Americans. He writes in his book on African Americans in Congress that it has been in recent years when a conservative agenda has prevailed that the CBC has come under scrutiny and had been questioned about its usefulness to both the African American and white community alike. He writes:

Today, many of the advances developed and supported by the Caucus are being eroded. Elements in society—black and white—are attempting to belittle us as unrepresentative of the black community. The age-old ploy of divide and conquer is used to dilute our strength because our enemies know that the Caucus is the only organization with the potential to mobilize the black community on a national basis for a political cause.[26]

Clay argues that the CBC is even more successful with its increase in membership. Had there been two dozen or more CBC members after World War II instead of two, says Clay, African Americans would have been included in many of the social programs that were in place after the war to help whites. Thus, Clay argues, the CBC provides representation for African Americans simply by its very existence. It serves to educate African Americans and non-African Americans, and it serves to fight for African Americans to be included in all programs. This work argues that individual CBC members understand the need to be committed to African Americans as a whole, but party politics and the legislative process prohibits them from doing so. Clay is correct in stating that the CBC, through its Brain Trusts, Issue Forums, and other forums, do serve to educate the American people about issues of concern to African Americans, but the desire of individual members to obtain committee seats, to support the Democratic party, and to represent increasingly diverse districts in terms of both class and race, renders the CBC as Caucus more symbolic in nature as oppose to producing substantive legislation that benefits African Americans as a whole. Indeed, as seen during the 1980s passage of legislation during the so-called drug war, CBC members were actors in the passage of very punitive legislation. Further, because the African American community is not united on issues such as crime, an incentive is not created among CBC members as a whole to advocate on behalf of an issue that may result in their Democratic colleagues losing congressional seats. According to a national opinion poll published by the Joint Center for Political and Economic Studies, in 1997 African Americans were divided on the question that asked whether there should be increased government spending on prisons and law enforcement with 51 percent believing that there should be more spending in these areas and 45 percent responding that there shouldn't be.[27] The criminal justice bills passed during the years this research covers address those two issues, more money for prisons and more law enforcement. Thus, a divided African American community may reflect a divided CBC on criminal justice issues. This is a long way from Congressman Diggs' pronouncement to Congress that "the issues and concerns of this caucus are not partisan ones . . . [the CBC's concerns include those of] citizens living hundreds of miles from our districts who look on us as Congressmen-at-large for black people and poor people in the United States."[28]

Barnett would agree with Clay to some extent. She argues that in addition to the CBC being a caucus within Congress, and thus should be understood as such, the CBC also acts as a collective body that articulates the interest of the African American community.[29] To understand the role of the CBC is to look at it as both a caucus within Congress and as an interest group with its primary constituency being African American people around the country. As a caucus, the CBC is one of many caucuses on Capitol Hill. For example, there is a Congressional Bicycle Caucus, a

Congressional Progressive Caucus, a Congressional Blue Dog Caucus, a women's caucus, etc. The CBC, however, is the only caucus with a specific mission of working on behalf of African Americans and disadvantaged groups. It is, then, a race-specific caucus, to some extent. Barker, Tate, and Jones "suggest that the *force of blackness* itself stimulates cohesion and identification among blacks in Congress. It remains as true today as it ever was, that as long as blacks are disadvantaged as a group, they must work as a group to remove those disadvantages."[30] In addition, CBC members may expect certain benefits in choosing to join the caucus, some of which may be more symbolic in nature. E.E. Schattsschneider tells us that among the benefits for joining an interest group include obtaining material benefits (monetary in nature, i.e., raising funds and awareness to issues impacting African Americans, and for reelection purposes), purposive (i.e., benefits associated with ideological or issue-oriented goals, that is to say that a CBC member who introduces legislation potentially have all CBC members as co-sponsors thus giving the member leverage), and solidarity (benefits come from being part of the group struggle to achieve policy goals).[31]

Clay would likely disagree with Barnett's assessment that the CBC must be seen for what it is, a collective group of members who are seeking leverage to support issues that are important to individual members, but they are insignificant to provide the fundamental changes needed to ensure that the African American community does not endure systemic problems such as unemployment, poor housing conditions, and a growing prison population.[32] Barnett's argument, however, is consistent with Robert Salisbury's Exchange Theory, which states that individuals undertake group relations based on their expectation that their participation will result in some payoff (i.e., exchange) for them.[33] Members of the CBC can make statements about being more concerned with increasing the size of the Democratic Party as opposed to increasing the size of the CBC and that they are not entering Congress to become anyone's conscious; however, those statements do not generally keep them from joining the CBC. Every elected Black Democrat to the U.S. Congress since the founding of the CBC has joined the CBC.

The formation of the CBC as a caucus in Congress presupposes that neither Democrats nor Republicans will look after the interests of African Americans without a body such as the CBC in Congress. Using mandatory minimums penalties as an example, both parties, including the first Democratic president elected since 1976, seemed to be hostile to the idea of eliminating or reducing mandatory minimum drug sentences. Further, the systemic problems faced by African American are not addressed within an institution that "is structured to repel fundamental social and economic change."[34] Thus, non-African American members of Congress may see the lack of progress in terms of moving out of poverty as individual failure among African Americans as opposed to systemic racism that created some of the conditions faced by African Americans. African American members have a personal experience and knowledge that it takes more than a few pieces of legislation to address issues facing African Americans. Thus, African American members of Congress use the Caucus as a means to set an agenda for Black America each Congress to ensure that members and the public are aware of some of the systemic issues. Members of Congress, even progressives, may not have the same legitimacy or understanding to articulate such issues. Or, they may not receive the same response from the African American community when they do attempt to discuss structural barriers to achievement. For example, when former Assistant Secretary of Labor and former Senator Daniel Patrick Moynihan issued a report on the state of the African American underclass, he came under fierce criticism at the time, and his report is still criticized today.[35] However, members of the CBC have held many forums on the state of African Americans, the African American underclass, the crisis among Black men, etc. . and receive no such criticisms because it is understood that African American members of Congress can discuss these controversial issues with a more comprehensive approach that does not simply revert back to personal responsibility as the reason for societal ills. However, as CBC members' districts become more diverse, even they may distance themselves from language that is couched in group rights as opposed to individualism.

As the CBC becomes more entrenched with institutional and party politics, it sacrifices its goals in advocating issues on behalf of African Americans and the disadvantaged in an effort to become more pragmatic. For example, in 1996 all but one CBC member (Congressman Sanford Bishop, D-GA) opposed legislation that put severe restrictions on welfare benefits. This legislation was supported by President Clinton and white Democrats alike. According to Tate, "while prominent White Democrats, notably in the Senate, would denounce the President's move to eliminate the 'safety net,' the Black members of Congress, including Senator Carol Moseley Braun, were notably muted in their opposition."[36] She writes that the CBC remained quiet, in part, because "they did not want to endanger the reelection of President Clinton" . . . and "their dependence on the power of the White House had increased sharply."[37] In addition, it becomes difficult to act as a caucus that represents African Americans as a whole when (1) individual members may have tougher reelections than others and (2) when the African American public is not united on an issue. To continue using the issue of welfare as an example, Tate also writes that "Black House legislators were also running for reelection themselves, and they found that blacks were divided with most in favor of welfare reform. Thus, they voted their conscience but kept quiet."[38] The latter reason for their silence after the vote is particularly important as African American congressional districts become more diverse in terms of their constituency. Tate also presents polling data in her book that shows that in 1984, almost 50 percent of those African Americans polled supported an increase in spending on the Food Stamp program with only 11 percent supporting a decrease in funding. In 1996, however, only 21 percent of those polled supported a decrease.[39] This indicates a less favorable attitude toward government spending on welfare programs. The question remains whether the CBC as an interest group can be effective on an issue such as mandatory minimums for crack cocaine when a get-tough-on-crime policy continues to win elections and thus is very popular among politicians. How does the CBC, as a collective group, convince its Democratic and Republican colleagues to take steps to eliminate mandatory minimums for crack cocaine crimes or to reduce the disparity between crack and powder cocaine?

The CBC as a collective group and its individual members must remain aware of the limitations of the caucus in bringing about the type of changes needed in the African American community. Progressive and redistribution politics can be detrimental to the career of a legislator, not necessary CBC members, but to their Democratic colleagues that the CBC must rely on for support. This brings about a debate about whether the CBC can be effective in a legislative body that seeks to minimize conflict.[40] On this point, Barnett also argued that African Americans are unlike other ethnic groups. Because White ethnic groups entered the country during a time of economic boom, they did use the political system to improve their socioeconomic position in society.[41] Therefore, the benefits they (White ethnic groups) may seek from the political system are tangible benefits such as maintaining roads, an economic safety net during hard times, jobs, etc. "For white ethnic groups there is no nationwide ideology that ranks specific groups. In contrast, racism is a pervasive ideology that ranks Blacks as a group below others because it assumes the inherent generic inferiority of Blacks."[42] As a result, they seek structural changes within the political system that collectively benefit the African American community as a whole. If the argument is that racism (both individual and institutional) had been an intrinsic part of American society, then it is the case, as Barnett notes, that seemingly non-racist policies are indeed racist. Such is the case with mandatory minimums. On this issue, then, Black leadership should be cognizant of historic racism in the American criminal justice system, and thus should oppose crime policies that do not address the long-term problems resulting from historic racism. This may prove to be difficult. Their colleagues in Congress, when debating issues, may distance themselves from dealing with symptoms of historical racism, believing that in the post–civil rights era, everyone has an equal chance, and thus the political body should not be used to remedy past grievances. A discussion of institutional racism is needed to explain this belief. Party politics that perpetuate institutional racism makes it challenging for the CBC to fully represent the African American public in accordance to its set mission. The irony is that while members of Congress do not openly say that race and past racism do indeed impact current conditions, within the debate on these issues, there is a subtle appeal to voters who wish not to support the progressive policies advocated by the collective CBC, policies such as the CBC Alternative Budget and the Hawkins-Humphrey full employment bill.

Institutional Racism and Legislative Ambiguities

Individual acts of racism such as burning African American churches, burning crosses in someone's yard, and other crimes now classified under the concept "Hate Crimes" have been addressed by way of the law. There is even legislation against harming someone because of his or her race, creed, religion, or color. However, a more intrinsic form of racism exists that is not addressed. Earlier in this chapter, we touched on Barnett's assessment of the need for structural changes within the system to truly address the plight of African Americans, but scholars such as Charles Hamilton and Robert Smith as well as Kwame Toure provide an analysis of institutional racism.

In their book on the struggles by African Americans to achieve full equality, Ture and Hamilton discuss the issue of institutional racism. They write:

> Racism is both overt and covert. It takes two, closely related forms: Individual whites acting against blacks, and acts by the total white community. We call these individual racism and institutional racism. The first consists of overt acts by individuals, which cause death, injury, and the violent destruction of property. This type can be recorded by television cameras; it can frequently be observed in the process of commission. The second type is less overt, far more subtle, less identifiable in terms of *specific* individuals committing the acts. But it is no less destructive of human life. The second type originates in the operation of established and respected forces in the society, and thus receives far less public condemnation than the first type.[43]

Smith argues that the above definition of institutional racism is acceptable, but that it has its limitations. Smith's point is that institutional racism does not have to be a situation where Whites are dominating Blacks simply because they feel superior, rather it can occur when the symptoms of institutional racism are ignored and are perpetuated by established institutions. He writes:

> . . . institutional racism is observed when the normal, accepted, routine patterns and practices of society's institutions have the *effect* or *consequence* of subordinating an individual or group or maintaining in place the *results* of past practice of now illegal overt racism. It is covert and unintended because to achieve the results the individuals involved need not consciously take into account race but need simply to go about the normal routines of their work, as required by an institution's standard operating procedure. Thus, institutional racism . . . Conforms to custom and law.[44]

Both definitions of institutional racism are very pertinent when considering legislation passed by a body such as Congress, particularly when the purpose of the legislation is to address issues such as high unemployment rates among African Americans. The specific examples of institutional racism highlighted below attempt to demonstrate what can be considered as institutional racism. The incidents all occur prior to 1986, the year the Anti-Drug legislation that contained mandatory minimum penalties for crack cocaine passed. The purpose is to demonstrate the political environment in which the CBC attempted to pass key legislation that would structurally and symbolically benefit the African American community.

The Hawkins-Humphrey Full Employment Bill

As has been mentioned, the CBC following the Mitchell strategy divided itself into a series of Brain Trusts to span across 13 fields of interest for the purpose of dealing with issues of concern to African Americans.[45] Congressman Gus Hawkins chaired the

Committee on Education and Labor, which is why he was given the task of crafting a full employment bill.[46] "HR 50, the Full Employment and Balanced Growth Act, better known as the Hawkins Humphrey Employment Act (he was coauthor of the bill with Senator Humphrey) . . . [in its original form] was a tough, no-nonsense piece of legislation calling for effective remedies to redress the woes of unemployment in the American economic system. It envisioned that the federal government as the employer of 'last resort,' mandating full employment even if the government had to create public service jobs through programs such as those created during the Great Depression."[47] Every CBC member co-sponsored the legislation. By the time the legislation finally passed, it was so watered down that it was deemed "utterly meaningless as a bill to aid the black unemployed."[48] The politics behind HR 50 is important to understand how institutional racism can result in meaningful legislation becoming mere symbolic legislation in its final form.

In discussing the Hawkins-Humphrey Act, Smith tells us that it is pivotal to understanding Black politics within an institutional body such as Congress. Smith says that during the mid-to-late 1960s when Dr. King was organizing the Poor People's campaign that had as its goal full employment for all Americans, King and the civil rights activist Bayard Rustin had debates about whether protesting or working within the system would accomplish the goal of full employment. Rustin believed that a biracial coalition working within the system would go further in achieving such goals.[49] The Humphrey-Hawkins act had a biracial coalition and the language surrounding the legislation was that it would benefit everyone, not simply African Americans. The coalition created to support the act was also progressive and consisted of people who believed that substantial changes could occur by working within the system. The full employment act would be one such change, in that it would guarantee full employment, a belief that is not necessarily consistent with the aforementioned beliefs that people fail to move beyond poverty because of individual deficiencies, not because there are no jobs available. In other words, this biracial, progressive coalition consisted of people who believed the American political system should guarantee jobs and that this substantial policy could pass by working *within* the system. Smith writes:

> The Humphrey-Hawkins Act may be seen as an application of Rustin's strategy or as limiting case study in the incorporationist theory of Browning, Marshall, and Tabb. Humphrey-Hawkins is a text-book case. Everything was done right, according to theory: There was the effort to develop a consensus, deracialized issue—full employment—that appealed across lines of class and color. There was the effort made at both the mass and elite level to mobilize the black community in support of the bill, and the effort to construct a broad multi-ethnic coalition. Finally, in the Carter Administration, blacks and the broad coalition constituted the governing majority in the executive branch as well as the Congress. Yet, in spite of this textbook case in institutional politics, the outcome of this legislative struggle for full employment was no more successful than the ill-fated struggle for the poor people's campaign.[50]

It is also important to highlight two key points. The legislation was drafted before Carter entered office, but African Americans put their support behind Carter, in part, because they believed he, a Democrat, would be very supportive of this issue. Carter, to quote Clay, was "perhaps the biggest enemy of the original bill's concept. He insisted on the inclusion of crippling provisions in exchange for his support."[51] The other important point to highlight is that even though the bill had multiracial support and was co-sponsored by 69 members (including the CBC), "the bill was viewed throughout the legislative struggle as a 'black bill' pushed by the Congressional Black Caucus in response to persistent recession level unemployment rates in the black community. Thus, despite all of the talk about the deracialized nature of the employment issue (i.e., that more whites are unemployed than blacks and, therefore, whites would benefit more from the bill than blacks) and the effort to construct a multiracial coalition in the Washington community, the bill was viewed as race-specific legislation—a black bill."[52] The chronic unemployment rate for African Americans was not alleviated as a result of the act and continued to increase in the administration following Carter's where there were overt racial overtures about African Americans, some of which will be discussed in an upcoming chapter. The Humphrey-Hawkins employment bill provides the type of example of institutional racism outlined by Smith and it also demonstrates the ambiguities of legislative achievement. In *Just Permanent Interests*, Clay says that the greatest accomplishment of Congressman Hawkins was this bill.

CBC Alternative Budget

Another effort on behalf of CBC members to introduce legislation to tackle structural unemployment and other chronic conditions faced by the African American community was the Alternative Budget. The CBC has introduced an alternative budget in many Congresses in some form, but has yet to pass any of them, nor has it garnered significant support from their House colleagues. The Caucus first introduced its alternative budget in 1981 in response to President Reagan's challenge to critics of his first budget proposal to come up with a viable alternative of their own.[53] House Democrats attempted to come up with a budget strategy, but it proved to be a watered-down version of Reagan's, leaving the CBC as "the most progressive organized bloc in Congress and social policies of the Reagan Administration have the Democratic Majority in Congress."[54] The Alternative Budgets incorporated provisions from the Humphrey-Hawkins act. According to Smith, "each Caucus budget proposal had as its centerpiece a major jobs program that would 'address the problems of structural unemployment which affects such a large segment of the black population in America.'"[55] To pay for the provisions in the Alternative Budget, the CBC proposed cuts in the defense budget and a tax hike on wealthy Americans and corporations. According to Smith, the CBC alternative budget was introduced five times between 1981 and 1987, and the most votes it received was 86 in 1983.[56] The CBC's alternative budget not only lacked support of the majority of their House colleagues and the Democratic leadership, but their quest to pass substantive legislation that would benefit African Americans was largely ignored by their colleagues and the press.[57] The high unemployment rates that existed when the Humphrey-Hawkins bill was considered continued to exist during the 1980s. Opposing the alternative budget was the equivalent to accepting the status quo. What is also interesting to note are two visions of the problem facing America. While the CBC saw the conditions in America being structural and a result of the denial of opportunities, their opponents "believed that federal spending for social and economic programs was the root cause of the financial ills of the country.[58] Thus, in stating that it is the programs and the bureaucracy but not the people, opponents of the CBC's efforts can make the claim that their opposition has nothing to do with race.[59]

The purpose of highlighting the Hawkins-Humprey full employment bill and the CBC's Alternative Budget is to demonstrate the impact institutional racism can have on initiatives designed to address ongoing societal ills. This, as Smith has stated, demonstrates the limits of institutional politics and it contributes to the lack of unity among CBC members as the body grows older and also becomes thoroughly incorporated into the system. An example is Congressman Williams Gray's (D-PA) support of the CBC Alternative Budget prior to his becoming Chair of the House Budget Committee, when he then opposed it, much to the disappointment of the CBC colleagues. Thus, CBC members inadvertently support institutional racism by supporting legislation that, to quote from Smith's definition of institutional racism again, "have the effect or consequence of subordinating an individual or group or maintaining in place the results of a past practice of now illegal overt racism."[60] This support is measured through roll call votes and personal interviews. It is important to note that the CBC has consistently introduced alternative budgets, with varying results, but never with it serving as the Democratic substitute.

CBC Representation and Party Politics

Manning Marable in *How Capitalism Underdeveloped Black America* argues that African Americans cannot receive the type of representation they need by way of traditional politics. Like Clay, he argues that historical racism hampered the achievements of African Americans. Unlike Clay, however, he argues that the acceptance of the two-party system, as it exists, is actually giving legitimacy to a system that is inherently racist. He writes:

> The instant the Black politician accepts the legitimacy of the system, the rules of the game, his/her critical faculties are destroyed permanently, and all that follows are absurdities. Black petty bourgeois politics is by definition an attempt to channel goods, services and jobs to black voters. In this endeavor, not a single white corporate executive or power broker would raise a veto. The Black Brahmin, the representative of the Black elite in politics, is praised for his responsible activities, or is perhaps criticized for being "too liberal," but all discourse takes place within the parameters of the system as it exists. After a period of years, the Black elected official actually believes that the meager level of services he/she provides for a constituency actually provides fundamental change for the Black masses.[61]

Marable would argue that the type of legislation needed to fight the root causes of crime is not the type of legislation Congress is willing to pass. Thus, for African

American leaders to support criminal justice legislation such as the Anti-Drug Act demonstrates a lack of leadership and a lack of willingness to understand or articulate to their colleagues structural racism in the criminal justice system. He writes that African Americans have long been subjected to incarceration in numbers highly disproportionate to their population. It is a means of a capitalist society to control and reserve a pool of black labor.[62] He argues that in recent decades it was conservative white America who pressured their elective officials to increase jail terms as a "desire to seek revenge and retribution."[63] That African American leaders would support these laws is an example of how the traditional political system can corrupt the values of African American leaders and the ability of these leaders to change the minds of their colleagues as well as the public through moral persuasion.

Ronald Walters and Robert Smith's book, *African American Leadership*, demonstrates that a number of scholarly opinions support similar conclusions. They contend that a political body such as Congress forces one to be an accommodationist, acting in accordance with other members of the legislative body so as not to be too creative or cause too much of a disturbance. African American members of Congress can be described as liberal integrationists. Most hold liberal ideas, but the system does not afford them the opportunity to advance liberal ideas, particularly if Congress and the public become weary of such ideas.[64]

As the CBC grows in size and as its members become more institutionalized (i.e., as they become ranking members or chairs of congressional committees) and as they become part of the Democratic apparatus within the system, challenges occur to the idea that there should be a continued advocacy for structural changes in the system. The issues advocated are the same as those that their congressional (non-CBC) colleagues advocate and those issues tend to be social security, prescription drugs, taxes, and issues that may fall under the distributive benefits category. Further, as a new and more diverse group of African Americans enter Congress, many members of the CBC may distance themselves from specific issues facing African Americans.

Also, as the districts CBC members represent become more diverse as a result of the decennial reapportionment, as individual members consider running for statewide offices in their respective states, and as individual members have a mixture of underclass and middle-class African American and white voters in their respective districts, there will be a tendency among some members of the CBC to distance themselves from race specific language.[65] Americans as a whole continue to believe in the idea of rugged individualism. Words such as "group rights" and terms such as "African Americans" seem to be divisive among some of the populace. Comments such as how can you be African American when you've never been to Africa or comments such as African Americans being divisive because of the reference to being African American can be heard throughout the public sphere. However, the CBC's stated mission is to fight on behalf of rights and equality for African Americans who have been discriminated against as a collective group. "For African Americans who acquiesce to Euro-American individualist ideas, their politics typically teeters between being either pragmatic (yet largely reactive and consistent with the dominant culture's political directives) or thoroughly delusive (often producing opportunists of the worst sort)."[66]

It is pragmatism that seems to have driven the support of some CBC members for the initial legislation that contained mandatory minimum penalties for crack cocaine. In addition, comments made by members of the CBC about the importance of electing Democrats, even if it means not supporting *issues* that the CBC would support, demonstrate that the CBC will have difficulty maintaining unity on interests that directly impact the African American community. Some CBC members also lament that because potential supporters see them as only advocating interests on behalf of African Americans, they are less likely to contact them on other issues.[67] For members seeking to obtain influence and prestige, the desire to distance themselves from collective benefits language and instead, operate within the parameter of euro-individualism can prevail.

The next section of this chapter focuses more specifically on structural characteristics that may pose a challenge to the unity of the CBC. These issues include the diversity of a member's district (i.e., whether his or her district is majority African American), seniority (i.e., the number of terms a member has served in the House of Representatives), leadership within the Democratic leadership hierarchy in Congress, and a member's position on a congressional committee.

Challenges to the Unity of the CBC

Understanding the makeup of individual districts position in the Democratic party and committee assignments are key to understanding challenges to the CBC to speak as one voice and to understanding the voting behavior of CBC members. African Americans have held key positions in the Democratic party and/or on Congressional committees, particularly over the course of the past several decades. Congressman Conyers, during the 96th Congress, chaired the Subcommittee on Crime. As more African Americans were elected to Congress, more served on the House Judiciary Committee. Their role in crafting, supporting, or opposing mandatory minimum laws will be further explored in a separate chapter. In reviewing the roll call vote of the bills that are explored, it should be interesting to see if other members took a cue from members of the House Judiciary Committee. It is important to state that the increased CBC membership, coupled with seniority and a desire of members to be on prestigious committees such as the Appropriations and Ways and Means Committees, can result in individual members becoming less interested in advocating for civil rights and social justice issues. As Pinney and Serra mentioned in an analysis of the CBC, "as African American leaders gain institutional responsibilities in the House by virtue of seniority, such as committee chairmanships, their support for CBC initiatives may become more tempered compared to their junior counterparts."[68] They go on to quote former Representative Gus Savage (D-IL) saying that "Black Committee chairmen don't act mainly as blacks, because the more dependent you are on white support for your positions, generally speaking, the less black you can act."[69] Further, "since 1992, black representatives have increasingly opted to serve on constituent committees that give them access to pork instead of policy and prestige committees to which members of the CBC have theretofore tended to gravitate."[70] As several members of the CBC mentioned during personal interviews during the early days of this research, there is no one voice in the CBC. CBC members represent districts that have a significant non-black population, thus they must do their best to represent those members as well. More than one CBC member continually expressed the view that there is no one voice in the CBC. Each member of the CBC has to vote in accordance to their districts and individual preferences. That these members expressed the view that there is no one CBC vote, one can surmise that there is no one substantive CBC strategy to correct unjust criminal and social justice policy within the CBC.

These challenges to the CBC render the Caucus ineffective in bringing about change to the mass base of African Americans because in pursuing positions in office, they often have to conform to the norm of getting elected. Smith writes: "Most Black leaders know that conditions of the Black underclass cannot be effectively addressed without changes in the structure of the national economy. Yet they act as if fundamental changes can come about as a result of playing the routine power games of Washington or city politics when clearly such changes, if possible, are only possible as a result of massive mobilization inside the Black community."[71] Moreover, as Smith also points out in his discussions of the CBC Alternative Budget, the CBC has a difficult time building coalitions among their colleagues who are more concerned with getting reelected. Many who are in the school of "politics is not enough" are concerned that the trappings of power (i.e., leadership positions) and the elections process (i.e., campaign fundraisers) will not address the serious problems faced by the African American community.

With just a few exceptions, every African American member who entered Congress joined the CBC.[72] There remains the challenge for the CBC to become a cohesive group when the solo membership requirement is to be an African American member of Congress. The CBC does not deny membership to conservative African Americans, those whose congressional districts contain less than 60 percent African Americans, or to those who are in a certain region of the country. With its membership being so diverse, how does the CBC remain united? How do individual members reconcile their personal motivations with the mission of the CBC, particularly if its support for African interests conflict with a desire to win support of non-African Americans, whether they are constituents or contributors to their campaigns. How does the CBC define itself given the political motivation of individual members? Robert Singh provides some additional insight in his book, *The Congressional Black Caucus: Racial Politics in Congress*. He outlines three perspectives of the CBC: "the Strategic Argument, the Ideological Case, and the Structural Explanation."

The Strategic Argument holds that the CBC is unable to offer perspective leadership because its top leadership is unable to articulate a strategy and goal among the rank and file members. Organizing these senior members of the CBC is key to establishing leadership and unity, thus a failure to organize this group creates disunity among the rank and file. This poses a challenge to the goal of successfully impacting change to the legislative agenda of Congress. On the issue of senior members of Congress, Singh says that it is difficult to be a member of a racially identifiable organization as one moves up the leadership and seniority ladder. He quotes Congressman Wynn (D-MD) as saying that he did not come to Congress to be anyone's conscience and Congressman John Lewis as saying that his goal is to better the lives of all Americans.[73]

The Ideological Perspective of the CBC, as outlined by Singh, maintains that the CBC will face challenges as a progressive race-conscious body seeking to bring about changes in a conservative, ideological environment. As Democrats seek to either take control or maintain control of Congress, the strategy to abandon liberal/progressive ideas becomes strong, thus the CBC becomes limited in persuading even members of their party to support progressive legislation.

The structural perspective maintains that racial majorities in a majoritarian system must adhere to the norm of the system. There are procedures and rules that a legislature must abide by—the CBC does not have power to divvy out resources that a legislator can get within the political system (i.e., pork programs). The CBC's influence, like other groups, is based on the institutional structure within which it operates.[74]

Singh argues that given that the CBC is a progressive racial minority within a moderate to conservative majoritarian system, it should give up its goals of lobbying on behalf of African Americans nationwide and focus, instead, on members' individual districts and utilize local patronage to articulate their ideas. In suggesting that CBC members should abandon their stated mission to work on behalf of African Americans and the disadvantaged nationally and instead work to serve their individual constituents only, Singh suggests that African Americans in Congress would be far more effective. Singh's suggestion fails to take into account that many issues that impact African Americans are systemic, thus offering benefits for individual constituents fails to address structural barriers to African American equality.

Using Singh's analysis, a group can actually be divided as its members obtain more seniority, a group that has limited impact on its own party because of its progressive mission/purpose, and a group that has little to offer in terms of punishment for members who stray from the Caucus position or incentives to maintain unity, will be challenged by individualist motives of its members, particularly if those motives stem from the type of district they represent or position within the party, or any other number of issues.

Diversity

Diversity includes the region a CBC member represents as well as the racial makeup of his or her district. A study that chronicles the diversity of the CBC is David Bositis' *The Congressional Black Caucus in the 103rd Congress*. During the redistricting process following the 1990 census, majority-minority districts were created in an effort to increase the number of African Americans in Congress (see Christina R. Rivers' The Congressional Black Caucus, Minority Rights, and the U.S. Supreme Court for a detailed account of the Voting Rights Act and the creation of majority-minority districts). This was a race-based policy designed to benefit African Americans collectively. Thus, members entering Congress at this time under this policy likely had an understanding of why the policy is necessary given past policies that denied African Americans equal access to the ballot and/or racial attitudes about African Americans that kept them from winning seats in Congress. Observing the political behavior of these members on issues that disproportionately and negatively impacted the African American community may be key to understanding if inclusion in the political system results in stronger race conscious behavior or pragmatic politics that emphasizes individual responsibility and the need to represent one's own district's constituents' desires as opposed to the desires of the African American community as a whole. During the 103rd Congress, not only did the size of the CBC nearly double, but the diversity in terms of age, region, and gender was such as had never been seen before. In addition, members of the CBC were rising into party positions, including Deputy Whip, freshman class president, and class parliamentarian.[75] Congresswoman Carrie Meek (D-FL), during the first year of her first term, was given a coveted seat on the House Appropriations Committee, the first freshman Democrat to hold that honor since the House Democratic Leader Richard Gephardt was elected to Congress.[76] These leadership positions and prestigious committee assignments may pose a challenge to keeping a cohesive coalition to adequately and effectively fight on behalf of those incarcerated as a result of mandatory minimum penalties for crack cocaine.

Two phenomena occurred in 1992: the election of a moderate southern Democrat (President Bill Clinton) and the election of 12 southern Democrats who did not come to office via a traditional liberal urban base. More importantly, an increase in the size of the CBC such as this gives members more influence when attempting to lobby non-CBC members as well as an enhanced incentive to lobby members. They are better able to bargain with non-CBC members using its 40 or so potential votes as a bargaining tool. These two dynamics would play out as Congress considered the president's crime bill and mandatory minimum legislation. As columnist Juan Williams pointed out in an article on the CBC, the new generation of CBC members was more independent minded and did not come into office on traditional civil rights issues. He writes "recent polling by the Joint Center has found that the new caucus members ran on the same issues that were at the top of White American's agenda: the economy, education, and crime."[77] Although this group of new members from the South was similar, they also had their differences. Congresswoman Eva Clayton of North Carolina, for example, was elected president of the freshman class. Her district is poor, rural, and half white and half black. As Williams points out, Clayton would consistently "have to deal with the tension between her commitment to the black caucus and her responsibilities to the new representatives who chose her as their leader."[78] In addition, with her district being split in terms of its racial makeup, close ties to many issues advocated by the CBC could prove to be detrimental. Congresswoman Cynthia McKinney, on the other hand, whose district in 1993 consisted of over 70 percent African American, expressed criticism of the CBC for not including southern African Americans in its agenda.

The CBC and Democratic Party Unity

There remains constant discussion among political pundits about the Democratic Party's taking African Americans for granted; that the Democratic Party relies on them for a sure vote. The LA Times reported in 1994 that President Bill Clinton's moderate "New Democrat" agenda with its focus on domestic issues such as crime and welfare was bringing about a racial divide within the Democratic coalition. "On an array of racially charged issues, tensions are sharpening between the administration and black leaders. Crime tops the list of disputes, with the Congressional Black Caucus and the Rev. Jesse

Jackson intensifying their full efforts to derail tough anti-crime legislation that Clinton urged Congress to complete quickly."[79]

President Clinton pushed for a crime bill that contained preventive measures but that was also fairly punitive in nature. The legislation also contained provisions to hire more law enforcement officers. Eleven CBC members voted against the rule to bring this bill to the House floor. Rather than working with these members to make the bill more in their favor, he sought to win the vote of conservatives by making the bill more punitive. This was viewed by many as an insult to many members of the CBC. Despite the obvious appeal to White moderates and conservatives, the mid-term elections held that year saw the loss of the Democratic majority in Congress. Democrats began to focus on winning back those seats. Their strategy to win back congressional seats was to continue to move toward the center, as opposed to adhering to progressive legislation that the CBC agenda calls for. Even with input from the CBC on criminal justice issues, Democrats in Congress and in the presidency use CBC members to help get out the African American vote (i.e., the promise that African Americans in Congress such as Congressman Rangel would chair a powerful committee if African Americans come out to vote).

Democrats also rely on the CBC to support its agenda, operating under the belief that much of the agenda is favorable to African Americans. When it comes to African American members of Congress needing the support of Democrats to put on the congressional agenda items such as mandatory minimums, the CBC may be ineffective regardless of the party in control of the House of Representatives. Democrats, it is important to remember, controlled Congress, at least the House of Representatives, during the 1980s when mandatory minimum laws from cocaine first passed, and they lost control of the Senate in 1982 and the presidency in 1980, and also the midterm elections of 1986 and the presidential election of 1988. This is important because it contributed to Democratic efforts to appear tough on crime. In addition, the CBC supported a Democratic president who until 2000 (as he was leaving office) refused to seriously address this issue. A race-conscious, progressive body cannot be effective in a conservative political environment to overturn legislation that may be detrimental to African Americans if the legislation (and the issue surrounding said legislation) appeals to White voters. "For a group with relatively few members, a near-complete one-party allegiance, a broad policy agenda, and distinctive ideological views, such an environment is not politically hospitable."[80]

CBC Voting Behavior

The studies on the CBC, although few in number, are mixed on the impact of the CBC as a collective group. Studies on voting cohesion indicate that the CBC is a highly cohesive voting bloc, but studies on Black leadership generally conclude that the CBC (1) has very little power in Congress and thus is more symbolic than a substantive caucus, and (2) members of the CBC are more interested in individualistic achievements rather than in acting collectively to respond to the issues affecting the African American community. Maintaining cohesiveness is very challenging as has been mentioned.

Perhaps, particularly as it relates to this research, the largest challenge in the number of rural members who entered Congress in 1993. When mandatory minimums for crack cocaine first passed, the CBC membership was dominated by members who represented large, urban centers in the North. By 1993 when several members began to openly express opposition to mandatory minimums for its impact on the incarceration rates of African Americans, rural America were was reaping profits from having prisons in their communities.[81] Pursuing jobs and economic development is a key priority among members of Congress, regardless of race. We will explore whether southern members were less likely to sponsor or co-sponsor legislation to reduce mandatory minimums; however, the rationale, beyond the scope of what was asked during the interview phase of this research and other comments gathered, will have to be left up to the reader.

Several scholars have written about how the racial makeup of a congressional district impacts a member's voting behavior. Most of the recent literature that examines the support of African American interests as measured by roll-call votes does so in the context of the creation of majority-minority districts. With little exception, the consensus seems to be that having more African Americans in Congress provides both descriptive and substantive representation. A few of these scholars are mentioned in this section of the research.

David Lublin in the *Paradox of Representation* argues that when African Americans and/or Latinos comprise 40 percent or more of a congressional district, the response to their interests increases substantially. He says that "interestingly, this threshold for responsiveness occurs at a much lower level than the 50-55 percent threshold generally required for the election of African American representatives."[82] In 1999, there were seven members of the Congressional Black Caucus with 40 percent of African Americans in their districts and 15 members of the CBC whose districts comprised of less than 55 percent of African Americans,[83] the threshold, according to Lublin, needed to ensure a victory.[84] If Lublin is correct, then these figures mean that there may be significant diversity within the caucus based solely on the percentage of African Americans in their districts. If the delegate approach is taken by members as opposed to the trustee approach, then divisions within the CBC can be expected.

Katherine Tate, in discussing the issues of representation, explains that it is difficult to truly put a member into one category (i.e., descriptive, substantive, symbolic) of representation because an institution such as Congress with its two-year election cycle, its constant bargaining and compromises, and the limited opportunity a member has to get one of several pieces of sponsored legislation passed, forces members to find other ways to offer representation that may seem symbolic to some while substantive to others in their districts. Tate says in one chapter that African American members of Congress are actually more liberal than the African American public. She says, for example, that the African American public was fairly conservative on welfare reform while the CBC almost unanimously opposed the legislation. Using data from the 1996 National Black Election Studies she writes: "The majority of Blacks (66 percent) favored the five-year life-time limit for welfare benefits for families. The vast majority (76 percent) also felt that welfare benefits should not be provided to immigrants immediately, but rather, immigrants should wait a year or more to receive them."[85] She mentions that the African American population seemed to be more conservative on the issue of crime as well, while the CBC seemed to take a more liberal position, particularly as it relates to the death penalty.[86] She writes: "In the 1996 survey, Blacks were asked where they stood on crime control on a scale from 1 to 7, where 1 was criminals should be apprehended and locked up, and seven was the government should do more to prevent crime. Blacks were roughly split between two extremes, with 45 percent favoring the tougher method of locking criminals up."[87] This idea that the CBC is more liberal than the African American public and that the CBC is, in essence, allowing elite opinion to drive public opinion is interesting, particularly when one is viewing the group as trustees for the African American public or as delegates for their individual districts. Again, this also may contribute to disunity within the CBC as members begin to express more moderate views as reflected by public opinion polling.

Some argue that without the increase of African Americans in Congress, the post-civil rights Congress would focus little on the issue of race. David Canon argues that not only do African American members of Congress provide representation for African Americans, but that they also seek biracial support prior to being elected and while serving in Congress, which means that they provide the necessary representation for Whites in their districts as well. He says there is a balancing act, and the biracial coalition is often sought only by members who appealed to Whites during their elections. He writes in explaining portions of his "supply-side theory" that

> . . . moderates who cultivate biracial themes and issue positions in their campaigns are expected to serve in the leadership, seek committee assignments that will aid both white and black constituents, address issues in the language of commonality, and engage in strong constituent service in both black and white communities . . . Black representatives who campaigned primarily in the African American community and see themselves as representing black interests will be less likely to serve in the leadership (because of the potential conflicts between the party's position and their role as the "conscious of the institution") and more likely to speak in the language of the politics of difference, focus on racial issues in legislation and committee preferences, and focus their constituency service efforts in the black community.[88]

In her study of African American leadership in Congress, Carol Swain explores the issue of whether the effectiveness of representation of Black interests in Congress is determined by the racial makeup of the District. She argues that in exploring the roll-call votes of members of Congress, African Americans can be properly represented by Blacks and non-Blacks alike in Congress. In other words, Swain argues that a White Democrat can and does provide representation for African Americans, as measured by roll-call votes.[89]

In an article on CBC voting behavior, Charles Jones hypothesizes that the CBC will exhibit higher levels of cohesion than other informal organizations in Congress because of a shared history of CBC members. Indeed, studies show that the CBC has a high rate of voting cohesiveness. Jones quotes a CBC member as saying that "the Black experience has put an extra responsibility on our shoulders."[90] Conventional wisdom is that a successful CBC is one that has a high level of voting cohesion and one that uses its voting bloc as leverage to influence policy. Jones explores roll-call votes in several categories to determine CBC voting cohesion. Among the categories were social, monetary, and external affairs. Social policy included education, benefits, housing, and law and order issues.[91] The Congresses (94th, 95th, and 96th) studied indicated that the CBC has the highest level of voting cohesion on social issues. There was a 100 percent cohesion level during the 95th Congress. Jones did not isolate any particular vote in the categories mentioned. A politically salient issue such as crime will create challenges to the unity of the CBC vote. Crime, as has been mentioned, is an issue that has been used by Democrats since the 1980s in order to garner votes, thus making it difficult for the CBC to unite around this issue, considering that the success of their party in winning congressional seats means success for CBC members in the form of chairing committees and subcommittees. It is an issue that has the African American community divided, as mentioned stated in the National Black Election Studies mentioned in Kathleen Tate's work, and because members with diverse districts are representing diverse regions of the country have to respond to different types of constituencies.

In an article on the congressional careers of CBC members, Alan Gerber makes the point that African Americans who are elected to Congress tend to maintain their seats for a longer period of time, which puts them in the position of having seniority on congressional committees. Theoretically, this seniority gives them more influence on committees and within the Democratic party. However, if the perception is that African Americans have power and are espousing a liberal agenda, they will continue to drive whites away from the party. He cites the Edsalls, who have studied the changes in party dynamics, as saying that "a consequence of the clear association of the Democratic Party and the Civil Rights movement is a backlash among some traditionally Democratic white voters."[92] Thus, the Democratic party will be torn between the agenda set forth by the CBC, and the need to cater to White conservatives. The significance of this article is that the majority of African Americans elected to Congress are Democrats, and thus their presence as a liberal group affects the public image of Democrats. Since the post–civil rights era, Republicans have painted Democrats as being too liberal or too supportive of big government programs. More importantly, as Gerber articulates in summarizing the position of Carmines and Stimson and the Edsalls on the issue of race and political parties, "if the decline in support of the Democratic Party among white voters is because of a perception of Democratic racial liberalism, the career of the African American House delegation will make it difficult to reverse this trend."[93] What this means is that African American legislators may have to temper their voting behavior and public criticism of Democrats who are not adhering to a progressive agenda to minimize the exit from the party of those voters who oppose the influence of a group such as the CBC. On the other side of this, Democrats may appear to be more conservative in their voting habits as a means to distance themselves from the perception that they are the party that upholds racial liberalism. These issues are a constant and American Americans and White legislators vote on politically salient issues.

By 1993, the CBC had many veteran members. As Gerber points out, the exit rate of the CBC in comparison to other House members (both Democrats and Republicans) has been much lower in the years studied (1974–1992). By 1993, there was still a handful of founding CBC members still in Congress. The year 1993 was also the year President Clinton began his first term. He was founder of the Democratic Leadership Council (DLC), which is a group that consists of moderate to conservative Democrats. President Clinton's continued appeal to conservative voters would become evident during major crime legislation lobbied for, the 1994 crime bill. CBC members, as Democrats, would have to weigh their decision making on roll call-votes on whether they should support the President or support the need to protect the interest of African Americans.

Alan Levy and Susan Stodinger in "Sources of Voting Cues for the Congressional Black Caucus" explore the hypothesis that the CBC will take more voting cues from one another than from the state delegation and party because ethnic and issue links are likely to be more determinative of voting behavior than geographic and other career advancement factors. What they found was that the CBC seemed to take its voting cues from their respective state (Democratic) party delegations just as often as they took cues from their fellow Caucus members. Also interesting is the authors' contentions that newer members of the CBC, because they are undergoing a socialization and learning process, may be compelled to take their voting cues from their respective state party delegation. The influx of new CBC members in 1993 will be analyzed in another section of this book to see if they were more likely to vote with the Caucus or the party on mandatory minimum penalties for crack cocaine. Levy and Stoudinger's article explores the 92nd Congress (1971–1972). There were several members who had served at least two terms in Congress by this time. It is important to note that even during the 92nd Congress, on social issues the CBC did not appear to be the dominant reference group for voting cues. Indeed, CBC members had a higher voting cohesiveness on social issues with their respective party delegation and with northern Democrats. The authors write "if black representatives hope to convert rhetoric and publicity in solid legislative accomplishments, they must begin to view the Caucus as a major source of voting cues, since this will enhance the possibility of cohesive and unified roll call behavior. Such unity will heighten the impact of the Caucus on the policy-making process, and more importantly may permit the Caucus to bargain and negotiate more effectively with other blocs in the House. . . Unity produces impact and unity can best be achieved if members look to the Caucus for voting cues and then act upon them."[94] The authors note that as the membership of the CBC grows, so will its diversity. Today, the CBC is much more diverse in terms of its makeup. The CBC's challenges will be to develop patterns of socialization so that its members view the Caucus as a major sources of voting cues, otherwise it will become an ineffective body with little impact on issues that impact public policy and the lives of African Americans.

Previously, Pinney and Serra found that the CBC exhibits a high degree of voting cohesion. They also suggest that the CBC is more united when there is a Republican president because there is less of an incentive or desire of the Caucus to support the president simply because he is a member of their party.[95] Overall, the study concludes that "while African American representatives are not always cohesive, they are more cohesive with the CBC on roll-call behavior than with their regional or state party delegations. Interestingly, the CBC's increased membership and diversity has not changed the overall homogeneity of the lot."[96] The suggestion by Giles and Jones that the CBC is likely to be more cohesive when there is a Republican in the White House may not prove to be the case. To appease a Republican president, a Democratically controlled House may pass legislation that is not what a progressive body such as the CBC would support. This creates a situation where individual CBC members have to weigh how their vote will affect their Democratic colleagues, their national constituency, and their individual districts. Their role as legislators may trump their role as representatives of a national Black constituency, and this may actually bring about a threat to CBC unity. As Democratic politicians attempt to win elections by catering to swing voters, which are primarily conservative Whites, progressive policies needed to address the issues of concern to African Americans may be sacrificed. This creates a conflict between the stated goals and mission of the CBC and the goals of Democrats in Congress, which is to win elections.

Challenges of Racism in the Two-Party System

Understanding the history of the two-party system is key to understanding how competition for White swing voters can compromise the interests of African Americans. When African American members of Congress have to interact with their fellow members of Congress, they often do so with the understanding that their actions can result in the loss of votes for the party they are tied to.

The Reconstruction era was one of great optimism for African Americans. African Americans in Congress and in state legislatures were heavily involved in crafting legislation to ensure full equality for all Americans. Some did so at a great risk to their personal lives. During Reconstruction, the White South—particularly southern Democrats—worked hard to undermine and overthrow the advancements of African Americans and the intrusion of the federal government, respectively. As Lerone Bennett tells us, the White South engaged in a reign of terror, while the White North and their Republican counterparts holding southern governorships turned a blind eye to the terror. It eventually resulted in a compromise that sacrificed the interests of African Americans. The well-known presidential election of 1876 (and the subsequent compromise of 1877) between Samuel Tilden and Rutherford B. Hayes was the beginning of the end to the progress African American leaders and their supporters made for civil, political, and human rights. African American interests and advancement were compromised for the sake of political expedience. The year 1877 was just 12 years after the end of the Civil War and two years after the passage of a major civil rights bill.

Bennett writes that the Civil Rights Act of 1875, which banned legal segregation "like the Civil Rights Act of 1964, signaled the last grasp of Northern idealism and the beginning of a period of white hysteria and reaction."[97] It is important to note that several signers of the U.S. Constitution wanted to abolish the institution of slavery, but because of opposition by slaveholding states in the South, a compromise was made. This is a constant theme that runs throughout the political history of the United States, one that African American leaders, at least those who founded the CBC, are cognizant of. When President Reagan began his presidential campaign in 1980 near Philadelphia, Mississippi, the place where three young civil rights workers were murdered during the 1960s, he advocated returning to states' rights. In 1986, just six years after his campaign, a more conservative political climate was underway and once again,

African Americans became the "sacrificial lambs" in the name of political expedience. Jesse Jackson Jr. articulates this point as well in his book that presidents and Congresses throughout history have used race to manipulate White voters. After detailing the history of the use of racially divisive terms during political campaigns, he writes:

> The conscious of modern-day conservative political resistant movement began in 1964 when "Mr. Conservative," Barry Goldwater, at the height of the civil rights movement, emphasized states' rights and local control as he won a mere fifty-two electoral votes—all of them from a solidly conservative Deep South . . . In 2000 Bush used a straight-out appeal to "conservatism" and strict "constructionalism": Gore's continuing "get tough on crime" appeal reflected the political success that both parties have had in identifying and linking "crime" and "welfare" in the public's mind with black people.[98]

The use of race to mobilize voters continues, which is why it is important for African American leaders to be united in opposing policies that disproportionately harm African Americans. The CBC's motto of "no permanent friends, no permanent enemies, just permanent interests" is an indication that the CBC understands that people and parties change their agenda items based on the mood of the political environment. As was mentioned, many Democrats during the 1990s switched to the Republican Party.[99] The CBC, which has in the past advocated for full employment (the Humprey-Hawkins bill), increased social spending (via their independent budgets), and an end to discrimination understood that if there is welfare dependency, it is because the issues they advocated for were not addressed by the legislative body. Yet, a Democratic president who encourages African American support was espousing the same type of rhetoric as a conservative Republican president. On this note, CBC member Jesse Jackson Jr. criticized President Clinton for a speech he gave to group of African American clergy in 1993 about the pathologies within the African American community, also stating that Dr. King did not die for Black men to be able to make babies and not care for them and to commit violence. Jackson writes:

> This is true, of course, but removing a sixty-year old floor beneath the poor and calling it "ending welfare as we know it," or placing a priority on balancing the budget rather than balancing the lives of unemployed and untrained poor people with jobs and adequate training, is not what King gave his life for either. Clinton made it clear that he knew jobs were the primary antidote to crime, but he offered no economic program of full employment and equal opportunity as a way out. President Clinton, leader of the wealthiest and most powerful government in the world, lectured black people about criminals, moral values, and degenerate behavior. He emotionally attacked the effects, but to correct the underlying causes offered only a passionate speech.[100]

In a political, economic, and social system where Whites have prevailed since the founding the country, any attempt to integrate a disadvantaged group will face obstacles. As Bennett writes, terrorist organizations during the Reconstruction era (i.e., the Klu Klux Klan) had as their fundamental purpose to restore White control and White domination of Black people.[101] He quotes from the testimony a governor of Alabama before a House Committee investigating the KKK as saying the following: "it came to be understood. . . That in this way [control over black people] Negroes might be made to toe the mark again, to do the bidding of the employer, to come up to a time a little more promptly, and do more work than they would otherwise do. It also soon became apparent that in this way the Negroes could be deterred from voting, as they naturally would."[102] Bennett writes: "The white conspirators wanted to take the black man's ballot so that they could take his bread. They wanted to depoliticize the black man so that they could dehumanize them."[103] African Americans and Republicans risked their lives to provide proper representation for African Americans. They were under constant death threats, further demonstrating that the struggles, even during reconstruction when the federal government occupied the South, were to be ongoing.

Nearly 100 years following Reconstruction, efforts continued to be underway to repress the African American vote and to make it difficult for African Americans to participate in the overall political process. In 1968, the United States Commission on Civil Rights issued a report about the political participation of African Americans in 10 southern states following the passage of the Voting Rights Act of 1965. The report found that both state and national organizations (Democratic and Republican) put procedures in place that made it difficult for African American candidates to run for office or to be part of the leadership for party organizations.[104] As was the case with Reconstruction, there was a disdain for federal intervention on behalf of African Americans by White southerners in power. This constant political battle, that, while in existence in the North, was most blatant and vocal in the South, shaped southerners' opinions about the federal government just as it shaped African American thought.[105] Thus, when President Reagan espoused states' rights and Republicans who took control of Congress during the 1990s pushed for a concept known as devolution (returning power to the states), it was within this framework that issues were crafted. This framework of southern rights and no federal intervention, based on the shared history of African Americans, should be one in which African American leaders organize against. Thus, the CBC, based on its mission, is at odds with a Democratic party that attempts to cater to voters who adhere to the aforementioned framework.[106]

In *Long Memory: The Black Experience in America,* Berry and Blassingame make the argument that the history of African Americans through their experiences in Africa, slavery, post slavery, and the present helped to develop the collective bond that African Americans continue to share today. They write: "Each generation, then, built on the lessons joined by the preceding ones about Africa, slavery, free negroes, economic and political oppression and opportunity, sexual myths and exploitation, the enduring value of church and school, white proscriptions and black protest, law and injustice, black nationalism, and military service."[107] The authors also tell us that since Reconstruction, African American politicians learned a very significant lesson about "the limits of coalition politics and the limits of officeholders they elected."[108] For example, politicians that were friendly to African American interests were at the same time against black control and empowerment.[109] Politicians friendly to Black interests also made compromises that were detrimental to African Americans for the purpose of political expedience. We assert that the African American vote and African American politicians were used in times of convenience and abandoned in times of White protests. The end of Reconstruction is an example of such disregard for African American freedoms. African Americans continued to support the Republican party, however, but became increasingly dismayed with the party's appeal to "white independents and southern liberal white Republicans."[110] In the words of Frederick Douglass at the 1883 Negro Convention, "If the Republican Party cannot stand for justice and fair play, it ought to go down."[111] Throughout the 1900s, African American politicians and scholars discussed the need for African Americans to vote independently and to not vote for the party out of habit. The realignment seen in the 1930s is an indication of the desire of African Americans to vote for a party that looks out for their interests. However, there remained cautionary voices about being loyal to one party. Berry and Blassingame write: "David Carthwright, in applauding the black shift to Roosevelt in 1936 as a sign of 'greater political maturity,' had warned in the pages of the *Crises* that blacks should not become tied to the Democratic Party. Continued support of Democrats would only result in another Negro political caste whose members will serve as perpetual decoys of the Negro masses."[112]

This history is part of the shared memory of African Americans, which in part, leads to the creation of a race-specific body in Congress such as the Congressional Black Caucus. In addition, the fact that every member of the CBC, with rare exception, is a member of the Democratic party shows that African Americans in Congress are tied to the Democrats in Congress and are looking out for the fate of the party as well as the interests of African Americans. The justification may be that African Americans will be better off under a Democratically controlled Congress, but in order to achieve that reality, CBC members are more hesitant to criticize their Democratic colleagues and president for fear that such criticism may harm the party.

There are those who argue that African Americans should look beyond the race connections they may have and focus on overcoming class divisions. In the *Declining Significance of Race,* William Julius Wilson indicates that the purpose of his book is to get African Americans and America to focus on the unique needs of the Black and disadvantaged poor. He states that when we view our problems as simply being a racial problem, we overlook the class stratification that exists in our community. The problem, he says, is that there is a middle-class bias to the policies advocated as a result. While many scholars, some of whom are included in this study, would underscore that African Americans, regardless of their class or status in society, experience racial discrimination that continues to prevent full equality, Wilson makes an important argument that one can draw upon when considering the issue of mandatory minimums. These laws targeted and impacted those in the inner cities, those individuals who have neither the power nor the clout to stop the massive incarceration of their youth.[113] Indeed, despite historic racism in the patrolling of African American communities by law enforcement officers and the incarceration of African Americans, middle- to upper-class professionals in Congress initially voted for criminal justice penalties that were discriminatory on its face and some admitted as much during the debate on these issues.

Wilson is not the only prominent scholar on African Americans who has written about the schism between race and class. Indeed, E. Franklin Frazier in *The Black Bourgeoisie* would make the same arguments. African Americans who moved up the socioeconomic ladder, even in times of overt racism, attempted to distance themselves from the African American have-nots. In fact, as Frazier writes, part of the education of the Black bourgeoisie was to distance themselves from the Black masses in terms of mannerisms and speech.[114] It leads one to the question of whether mandatory minimums for crack cocaine continue to exist 20 years after they became public policy and despite broad testimony that they are discriminatory and ineffective because the affected population is predominantly disadvantaged African Americans. President Clinton, as a moderate Democrat, seemed to understand the portion of the African American constituency that he needed to attend to most when he vowed to "End welfare as we know it," but when it came to Affirmative Action, he wanted to "mend it, not end it." President Clinton had a series of forums on race to satisfy the middle-class African Americans that were concerned about the proverbial glass ceiling, but when it came to the issue of the disparity in sentencing between crack and powder cocaine, he was extremely reluctant to support the elimination of those laws. In 1997, Attorney General Reno recommended that the disparity between powder and crack cocaine should be reduced. The CBC criticized President Clinton for not only his lukewarm support for the recommendation, but also because he did not recommend to Congress that the disparity between the two forms of the same drug be eliminated altogether.[115] In 1998, Congresswoman Maxine Waters, then Chair of the CBC, sent a letter to President Clinton criticizing him for (1) not supporting recommendations that did not go far enough in eliminating the disparity between powder and crack and (2) for claiming that he had consulted with the CBC on the sentencing recommendations. She issued a "Dear Colleague" letter essentially accusing President Clinton of misleading the public.[116]

Chronic conditions of poverty and joblessness lead Americans as a whole to believe that African Americans, particularly those living in inner cities' are uneducated, lazy, and criminals and thus deserve to be targeted by police and locked up. As Stephen and Abigail Thernstrom write in their book on race in modern America, "We speak of 'black crime' as a convenient shorthand, hard to avoid. And yet, unlike 'black poverty' it is a loaded phrase, implying some sort of innate predisposition to engage in illegal activity. As such it seems to echo racist assumptions about blacks being primitive people, gripped by passions, more likely to commit crimes unless controlled by white authorities."[117] They go on to discuss several public opinion surveys about the belief that African American are more prone to commit crimes. According to their evaluation of the survey results, African Americans tend to agree with the statements about Black criminal pathology. While the polls used by the Thernstrom's demonstrate a belief by the majority of Blacks believe that their fellow African Americans are "aggressive or violent," the results are misleading. These polls, when just taken at face value, can be a convenient excuse for African American politicians to support tough criminal justice policies. The Thernstroms cite a poll that was taken after the LA riots that concludes that 46 percent of blacks feel unsafe in their neighborhood and a 1992 poll by Gallop and Newsweek that shows 91 percent of African Americans concluded that crime was "one of the 'more urgent' problems facing their communities.[118] The translation is that African Americans support law enforcement tactics and tough jail sentences. What polls do not take into account is that while African Americans may support fighting crimes, they do not support the types of incarceration and targeting that occurs and such polls do not reflect alternative measures that African Americans may support.

Nevertheless, it is these types of polls that politicians, as was mentioned, used to justify a get tough on crime policy. It was these polls that President Clinton used to justify his refusal to recommend to Congress that mandatory minimum penalties be eliminated and/or the disparity between power and crack are eliminated. President Clinton seemed to understand the apparent split among African Americans on crime policy. The National Urban League's "The State of Black America, 1996" explains the paradox that African Americans are both the victims of crime and the victims of injustice by law enforcement and criminal justice policies. African Americans express anger and outrage over crime, which the poll results capture, but they are equally opposed to discriminatory treatment and the lack of efforts and resources they should go into solving the root causes of crime.[119] More polling data will be presented throughout this book.

The founding members of the CBC as well as Dr. King and other prominent African American leaders during the 1960s believed that the root causes of poverty and crime must be addressed by providing jobs and decent education opportunities, not by a full-scale incarceration of young people. Dr. King's advocacy of a Bill of Rights for the Disadvantaged was one of many demonstrations of his belief that several alternatives to reducing crime and poverty rates in African American communities and in white communities.[120]

Conclusion

The purpose of this chapter was to understand present and historical challenges African American leaders face as they attempt to represent African Americans as a collective group. It also shows how race has been a controversial issue within Congress and the American two-party system. Because race shapes the political opinion of White Americans as well as African Americans, the CBC in seeking to advocate issues to help African Americans will find obstacles from their fellow party members and from their non-Black constituents. While this chapter does not exhaust the literature on African Americans in Congress and race in the two-party system, it does offer challenges African American members face as legislators and as party members. The legislative process rewards variables such as seniority, party identity, and pragmatism while it discourages racial group identity and consciousness and the need to make structural changes to address poverty, homelessness, unemployment, and other issues that disproportionately impact the African American community. The next chapter provides an insight of the CBC views on race, crime and the Democratic party in their own words.

Keyterms

Endnotes

1 Champagne, Richard, and Rieselbach, Leroy. "The Evolving Congressional Black Caucus: The Reagan-Bush Years," in Champagne, Richard, and Rieselbach, Leroy. "The Evolving Congressional Black Caucus: The Reagan-Bush Years." In Perry, Huey & Parent, Wayne, eds.)*Blacks and the American Political System*, Gainesville, FL, University Press of Florida, 1995, p. 130.

2 Ibid.

3 Clay, William J., *Just Permanent Interests: Black Americans in Congress: Black Americans in Congress 1870-1991* (New York: Penguin USA, 1992), p. 117.

4 Barker, Luscious, Mack Jones, and Katherine Tate, *African Americans and the American Political System,* 4th edition (Upper Saddle River, NJ: Prentice Hall, 1999), p. 278.

5 Clay, p. 121.

6 Clay, p. 117.

7 At the beginning of every Congress, the CBC chooses its leadership. The CBC also has weekly Wednesday lunches (when Congress is in session) where members discuss key agenda items. In recent Congresses, the chair's position has been highly contested. The individuals who ran for the chair's position have varying ideas on the direction of the Caucus should go. Nevertheless, the election process and the structure of the group is an indication that the CBC continues to believe in its mission and in a desire to maintain cohesiveness.

8 Clay, pp. 178–179.

9 Barnett, pp. 32–38.

10 Ibid., p. 37.

11 Ibid.

12 Clay, p. 269.

13 Clay, p. 269.

14 Ibid., pp. 269–270.

15 Barnett, p. 40.

16 Barnett, p. 39.

17 Ibid.

18 Barnett, p. 40.

19 Jones, Charles. "Testing a Legislative Strategy: The Congressional Black Caucus's Action-Alert Communications Network," *Legislative Studies Quarterly*, XII, 4, November 1987, p. 523.

20 Ibid.

21 Barnett, p. 37.

22 See Tate, Katherine. *Black Faces in the Mirror: African Americans and Their Representatives in Congress*. Princeton, NJ: Princeton University Press, 2003, p. 67. Chapter 4; and Fenno, Richard F. Going Home: Black Representatives and Their Constituents. Chicago: The University of Chicago Press, 2003.

23 Tate, p.13.

24 Ibid.

25 Barnett, p. 31. (Please note, since the publication of Barnett's book, there have been two six African American senators—Carol Moseley Braun and Barack Obama, both were members of the CBC and, incidentally, both ran for the presidency.) Roland Burris (D-IL) was appointed to complete Barack Obama's term in the Senate after his election to the Office of the Presidency. In addition, William Maurice "Mo" Cowan (D-MA) was appointed in 2013 when Senator John Kerry was nominated to serve as Secretary of State in President Obama's cabinet. Further, Tim Scott (R-SC) served in the United States House of Representatives prior to his appointment to serve out a Senate seat vacated by Senator Jim DeMint in 2013. Corey Booker (D-NJ) was elected in a special election to serve in the United States Senate. Scott and Booker are serving in the United States Senate (as of 2014), which is historic in that two African Americans are serving in the United States Senate at the same time.

26 Clay, p. 342.

27 Bositis, David A, "1997 National Opinion Poll-Politics," (Washington, DC: The Joint Center for Political and Economic Studies), 1997, pp 6, 20).

28 Champagne and Riselbach, pp. 130–131.

29 Barnett, p. 30.

30 Barker, Tate, and Jones, p. 288.

31 The brief reference to interest group formulation is important because it provides an understanding of why people join groups and why groups are formed. While Elmer E. Schattsschneider (*The Semi-Sovereign People: A Realist View of Democracy in America,* Florence, KY, Wadsworth Publishing, 1975, Mancus Olsen (*The Logic of Collective Action*), Cambridge, MA, Harvard University Press, 1971, and Jefferey Berry (*The Interest Group Society), White Plains, NY, Longman Publishing Group (now combined with Allyn and Bacon), 1997,* focus on public interest groups that the average citizen can join, the CBC in declaring itself representative of all African Americans, is a de facto interest group. David Truman's *The Governing Process,* New York, Knopf, 1971, offers the Disturbance Theory, which postulates that the creation of interest groups are the results of two distinct processes that occur in society: the tendency of all societies to become more complex and the existence of some (nonspecific) societal disturbance that motivates individuals for collective action. Slavery, Jim Crow laws, and overt and covert discrimination and segregation fall under one long continuum of societal disturbance that mandates collective action among African American members of Congress.

32 Barnett, p. 30.

33 Salisbury, Robert, "An Exchange Theory of Interest Groups," *Midwest Journal of Political Science*, Vol XIII (Feb. 1969), pp. 1–32.

34 Barker, Jones, and Tate, *African Americans and the American Political System,* 4th ed., p. 54.

35 Ibid, p. 109.

36 Tate, p. 89.

37 Ibid., p. 89.

38 Ibid.,

39 Ibid., p. 92.

40 Kingdon, John. *Congressman's Voting Decisions*, 3rd edition. Ann Arbor:: The University of Michigan Press, 1989.

41 Barnett, *Public Policy for the Black Community: Strategies and Perspectives* (Port Washington, NY: Alfred Knopf, 1976), p. 9.

42 Ibid., p. 13.

43 Ture, Kwame, and Charles Hamilton. *Black Power: the Politics of Liberation.* New York: Vintage Books, 1992, 1967 (reissued in 1992 with a new afterword), p. 4.

44 Smith, Robert. *Racism in the Post Civil Rights Era: Now You See it, Now You Don't* (Albany: State University of New York Press, 1995), p. 33.

45 Clay, p. 369.

46 Smith, Robert. *We Have No Leaders: African Americans in the Post-Civil Rights Era.*, Albany, NY, State University of New York Press (September 1996), p. 192.

47 Clay, p. 95.

48 Barnett, *The Congressional Black Caucus*, p. 45.

49 Ibid., pp. 189–191.

50 Smith, *Leaders,* pp. 191–192

51 Clay, p. 95.

52 Smith, *Leaders*, pp. 206–207

53 Smith, Robert. "Politics Is Not Enough: The Institutionalization of the African American freedom Movement."In Ralph Gomes and Linda Faye Williams, eds., *From Exclusion to Inclusion: The Long Struggle for African American Political Power*. Westport, CT: Praeger, p. 113.

54 Ibid., p. 114.

55 Ibid.

56 Ibid., p. 115.

57 Ibid., pp. 116–117.

58 Clay, p. 279.

59 Gomes and Williams, pp. 117–121.

60 Smith, *Racism in the Post Civil Rights Era*, p. 33

61 Marable, Manning *How Capitalism Underdeveloped Black America*, updated edition (Cambridge, MA: South End Press, 2000), pp. 170–171.

62 Ibid., p.126 .

63 Ibid.

64 Walters, Ronald, and Robert Smith, *African American Leadership* (New York: State University of New York, 1999).

65 Dawson, Michael C., *Black Visions: The Roots of Contemporary African American Political Ideologies* (Chicago: The University of Chicago Press, 2001); also see Darryl Harris' "The Duality Complex."

66 Harris, Darryl, "The Duality Complex: An Unresolved Paradox in American Politics," *Journal of Black Studies,* (July 1997), p. 789.

67 Wallison, Ethan, "Black Caucus Faces a Changing of the Guard: Group Becomes More Mainstream on Several Fronts, Which Brings its Trade-Offs," Roll Call, Monday, September 9, 2002.

68 Pinney, Neil, and George Serra. "A Voice for Black Interests: Congressional Black Caucus Cohesion and Bill Sponsorship." *Congress and the Presidency*, Washington, DC (Spring 2002): 75.

69 Ibid.

70 Derfer, Jeremy, "The New Black Caucus," *The American Prospect*, Princeton, March 27–April 2000.

71 Smith, "Politics Is Not Enough," p. 119.

72 Senator Edward Brooke (R-MA) and Congressman J.C. Watts (R-OK) did not join the CBC. As a result of the November 2010 election, the 112th Congress sat two African American Republicans, Allen West (R-FL) and Tim Scott (R-SC). West joined the CBC, while Scott opted not to join the group. (See also "Is There a Place for Republicans in the Congressional Black Caucus?", The Root, http://www.theroot.com/articles/politics/2010/09/will_a_black_republican_join_the_congressional_black_caucus_come_november_3.html September 17, 2010, accessed on May 20, 2014.

73 Singh, Robert, *The Congressional Black Caucus; Racial Politics in the United States' Congress* (Thousand Oaks, CA: Sage Publications, 1998).

74 Ibid.

75 Bositis, David. *The Congressional Black Caucus in the 103rd Congress*. Washington, DC: The Joint Center for Political and Economic Studies, 1994, pp. 20–21.

76 Ibid., p. 117.

77 Williams, Juan,"From Caucus to Coalition: Can the Black Freshman Class in Congress Shape the Clinton Program?" *The Washington Post*, Sunday, January 10, 1993, C2.

78 Ibid.

79 Brownstein, Ronald. "Clinton's New Democrat Agenda Reopens Racial Divisions; President's Ideas on Crime and Welfare Don't Sit Well with Blacks in Congress. Liberals' Dissatisfaction May be Rising." February 9, 1994, Wednesday, Part A, Page 5, Column 1.

80 Singh, p. 17.

81 There remains a debate as to whether rural America has actually benefited from prison construction. Indeed, there has been an increase in prison construction since the 1980s. According to the Sentencing Project, rural prison construction increased by 8.1 percent between 1985 to 1995, and for every 100 inmates, 35 jobs were created. Yet, the authors of the Sentencing Project publication assert that rural communities did not receive an economic boom as a result of the prison construction. See "Big Prisons, Small Towns: Prison Economics in Rural America," published by the Sentencing Project and authored by Ryan King Marc Maur and Tracy Huling, Feb. 2003. Also for additional insight on the prison boom in rural America, see a PBS documentary entitled *Prison Town, USA* by Katie Galloway and Po Kitchens. For additional perspectives written 20 years after the prison boom began, see the following two *New York Times* articles: "Plan to Close Prison Stirs Anxieties in Rural Towns," Fernanda Santos, January 27, 2008, and "Its Mill Days Gone (And Not Coming Back), a Small Town Tries Plans B &C," Katie Zezima, September 2, 2007.

82 Lublin, David. *The Paradox of Representation: Racial Gerrymandering and Minority Interests in Congress,* (Princeton, NJ: Princeton University Press, 1997), p. 73.

83 Tate, Katherine, *Black Faces in the Mirror: African American and Their Representatives in Congress,* p. 67.

84 Congressman Stokes also cites this critical 55 percent threshold. This number is used to select CBC members to participate in this study. In the interview chapter, the researchers will remain aware of Lublin's argument that districts with less than 40 percent African Americans in them, the majority of Congressional districts, are the least responsive to African American interests. This researcher will explore whether African Americans who represent districts that are less than 40 percent African American are also least responsive to issues affecting African Americans as a whole.

85 Tate, p. 93.

86 Ibid.

87 Ibid.

88 Canon, David, *Race, Redistricting, and Representation: The Unintended Consequence of Black Majority Districts.* (Chicago and London: University of Chicago Press, 1999), pp. 144–145.

89 Swain, Carol, *Black Faces, Black Interests: The Representation of African Americans in Congress* (Cambridge, MA: Harvard University Press, 1993). Swain's conclusion has drawn much criticism among scholars who study race and representation. Among the criticism is that representation is very broad and thus cannot be measured simply by looking at roll call votes. Some, such as Whitby in *The Color of Representation*, argue that it is the presence of more African Americans that came about as the result of redistricting that provides for a discussion of issues impacting African Americans, even if sufficient legislation is prevented from reaching the House floor.

90 Jones, Charles, "United We Stand, Divided We Fall: Analysis of the CBC's Voting Behavior, 1975–1980," *Phylon: The Review of Race and Culture,* 48(1) (1987), 27.

91 Jones, p. 29

92 Gerber, Alan, "African Americans' Congressional Careers and the Democratic Delegation," *Journal of Politics,* (August 1996), 841.

93 Ibid, p. 842.

94 Levy and Stoudinger, p. 43.

95 Pinney and Serra, "The Congressional Black Caucus and Vote Cohesion: Placing the Caucus Within House Voting Patterns," *Political Science Quarterly*, 52(3) (September 1999), 598.

96 Ibid.

97 Bennett, Jr., Lerone, *Black Power USA: The Human Side of Reconstruction 1867–1877*, p. 395.

98 Jackson, Jr., Jesse with Frank E. Watkins, *A More Perfect Union: Advancing New American Rights,* (New York: Welcome Rain Publishers, 2001), p. 206.

99 Earl and Merle Black are key sources on the phenomena of party-switching during the 1990s. They expand their research in a book entitled *The Rise of Southern Republicans,* Cambridge, MA, Belknap Press of Harvard University Press, 2003. This book provides a thorough examination of racial and party politics over the past five decades.

100 Jackson and Watkins, p. 218.

101 Bennett, p. 364.

102 Ibid., p. 365.

103 Ibid., p. 365.

104 *Political Participation in the United States: Report for the United States Commission on Civil Rights* (Washington, DC: United States Government Printing Office, 1968).

105 In *Race, Class and Poverty,* Paul Lewinson argues that southern political thought is shaped by the presence of African Americans in the political system. Race impacted every aspect of southern life in the pre and post Civil War years. For the poor White southerner, the fact that he was elevated above African Americans empowered him, thus efforts to fully integrate African Americans met with a steady stream of opposition. African American leaders with a predominantly Black population had to be cognizant of this in their fight for equality and African American members of Congress today with a more diverse population, have to still be cognizant of this. As they consider legislation, they begin to consider the views of groups that have fought against African American equality, which makes providing African American leadership more difficult (*Race Class and Party: A History of Negro Suffrage and White Politics in the South*, New York: Oxford University Press, 1932).

106 Hacker, Andrew. *Two Nations: Black, White, Separate, Hostile, Unequal*. New York: Ballantine, 1992. Myrdal, Gunnar. *An American Dilemma: The Negro Problem in American Democracy*. Transaction Publishers, Piscataway, NJ, 1995. These are two key books used to understand the role race plays in shaping the political thought of both African Americans and whites. The two books explain that Whites have long feared and felt African Americans to be inferior, which explains why they could uphold the principles of the Constitution at the same time African Americans were enslaved, under strict segregation laws, and continue to experience racial inequities stemming from the racial caste system that has long existed in the country. African Americans are forever conscious about how they are viewed by White Americans. Hacker points out that several polls explain the varying viewpoints. On the issue of crime, Hacker argues that White stereotypes of African American males being sexual predators and violent criminals impact their views on crime. He says Willie Horton was a big issue because it played on the stereotype of African American males having a constant desire to rape White women. Again, these beliefs shape public thought, which contributes to the reason Congress overwhelmingly voted for legislation that would punish crack users more harshly than users of any other drug. The images of African American violence influenced White political thought.

107 Berry, Mary Frances, and John W. Blassingame, *Long Memory: The Black Experience in America* (Oxford: Oxford University Press, 1982), pp. x-xi.

108 Ibid., p. 154.

109 This is similar to the argument made by Ture and Hamilton in *Black Power: The Politics of Liberation*. They write that African Americans must understand that in many cases, coalition politics does not benefit them. They argue that African Americans are often "allying with forces clearly not consistent with the long-term progress of blacks: in fact, the whites enter alliance in many cases to impede that progress," (p. 72).

110 Berry and Blassingame, p. 166.

111 Ibid.

112 Ibid., p. 179.

113 In addition the literature mentioned in a separate chapter, and an article from the *National Journal* entitled "Targeting Harlem, Not Hollywood" also discusses the unequal treatment/targeting those in inner cities as opposed to the suburbs. [W. John Moore, "The Weekly on Politics and Government," National Journal, (February 11, 1995), p. 288]

114 Frazier, E. Franklin, *Black Bourgeosie*, (New York:Free Press Paperbacks, 1957) pp. 77–78.

115 Holmes, Steven A., "Black Lawmakers Criticize Clinton Over Cocaine Sentencing," *The New York Times* (National Edition) (Thursday, July 24, 1997), A15.

116 A copy of the "Dear Colleague Letter" dated July 22, 1998 is in Appendix 2.

117 Thernstrom, Stephan, and Abigail Thernstrom, *America in Black and White: One Nation, Indivisible* (New York: Simon and Shuster, 1997), p. 259.

118 Ibid., p. 260.

119 Stone, Christopher E., *The State of Black America* (Washington, DC: The National Urban League, January 1996).

120 A discussion of the Bill of Rights for the Disadvantaged and a discussion of why African American leaders should not support compromise on these issues can be found in Chapter 8 of *Why We Can't Wait* (New York: Harper and Row, 1963).

ACTIVITY 1
Putting yourself into the role of a CBC member...

1969 - Now

Instructions:

In the space above, pretending that you are an African American member of Congress, please describe why it might have been important to create the CBC. Please consider politics, the social climate of 1969, and anything else you think is important in your response.

A Chapter 2 Exercise

[Please tear out your completed response so you can turn it in to the instructor]

ACTIVITY 2

In the boxes below, please name and briefly describe the three phases
of the CBC . . .

A Chapter 2 Exercise

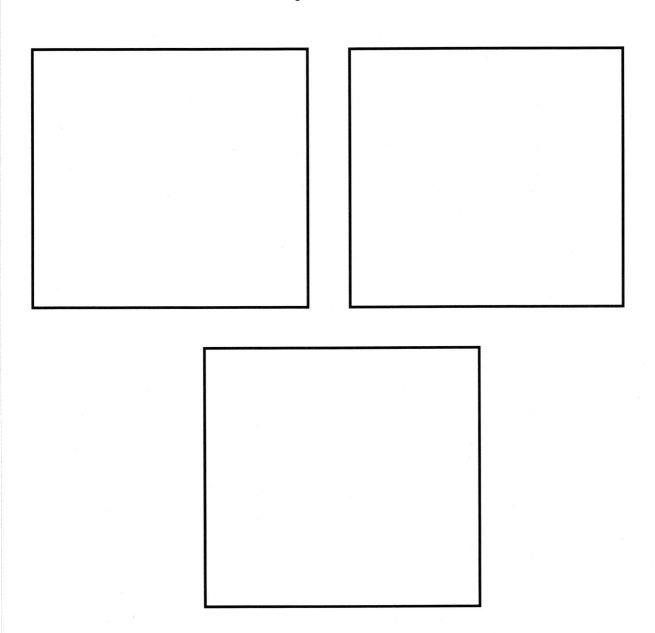

[Please tear out your completed response so you can turn it in to the instructor]

ACTIVITY 3

Applying a book concept to a real-life issue...

Institutional Racism

Drug Legislation

Instructions:

Part 1: Within the institutional racism box, please define institutional racism, based on that specific section of the chapter and using any outside research using the Internet.

Part 2: Within the drug legislation box, please describe how you think drug legislation during the 1980s might be connected to institutional racism. The chapter provides some examples to help you.

A Chapter 2 Exercise

[Please tear out your completed response so you can turn it in to the instructor]

3

The CBC and the Democratic Party: Personal Reflections of CBC Members

Chapter 3 Synopsis: This chapter provides an examination of the CBC's connections with the Democratic party. The CBC has primarily consisted of Democratic members. As such, in addition to being concerned about the interests of the African American community, the group also has to be concerned about the strength of its party, as measured by successful reelections. This means that the CBC must engage in pragmatic politics. If a Democratic party member supports maintaining the crack/powder disparity, the CBC may seek to modify its criticism so as not to damage the election prospects of its party members. This chapter also explores the challenges a racially identified group has in a Congress where both Democrats and Republicans use racial politics in political campaigns.

Based on personal interviews with CBC members serving in the 107th Congress, the authors created a political behavior typology of CBC members based on level of responsiveness to African American interests on mandatory minimum penalties for crack cocaine and attitudes and commitment to the Democratic party. For example, in our typology it is possible to be placed in a passive trustee, passive delegate, active trustee, and active delegate category. In our typology, a CBC member would be placed in the active-trustee category if he or she has more than 55 percent African Americans in his or her congressional district, sponsored or co-sponsored legislation on mandatory minimums for crack cocaine, believed that the CBC should make the issue of mandatory minimums a top priority for the group, and that Democrats should make the issue a priority. A CBC member would be classified as an active-delegate if he or she had less than 55 percent of an African American population in his or her congressional districts, sponsored or co-sponsored legislation on mandatory minimums for crack cocaine, and believes that both the CBC and the Democratic party should make this issue a top priority. This member would be categorized as an active delegate because he or she co-sponsors legislation dealing with this issue, wants it to be a top priority, but does not have the number of African Americans in his or her district that would result in him or her doing more to advocate against this policy. (It is important to note that this typology is a very loose variation of scholar James David Barber's four types of presidential character as articulated in *The Presidential Character: Predicting Performance in the White House* and the delegate versus trustee model of representation. A trustee model, as expressed by English theorist and politician Edmund Burke (1729–1797), articulates the idea that elected officials, while listening to and representing the best interest of their constituents, should ultimately determine what is the best interest for their constituents.[1] A delegate, on the other hand, has an obligation to determine what is in the best interests of their constituents by directly responding to what said constituents express what is best for them.[2] So the former is a model of representation putting the elected official at the center of decision making, and the latter is a model of representation putting the constituent at the center of decision making.

Since African Americans got the franchise after the Civil War, they have had a tenuous relationship with both the Republican and Democratic parties. They began as Republicans, the party of Abraham Lincoln. However, because of measures to keep African Americans from voting in the post–Reconstruction era, African Americans were absent from Congress for decades. In fact, Congressman George H. White of North Carolina was the last African American Congressman elected during this era when he left in 1901, and he was a member of the Republican Party. It would be approximately

90 years later when North Carolina would send another African American member to Congress; this time it would be Congresswoman Eva Clayton of the Democratic Party. However, African Americans did make a return to Congress during the 1920s, and as Democratic presidents such as Franklin Delano Roosevelt began to attract the African American vote, the Democratic party would see additional African Americans joining the Democratic ranks in the House of Representatives. By the 103rd Congress (1993–1994), African Americans would see record numbers in Congress (39) and all but one were members of the Democratic party. Congressman Gary Franks, already a sitting member of Congress by the 103rd Congress, was a member of the Republican party. He would be joined by Republican J.C. Watts in a subsequent Congress. Given that the CBC was firmly committed to the Democratic party, it is important to explore their personal observations about the political and legislative behavior on mandatory minimums before moving forward to more specific legislative action that will be included in the next two chapters of this book.

By the late 1990s and early 2000s, much had been written about the enormous prison population and how drug policies crafted during the 1980s, particularly mandatory minimums for crack cocaine, had contributed to the large number of first-time, nonviolent drug offenders entering the prison population. During the 107th Congress, several CBC members were interviewed to obtain their views on mandatory minimum laws for crack and on the ideological leanings of the CBC and the Democratic party. During this Congress, there were 38 CBC members, including two newly elected members.[3] In addition, there were a total of 12 new CBC members since the 1995 vote on mandatory minimum penalties for crack cocaine was taken. Like the CBC members who entered Congress at the beginning of the 103rd Congress, these members represented diversity in terms of gender and region.

CBC Ideology

Despite its diversity, members of the CBC are considered to be ideologically liberal. In other words, regardless of what roll-call votes, legislation introduced and co-sponsored and other mechanisms used by scholars to measure ideology tell us, where do individual members of the CBC identify themselves on the issue of ideology? The CBC has received high marks from Americans for Democratic Action, a liberal political organization that looks at the voting records of members of Congress and provides a rating for members based on whether they are considered liberal by the organization's standard. However, when one isolates the CBC's vote on criminal justice issues, members do not vote as a cohesive group. Politically salient issues such as crime, used by Democrats to win white voters who left the Democratic party because of an impression that Democrats had become too liberal on crime and welfare issues, contributes to the cleavage within the CBC.[4] The CBC, in general, and during the 107th Congress, in particular, consists of Democrats. Loyalty to the party and loyalty to the Caucus are weighed when considering these issues.

Interviews of CBC Members

To help grasp the complexity and importance of the CBC culture and other nuances associated with drug policies, the authors completed field research in order to interview several CBC members; some were members when the majority of votes addressed in this manuscript were taken, while other members have joined the CBC since this relevant legislation was introduced. Based on this level of detail, the findings with respect to attitudes and impact are clearer. Data were collected with voluntary consent of those respondents interviewed.

During the 107th Congress, 15 of the 38 members of the CBC were interviewed by one of the authors of this book. The interviews took place over the course of five months from December 2002 throughout April of 2003.[5] The members interviewed consisted of 10 men and five women and represented regional diversity. At least one member from the Northeast, Midwest, South, West, and Southwest participated in the interviews, and at least one member who served in Congress during the 1980s, 1990s, and 2000s participated in the interviews. In addition, there were members among this group who served as the Chair of the CBC at some point during their congressional career. Further, the members interviewed represent congressional districts that have as few as 42 percent of African Americans to as many as 66 percent. The interviewees were asked a variety of questions to determine their views on the legislative process, crime, political behavior of Democrats, racial attitudes toward mandatory minimums for crack cocaine, and the stated impact mandatory minimums for crack cocaine has had on their congressional districts. A questionnaire was given to each member at the beginning of the interview and members responded to the questions as they were read by the researcher. These interview results come directly from the members and, thus, do not reflect staff bias. With two exceptions, there was no staff present when the interviews took place. There were 14 questions on the survey; some were open-ended and some were closed-ended.

The results were divided into six categories. The first category addressed CBC attitudes toward mandatory minimum penalties. The second category addressed CBC attitudes toward the legislative process. The third category addressed CBC attitudes toward Democratic political behavior. The fourth category addressed CBC and Democratic ideological shifts. The fifth category addressed the self-reported effectiveness of the CBC. The final category addressed the CBC's views on interest groups. Following these categories is a typology based on the level of representation of African American interests and attitudes and commitment to Democratic unity.

The fact that CBC members join an exclusive, race-identified body indicates a degree of commitment to representing the African American community as a whole. When Congressman Rangel rejected the application of a White member who wanted to join the CBC in 1975, he said, "the Caucus symbolizes black political development in this country. We feel that maintaining this symbolism . . . . Is critical at this juncture in our development . . . . ."[6] His reasoning was that "just as separate caucuses of Democrats and Republicans 'have unique interests to protect and project and would not include non-party members in their respective groups, we, too, have the same needs and concerns.'[7] Members are considered to have a high level of responsiveness to African American interests if they represent a district that consists of more than 55 percent or more of African Americans.

According to Lublin, members with 40 percent of African Americans in their congressional districts are more conscious and responsible to the needs of African Americans, and their responsiveness increases as the percentage of African Americans in their districts increases. Further, those members with a significant percentage of African Americans in their districts are more restrained in efforts to run deracialized campaigns, thus they tend to support black issues.[8] Further, a caucus that is exclusively Democratic has party ties that they must maintain. The degree to which they maintain these ties, as measured by support or opposition to legislation and a self-reported belief that Democrats should make this a top agenda item, puts members in a category of either low or high Democratic unity. A CBC member with over 55 percent of African Americans in his or her district and who believes that Democrats should make mandatory minimum penalties for crack cocaine a top agenda item would be considered, for the purpose of this newly created typology, to have a high level of representation of African American interests as a low level of Democratic unity. Below the responses of CBC members to the questionnaire is a description of each category within the typology.

CBC Attitudes on Mandatory Minimum Penalties for Crack Cocaine

In response to whether a member supported or opposed mandatory minimum penalties in general and mandatory minimums for crack in particular as well as the disparity between the treatment of those convicted of crack versus powder cocaine, each of the members interviewed oppose mandatory minimums in general and mandatory minimums for crack specifically. Further, all believed that the law is discriminatory against African Americans. However, one member who represents a southwestern state with less than a 45 percent African American population in his or her congressional district somewhat justified the disparity because, in the member's opinion, crack cocaine use creates a more violent behavior than powder cocaine. The member stated that people using powder cocaine can continue to work each day without significant behavioral problems. Even so, this particular member did believe that the laws were discriminatory and opposed the laws.

In contrast, a member who represents a large, urban district in the Midwest that has an African American population of approximately 60 percent said in response to the legal disparity of the treatment the following:

I think this is one of the real mysteries of our nation. It is also one of the inconsistencies. It's also part of the oppressive nature and the inability of our society to actually treat each and every one as being equal. The reality is, you look at those drugs that are the drugs of choice for which population—poor people, minorities, individuals who do not have much resources obviously use that which is cheapest or that which can be obtained. So crack cocaine is the drug of choice for many of them because that's what they can get. Powder is the drug of choice for individuals who are in a different socioeconomic category which in many instances put them in a different race category. The most that you can say is that this is blatantly unfair. But if you get right down to the bottom of it, I mean it's hard to find any logical explanation. I've never been able to find one. So I think it is just blatantly unfair.[9]

The two perspectives above highlight a contrast between someone who has a historic sense of race in the criminal justice system and race in America and someone who accepts reports that people who use crack are more dangerous than those who use powder. The individual who cited the reports also said that he is from a tough law-and-order environment that does not accept excuses for crime. Besides, the member went on to say, African Americans know that the law is discriminatory, yet they continue to use crack.

When asked if they believed that mandatory minimum penalties have impacted their respective states in general and congressional districts in particular, all of the members except for one responded that the legislation has had a tremendous impact on their state. The member who represents the Southwest district was unsure if it impacted his or her state.

Self-reported Impact on Congressional Districts

With regard to the specific impact on one's congressional district, all but one member stated that mandatory minimum penalties have impacted his or her congressional district. The responses ranged from members reporting a decrease in population resulting from the incarceration of men and women, which leaves children without mothers and fathers, an increase in tax burdens due to prison construction, young people being taken out of the community for years at a time, which leads to destabilization, young people returning to the community without having been educated and trained, causing additional problems, and felony disenfranchisement. One member lamented that so many prisons have been built in his district that as soon as they are built, they are filled to double their capacity. Members felt strongly that this legislation has impacted African Americans in their respective states and districts.

The self-reported impact of this legislation on African Americans in their districts coupled with the fact that all of the members stated that they believe that these laws are discriminatory against African Americans, tells us that CBC members are very conscious of racial discrimination in the criminal justice system, which puts them at odds, at least symbolically, with the Democratic leadership that refuses to address this issue. However, even within the CBC, there is some level of disagreement about whether the law remains justifiable. For example, among those interviewed, two believed that mandatory minimums are discriminatory against African Americans; however, they offered a qualification to the response. One of the two commented that it appeared to be, but that there was a justification for it. Another member from the South commented that it is discriminatory against African Americans, but that he is not sure if the intent of the law was to be discriminatory.

CBC Attitudes Toward the Legislative Process

During the interviews, CBC members were asked if they would oppose comprehensive bills if they contained mandatory minimums for crack cocaine. This question was asked because the Anti-Drug Abuse Acts of 1986 and 1988 were comprehensive bills that contained this penalty. The question also asked if the member believes that the CBC should oppose such comprehensive bills if they contain provisions that would be especially harmful to the African American community. In this two-part question, all of those responded said that they would as individuals oppose such bills. The differences in responses came from the second part of the question. There was no consensus as to whether the CBC as a group should oppose such bills. Below is a sample of the responses:

A member who represents a large, urban district in the Midwest that has an African American population of approximately 60 percent said:

> Well, I would say yes, but you have to also understand that the CBC is not monolithic. Members of the Congressional Black Caucus represent other population groups, almost as much as they represent African Americans. You don't have to have an African American or a predominantly African American district to get elected. Take for example J.C. Watts, who is not a member of the Caucus, but his district has few Blacks or Julia Carson from Indiana whose district is not nearly 50 percent African American or any other districts where there are no more than 50 percent African Americans. My district is probably no more than 57 or 58 percent African American. So, there are no monolithic African American districts and I think that politicians do what they need to do to represent their districts in order to get elected and reelected . . . Yes, I think that the Caucus, if it would, should take a position that there ought to be enough agreement within the Caucus to agree on this issue there are many issues that you will not be able to get unanimous thought of the CBC . . . But there is an old saying: Where I sit on the turtle is where I stand. People come from different parts of the country with different districts and their thinking is shaped by the environment from which they come.[10]

A member who represents a southern district that is just 13 percent rural with an African American population of 45 percent concurred with the statement that the CBC does not vote, rather, individual members of the CBC vote. Thus, when we are asking a question about how the CBC voted on an issue, we should keep in mind that there is no CBC vote. To be fair, the member did state that the CBC, given the impact of the sentencing laws on the African American community, has tried to coalesce around this issue, but there remain various views on drug policy within the CBC. It is interesting that the above member serves on the House Judiciary Committee (during the 107th

Congress), which provides the member with intimate knowledge on this issue, and that he has strong views about this issue as indicated via floor statements and this personal interview, yet, he does not feel the urgency of persuading CBC members to unite in their voting behavior on this issue.[11]

A CBC member who represents an urban, economically depressed district in the Northeast that has an African American congressional population of 58 percent said that the CBC should oppose this law and any law, whether intentional or unintentional, that discriminates against a particular group. He said it is an issue of fairness. These comments were echoed by other members, including one who represents a large, urban district in the Midwest with 66 percent of its population consisting of African Americans. S/He said that the African American community has long suffered from inequities in every aspect of the criminal justice system; therefore, the CBC should speak out against the laws. The responses to this question can be divided among those who believe that the CBC should oppose such comprehensive bills supports the idea of members making the decision based on the politics of their respective congressional districts and those who believe the CBC should oppose the bills because African Americans as a whole are disproportionately impacted by them and do not receive fairness and justice in the criminal justice system. The latter group believes that achieving equity and fairness should be more important than reelection concerns or upsetting the unity of the Democratic party.

Because CBC members believe these laws are discriminatory against African Americans and believe that the 100:1 disparity is unjustified, they were asked about the Democratic party's rationale in introducing and supporting this legislation. Most members (60 percent) are unsure of the rationale for the law. Among those who are unsure, there seemed to be a belief that racism had more to do with the passage of the laws. Some members commented that the negative view of African American males by the American public led to the harsh laws, but they did not want to go as far as saying this is the reason members passed the laws. One member stated that he actually sought to find out by asking his colleagues who were in Congress at the time, but he has never been given a straight answer. A member who represents a district in the Southwest insisted that the differences between crack and powder cocaine were the reason for the disparity, and a member in the Northeast with a sizable African American population also conceded that crack had an intense high, thus, like alcohol during pre-prohibition era, society responded to the perceptions about the drug itself. Those who responded with a "no" to this question believed that race had more to do with the disparity than anything else. This view was prevalent. The CBC is, after all, conscious of how race and racism impact legislation.

CBC Attitudes about Democratic Political Behavior

Given the belief among respondents that racism, whether it was overt or covert, had a lot to do with the passage of the law, and given that it was Democrats who introduced and supported legislation containing harsh penalties, it is important to assess whether the Democratic leadership consulted a body established to protect the interests of disadvantaged groups and African Americans when considering this legislation. A question was asked to those interviewed about whether the Party leadership consulted the CBC on the United States Sentencing Commission's 1995 recommendation to eliminate the 100:1 disparity and to eliminate mandatory minimum penalties for simple possession of crack cocaine. As this vote took place just days after the Million Man March, it is inferred that the Democratic leadership would be more cognizant of consulting with African Americans in Congress.

The majority of respondents (53 percent) said that the Democratic leadership did not consult with them about the vote. Two members stated that the Democrats did consult with the CBC. Most of the remainder entered Congress after the 1995 vote, although one of the respondents was unsure about whether the Democratic leadership consulted with the CBC on this issue. What is significant is that the member who made this comment is a former Chair of the Congressional Black Caucus. The Chair of the Caucus, as is the leader of any organization, is expected to relay information to its members and to act as a liaison between members of the organization and outside groups. An upcoming chapter used the vote of the Chair of the CBC as a variable to assess group cohesion because it is believed that members will take its cue on how to vote from the Chair of the Caucus.

The member from the Northeast with more than 60 percent African Americans in his district who said the Democratic leadership did consult with the CBC believes that if the amendment had lowered the threshold for powder cocaine, then Democrats would have voted for it. He said even if Democrats agreed that lowering the threshold may be good policy, they were concerned about doing so because a potential 30-second campaign commercial can paint the member as being soft on crime, as opposed to the commercial showing the differences in treatment of the law being justifiable in enacting a change. Along the line of those same thoughts, a member from the Deep South said that there were many meetings but the CBC was voted down. S/He said that Democrats were afraid of the liberal label. A member from a southern district with an African American population of less than 60 percent responded that the Democratic leadership did not consult with the CBC, but that the CBC raised the issue with the White House. The White House, this member said, took the position that the threshold for powder cocaine should be lowered rather than the threshold for crack cocaine raised.

The comments on this point are astonishing considering that the CBC is a strong Democratic caucus that has a special concern about this legislation given its impact on the African American community. Yet, the Democratic leadership chose not to engage the CBC on this issue. It was an issue where politics rather than policy would dominate. A similar example is useful here. During the 1980s, Congress passed a law that would reform Medicare. Many seniors believed the reforms would be costly to them. Members of Congress, nevertheless, overwhelmingly passed the legislation and President Reagan signed it into law. There was massive protest among seniors about the Medicare Catastrophic Coverage Act. Fearing a backlash among seniors in their congressional districts, 16 months after the legislation passed, it was repealed.

As *The New York Times* reported, "In an action that tinged with bitterness and disappointment, the negotiators responded to the protests of thousands of elderly people, who resented the surtax they paid for the benefits many already received as retirees."[12] Seniors seem to be a greater key constituency than the hundreds of thousands of African Americans that manifested their position during the Million Man March. African Americans would continue to suffer under the mandatory minimum legislation for crack cocaine.

CBC Ideology versus the Democratic Party

Members were asked about the perceptions that Democrats have moved from being liberal on criminal justice issues to taking a conservative tough on crime and law and order position. The member was asked if he/she agreed or disagreed first that the change occurred and then second with the change in ideology on crime by Democrats. Members were also asked if Democrats should make mandatory minimums for crack cocaine a top agenda item and if the CBC should as well.

A three-part question was asked so that members could respond within the context outlined in the previous two sentences. The question asks about the rationale of Democrats in passing tough-on-crime laws, and now that time has shown its impact on the African American community, whether Democrats and the CBC should make it a top agenda item to address the discriminatory impact.

There was no consensus among the respondents as to whether Democrats supported tough crime legislation so as not to appear to be soft on crime. Forty percent disagreed that Democrats supported the legislation to show that they are tougher on crime than Republicans, while 33 percent agreed. Twenty-seven percent said that it depends because the environment in which the legislation was debated has to be considered. Interestingly, each of the respondents preferred prevention and rehabilitation over punishment. A member who represents a district in the Midwest with more than 60 percent of African Americans expressed the typical view that warehousing people, particularly nonviolent offenders, will not reduce crime. Another typical response was that preventive programs and education are more effective tools to fight crime than incarcerating people. The contrast between non-CBC Democrats supporting the use of a tough law-and-order approach to fighting crime and CBC preference to use prevention programs and education to fight crime demonstrates the challenges of the CBC to successfully push for agenda items that support the African American community. It also creates a division between those who support preventive measures, but who also believe that party unity is important. This latter group, therefore, believes that Democrats should not be forced to abandon tough law-and-order tools, even if those tools lead to the massive incarceration of African Americans.

When asked, as part of the three-part question, whether Democrats should make it a top agenda item, over 67 percent of the respondents said yes, while 27 percent said no, and one respondent said it depends on other issues that are equally important such as homeland security. With only two disagreements, the respondents overwhelmingly stated that the CBC should make it a top agenda item. The reasons given as to why the CBC should make it a top issue include the discriminatory nature of laws (many members stated that the CBC uniquely understands discrimination), that the laws have had such an impact on the African American community, and that the CBC is more sensitive to unfairness. It is important to note that members stated that it should be *a* top issue with the CBC, not *the* top issue.

One member who represents a Northeast district with an African American population of more than 60 percent disagreed somewhat with the characterization that Democrats are sounding somewhat tougher on crime in an effort to win votes. This member said that over the last 10 years, it has been Democrats who favored 100,000 more cops in the streets, but Democrats also pushed for more drug rehabilitation measures. He went on to say that gun control and more cops on the streets are now Democratic issues. Republicans had accused Democrats of stealing their issues. The member agreed, however, that on "wedge" issues, Democrats have changed their stance over the past 10 years. The member agreed that both Democrats and the CBC should make this a top agenda because it is time for a policy change. Overcrowded prisons have wreaked havoc on the community and on state budgets.

A member who represents a Midwestern district with an African American population of less than 50 percent somewhat disagreed with the part of the question about the perception that Democrats have moved from being liberal on criminal justice issues to taking a conservative tough on crime and law-and-order position, but added that if there are Democrats that want to engage in tough on crime rhetoric, then they should leave the party. S/he says that this type of rhetoric is damaging to our base, instead of showing compassion. S/He added that she/he would oppose any Democrat that wants to continue with the system of "locking people up." The member agreed that Democrats and the CBC should make this a top agenda item.

This member did agree that Democrats should make the issue of mandatory minimums for crack a top agenda item and that the CBC should as well because the Caucus is more sensitive to the unfairness of the law.

Another member from a southern district that contains approximately 50 percent African American agreed that there is a trend; that Democrats are becoming less tolerant/less empathetic in terms of the effectiveness of treatment and rehabilitation. This member went on to lament that Democrats do not seem to be willing to devote resources to where they are needed. This member also stated that the CBC should definitely make this a top issue and once the CBC does, individual Democrats will realize the inequities and join the CBC in the fight to eliminate the disparities. S/he said that neither the Democratic nor the Republican Party would make this an issue.

Another question asked if the CBC's growth in any way changed its mission. It also asked if the member considers his views to be liberal, moderate, or conservative in general and specifically on crime. On this question, there is a general consensus that the Congressional Black Caucus is more moderate as well as diverse today than it was prior to the 103rd Congress. Some members view this as a positive, while others viewed both the growth and the moderate ideology as a negative because it has become more difficult for the CBC to stand united on issues. Some members mentioned that there are among their colleagues those who are more concerned about getting on television by espousing issues different from what the CBC would support as opposed to seriously dealing with issues that plague African Americans. Further, many members said that the CBC is no longer a monolithic group because of its growth. One southern member stated that there is a different culture in the South that leans people toward a more conservative position on many issues, while a northeast Democrat mentioned that CBC members no longer represent majority African American constituencies and thus have to represent the interests of other groups as well. A member representing a northeast district says that overall, the CBC remains a liberal body and continues to stand for the principles on which the CBC was founded.

When members were asked to state whether they were liberal, moderate, or conservative, they were not given a definition of the terms. They provided an answer based on their own definition of the terms. However, the question was asked with the assumption that members viewed the terms "liberal" and "conservative" as it is generally views by the general public. The term *liberal* is used to refer to those who support greater government intervention to solve social and economic problems.[13] In contrast, conservative generally refers to those who oppose governmental intervention to solve social problems.[14] It is interesting to note that many of the members interviewed regardless of the region they represented, seniority, or percentage of African Americans in their respective districts did not consider themselves to be liberal, some also chose the moderate label, although their voting record would indicate otherwise. More members said that how they vote on an issue depends on the issue in question or on the type of crime addressed, and thus they would consider themselves to be liberal, conservative, and moderate. The question provides an opportunity for members to rank their individual ideology, and their views on crime; the response for each member are shown in Tables 3.1 and 3.2. This is one way to demonstrate the growing diversity of the CBC, which may pose significant problems in adequately addressing the subject of our research.

The self-identification of CBC members is an indicator of the ongoing struggle of the CBC to speak as a united voice. Again, the CBC has had to deal with internal difficulties since its inception. Over 30 years after the CBC was founded, it seems to be moving further away from (1) a progressive agenda and mission and (2) a cohesive body. As the responses to the questionnaire indicate, CBC members have broad concerns and interests, and a constituency that is not all African American, which contributes to the diversity of ideas. One northeastern member, for example, responded that the CBC is more conservative because the country is more conservative. Thus the

Table 3.1   Ideology: CBC Self-Identification

Liberal	Moderate	Conservative	Other/depends*
5	4	0	6

*One individual in this category mentioned that he is a progressive, while all others mentioned that they are moderate-conservative, depending on the issue.

Table 3.2 Crime Ideology: CBC Self-Identification			
Liberal	**Moderate**	**Conservative**	**Other/depends***
4	4	0	7

*These members mentioned that it depends on the crime, while they may have a liberal stance with regard to the death penalty, there are other crimes such as identity theft and child pornography that they would take a conservative (tough sentences) stance on.

political environment in which we live forces a progressive body such as the CBC to adapt. Adapting in a conservative environment where members of one's party are trying to win votes creates divisions. It seems that national Democratic leaders are boldly willing to support these divisions. For example, consider Ron Walter's discussion of Clinton's actions on welfare reform during his presidency. It shows that the president started picking up the personal responsibility mantra of the right, without adequately addressing structural issues that leads to a "permanent underclass." Although the CBC was in opposition to the Personal Responsibility and Work Opportunity Reconciliation Act of 1996, "Clinton's efforts on behalf of PRWORA were widely thought to have helped decrease the voter alienation which led to the Democratic defeat in 1994 and insulate Clinton from charges that he was continuing the Liberal policies of former Democratic administrations."[15] Just as some Clinton administration officials resigned after he signed this bill in 1996, CBC members should have held the president and the party's feet to the fire, but like good soldiers, they campaigned for the party. The national Democratic party is long past pushing an agenda that progressives and the CBC want, and the CBC is long past the days of holding the party accountable with strategies such as we saw with Mitchell, Fauntroy, and Powell. Ron Walters includes a poll on Black/White Responses to Political Values with the Democratic Party. On the position of whether African Americans have improved in recent years, 52 percent of the Black respondents agreed that they have, while 71 percent of the White respondents agreed. On the question of whether racial discrimination is the reason Blacks can't get ahead, 62 percent of Blacks agreed, while 37 percent of Whites agreed. On the question of whether Blacks are responsible for their own conditions, 31 percent of Blacks agreed while 37 percent of Whites agreed.[16] Democrats will look at these polling numbers and take such actions that may appeal to the White respondents. President Clinton's flirting with the center demonstrates the point. Speaker of the House Pelosi's insistence that Conyers not discuss impeachment during the 2006 midterm elections is another example, in addition to her insisting that Congressman William Jefferson leave the House Ways and Means Committee following allegations of wrongdoing. Further, Pelosi's (as minority leader) unwillingness to give Cynthia McKinney back some seniority upon her return to the House of Representatives in 2005 also demonstrates where the leadership stands on controversial issues involving race. The point of this discussion is to demonstrate that when a caucus is divided, the Democratic leadership often feels no threat of substantial public criticism from the caucus when a member is treated unfairly or when an issue is not addressed.

CBC and Its Effectiveness

A survey question administered by one of the authors asked members to assess the effectiveness of the CBC in articulating this issue (mandatory minimums for crack cocaine) to their colleagues and to the American public. This is a fixed choice question that provided the following choices: (1) not very effective, (2) somewhat effective, (3) reasonably effective, (4) very effective, and (5) extremely effective. The question is important in that members themselves are given the opportunity to rate the Caucus in terms of how effective they believe the CBC had been in articulating the negative impact policy is having on its core constituency. It is a political efficacy question, meaning it is an attempt to assess whether members believe that the CBC can have an impact on legislation and issues. Once again, there is no consensus on this issue. A third of the respondents stated that the CBC has been effective in articulating this issue to their colleagues and to the public, a third answered reasonably effective, 20 percent answered very effective, and the rest answered not very effective or somewhat effective. One member said that the Caucus had been effective, but did not wish to choose a degree of effectiveness. This member, who represents a western district with an African American population of less than 35 percent, believes that the Bush administration provided a roadblock to how effective the CBC can be on this and other issues. It should be noted that in a previous question, this member stated that this should not necessarily be a top issue among Democrats and that there are so many other issues that the CBC should focus on, issues such as education funding, healthcare, and the budget. Thus, on the one hand, this member seems to criticize the Republican administration for not listening to the CBC on these issues, but on the other hand, the member does not believe it is necessarily an issue that Democrats and the CBC should concern themselves with if the political environment is not right and if there are more pressing issues. A member who represents a Midwest district believes the effectiveness of the CBC varies by Congress. In other words, a Congress that is in session when there is a Democrat in the White House will see a more effective CBC and/or the CBC is more effective, or at least have a stronger voice, when the House of Representatives is controlled by Democrats as opposed to Republicans.

Another member representing a large urban population with approximately 60 percent of African Americans in his/her congressional district also said the CBC has been effective but for different reasons than the member mentioned above.[17] The member basically took a viewpoint that because of racism in this country, it is the CBC that has been in the forefront of articulating these issues because members of the group have a better understanding and experience with racism. The member declared:

> I'd say a 4 (very effective). The CBC has so many things to try to talk about, to educate people about, to deal with. All of the regular things, because everything that is regular builds on your neighborhood, your area, your district, too, so you've got to deal with that and then you have special nuances that exists as a result

of slavery and oppression, discrimination—all of the things that African Americans have experiences which come together to make us who we are—and so we are still in the process of trying to overcome. So given all of that, I think the CBC does an outstanding job of raising issues, articulating them, processing and looking out for the interests of the population. We are primarily charged with that responsibility.

A northeastern member who has stated in a previous question that these laws have had a tremendous impact on his/her congressional district due to the widespread incarceration of African Americans believes that without the CBC in place to bring to the attention of their colleagues and the public these disparities that are race driven, that there would likely not be as many groups speaking out against these types of issues.

The CBC's Views on Interest Groups Surrounding Mandatory Minimum Penalties

Members were asked an open-ended question to invite them to name the groups that have contacted them about this issue. The purpose of this question was simply to get an understanding of whether outside groups lobbied the CBC members on this issue. Given that the CBC represents the group that is disproportionately impacted by these laws, it is assumed that interest groups would contact them frequently in an effort to garner support and coordination in overturning mandatory minimum penalties for crack cocaine. Most members had a hard time with this question.[18] Perhaps this is one of the more surprising questions, because although, particularly since 1993, there have been a few hearings and many public forums sponsored by various organizations not affiliated with Congress, and it has been mentioned at public marches such as the Redeem the Dream March sponsored by Martin Luther King III and others, CBC members had a difficult time answering this question. Only six members mentioned groups such as the NAACP, the Rainbow Push Coalition, the National Urban League, and/or the American Civil Liberties Union, groups that have been out front in at least articulating this issue. There were several members who said no one had contacted them recently, one member who said no one and reminded me again that s/he has a small African American population in his/her district (this was a constant reminder as the survey instrument was being administered), and one member who said that I am the first to contact him/her about it. Several members did mention that local groups, such as social workers, ministers, and even judges and state sentencing commissions have contacted them about this issue.

An additional question asked the members to name some organizations that most effectively represent Black criminal justice issues. The purpose of this question is to understand if there is a consistent group of people that the CBC is aware of that they can turn to gather statistics and support. Given the historical treatment of African Americans in the criminal justice system, it is likely that organizations such as the

National Black Police Association, the National Organization for Black Law Enforcement Officers (NOBLE), or the National Black Lawyers Association would have the ear of the CBC as they concern themselves with the treatment of African Americans in every aspect of law enforcement. There were several members who could not answer this question. Of those who did answer, the responses included the Leadership Conference on Civil Rights, the NAACP, the NAACP Defense Fund, the National Association of Blacks in the Criminal Justice, and former mayor of New York Ed Koch.[19] Not surprising, the member who is a former judge and prosecutor provided several organizations such as the National Bar Association, the NAACP Legal Defense Fund, the Mississippi Legal Project, the ACLU, the National Black Prosecutors Association, and the Public Defenders Association.

A closed-ended question asked about the effectiveness of traditional and nontraditional organizations in promoting better criminal justice policies. Given its mission, it was assumed that the CBC would likely rank traditional civil rights organizations higher than nontraditional rights organizations because of the heavy focus these organizations place on issues that impact the African American community. Table 3.3 describes the CBC's attitudes about the effectiveness of the organizations.

The numbers in Table 3.3 represent the number of responses each category received by CBC members. For example, the first box shows that the NAACP received just one response that it was effective, three that it is somewhat effective, and so on. Based on members, responses, nontraditional civil rights organizations, particularly the ACLU and the Sentencing Project, are very effective or extremely effective in articulating this issue, while traditional civil rights groups such as the NAACP and the Leadership Conference on Civil Rights and the National Urban League are deemed to be, at best, reasonably effective by the majority of the respondents.

Categorizing Members' Responses

The interviewees are placed in a typology based on the level of responsiveness to African American interests on mandatory minimum penalties for crack cocaine and attitudes and commitment to Democratic unity. The following categories are used to place members in a typology:

RESPONSIVENESS TO AFRICAN AMERICAN INTERESTS HIGH — DEMOCRATIC UNITY LOW

These members have more than 55 percent African Americans in their congressional districts, sponsored/co-sponsored legislation on mandatory minimums for crack during the 107th Congress, believe that the CBC should make the issue a top priority, and that Democrats should make this issue a top priority. These members are categorized as "active-trustee,"[20] meaning that they see African Americans as a core constituency of all CBC members regardless of which district individual African Americans reside in, and they believe that this constituency should come before the desire to ensure unity within the Democratic Party.

TABLE 3.3 CBC Self-Reported Attitude about the Effectiveness of Traditional and Nontraditional Civil Rights Organizations						
	Not Very Effective	**Somewhat Effective**	**Reasonably Effective**	**Very Effective**	**Extremely Effective**	**Do Not Know/ No Answer**
Interest Group						
NAACP	1	3	2	5	2	1
The Leadership Conference on Civil Rights	1	1	4	6	1	2
The National Urban League	3	3	3	5	0	1
ACLU	0	1	1	8	4	1
Families Against Mandatory Minimums	0	0	5	4	1	5
The Sentencing Project	0	1	2	3	6	3
National Black Police Association	1	4	5	2	1	2
The Black Leadership Forum	1	3	6	3	0	2
The Black Leadership Roundtable	1	4	5	2	0	3

RESPONSIVENESS TO AFRICAN AMERICAN INTERESTS HIGH — DEMOCRATIC UNITY HIGH

These members have more than 55 percent of an African American population in their districts, sponsored/co-sponsored legislation on mandatory minimums during the 107th Congress, believe the CBC should make the issue a top priority, but do not believe the Democratic Party should make it an issue. These members are categorized as "passive trustee," meaning that they believe the CBC represents a national constituency, but that the Democratic Party should not be pressured to take risks.

RESPONSIVENESS TO AFRICAN AMERICAN INTERESTS LOW — DEMOCRATIC UNITY LOW

These members have less than 55 percent of an African American population in their congressional districts, did sponsor/co-sponsor legislation on mandatory minimums for crack during the 107th Congress, and believe that both the CBC and the Democratic Party should make this issue a top priority. These members are characterized as "active-delegate" because they co-sponsor legislation, believe this should be a top priority, but do not have the number of African Americans in their district that would result in their doing more to advocate against this policy.

RESPONSIVENESS TO AFRICAN AMERICAN INTERESTS LOW — DEMOCRATIC UNITY HIGH

Theses members have less than 55 percent of African Americans in their congressional districts, did not sponsor/co-sponsor legislation on mandatory minimums for crack during the 107th Congress, believe that the CBC should make this a top priority, but not the Democratic Party. The "passive-delegate" has a low percentage of African Americans in his or her congressional district.

Bill Sponsorship/Co-Sponsorship

During the 107th Congress, four bills were introduced in the House of Representatives regarding mandatory minimum sentences for crack and powder cocaine. The bill that contained the most co-sponsors (44) and the most CBC sponsors was HR 1978, introduced by Congresswoman Maxine Waters (D-CA). This legislation would have eliminated mandatory minimum penalties for crack cocaine.[21] All but three of the CBC members interviewed when first preparing this study co-sponsored this legislation. Two among the three have more than 55 percent of African Americans in their congressional districts, and one has less than 55 percent. Another bill introduced in the 107th

Table 3.4 Responsiveness to African American Interests		
Democratic Unity	**High**	**Low**
High	Passive Trustee	Passive Delegate
Low	Active Trustee	Active Delegate

Congress was introduced by Congressman Rangel. HR 687 is similar to legislation he's introduced each Congress since the 103rd. It contains only three co-sponsors. Of the three, only one is a CBC member and none of the co-sponsors are CBC members interviewed by the authors. A third bill was introduced by CBC member Congressman Al Wynn. HR 765 would make retroactive the safety valve legislation passed in 1994 as part of the crime bill.[22] This bill contained 23 co-sponsors. Six of the co-sponsors were interviewed as part of this original study. These CBC co-sponsors represent districts that are predominantly African American and those with less than 55 percent of African Americans, and those districts in each region of the country, except for the South. A fourth bill was introduced by a non-CBC member. HR 4024 would have lowered the penalty for powder cocaine to the level that currently exists for crack cocaine, thus requiring a mandatory minimum penalty for 5 grams of powder cocaine as well. This legislation contained 19 co-sponsors. Only four of the 15 members interviewed for this original research co-sponsored this legislation. Three of those members represent districts with less than 55 percent African American. Congresswoman Waters' legislation received the strongest amount of support as measured by co-sponsors. It was co-sponsored by a total number of 28 CBC members. The legislation was referred to a committee and never received a hearing.

As has been mentioned, efforts were made by CBC members during the Clinton administration to modify mandatory minimums for crack cocaine laws, but those efforts failed. By the time the 107th Congress concluded on January 2, 2003, the prison population would reach 2 million, more than 750,000 of which were African American men. Further, approximately 80 percent of those convicted of drug offenses were African Americans and Hispanic.[23]

The interview data demonstrates the difficulty to form a consensus on the issue of mandatory minimums. It also demonstrates that members who represent predominantly White (or non-majority Black districts) are more accepting of these laws, arguing that their law and order constituents would expect them to support it. The data also demonstrate a degree of pragmatism among CBC members. Many are reluctant to force the Democratic party to address this issue. There is an understanding that the party would look soft on crime, and thus lose elections. As the reader will recall, these laws made it to the agenda in the first place because of the perception that Democrats were weak on crime. This chapter continues to confirm the overall premise of this book and that is that ties to the Democratic party has allowed these oppressive criminal justice laws to reach the height of the congressional agenda and to remain a part of policy for over more than 20 years. The diversity of congressional districts and a clear ideological division makes it difficult for the CBC to come together on behalf of their core constituency, as outlined in the mission statement of the CBC. The constituency is not just African Americans, but also the poor and disfranchised. These laws have hit the poor and disenfranchised.

When Democrats took over the majority in Congress, beginning in 2006 with the 110th Congress, CBC members gained power,[24] we will analyze the bills introduced and/or co-sponsored by the CBC and others members at the beginning of the Congress. Further, while Congressman Conyers, as a result of Democrats regaining the majority in the House of Representatives in November 2006, chairs the House Judiciary

Committee, we will explore whether he has been able to get a bill through committee and onto the Floor of the House of Representatives for a vote.

Conclusion

In this chapter, we observe that the response to the survey questions is an indication that the CBC is not a monolithic group. The majority of members thought that harsh sentencing laws should be reformed. There was also a belief that the negative image of African American males had a role in the crafting of the legislation. The responses also indicate that some members were willing to give the Democratic party the benefit of the doubt in that they did not believe that the party supported these laws simply to show that the party was "tough on crime." It is of interest to note that several members did not know how the 100:1 disparity came about in the first place. However, this could be because several of those interviewed were not in Congress in 1986.

Keyterms

Endnotes

1 Patterson, Thomas E., *We the People: A Concise Introduction to American Politics*, 6th edition, New York: McGraw-Hill, 2006. pp 64–65.

2 Ibid. p.67.

3 Congressman William Lacy Clay from Missouri and Congresswoman Diane E. Watson from California.

4 As Paul Frymer discusses in his book and as is discussed in this work, Democratic party leaders fear that any appeals to African American voters, whether it is to focus on crime prevention measures or Affirmative Action, will lead to election defeats of Democrats. Thus, there is an effort on behalf of the party leadership to distance the party from racial issues, and, as this research argues, to enhance its language on the need to have strong law enforcement as an overt appeal to White voters, regardless of the outcome of these policies on African American voters.

5 Please note, while the interviews began at the closing of the 107th Congress, they ended during the first session of the 108th Congress. All members interviewed served in the 107th Congress. The 107th Congress was selected because, in part, it marked the fifteenth anniversary since legislation passed creating the 100-1 disparity between powder and crack, and because the CBC during that Congress still consisted of members who were in Congress in 1986–1995 when key votes were held and during the post–1993 Congress when members began introducing legislation to eliminate or substantially reduce the disparity.

6 Barker, Tate, and Jones, *African Americans and the American Political System*, p. 288.

7 Ibid., pp. 288–289.

8 This discussion takes place in another chapter of this paper. David Lublin's *The Paradox of Representation: Racial Gerrymandering and Minority Interests in Congress* and Katherine Tate's *Black Faces in the Mirror* are among the literature used to discuss this issue.

9 Danny Davis, United States 107th Congress (Democrat-IL), Personal Interview. Congressman Davis' Office. March 2003.

10 Ibid.

11 This individual would later become chairman of the Congressional Black Caucus. Among the priorities for the Congress, the member served as Chair, including ending racial injustice in the criminal justice system in general and ending arbitrary mandatory minimums in particular were among them. These priorities are in the appendix.

12 Martin Tolchin, "Conferees Agree to Repeal Disputed Medicare Program," *The New York Times* (November 18, 1989.).

13 Barker, Jones, and Tate, p. 57.

14 Ibid., p. 98.

15 Walters, Ronald W., *White Nationalism: Black Interests* (Detroit, MI: Wayne State University Press, 2004), p. 160.

16 Ibid., pp. 95–96.

17 The authors made efforts to respect anonymity of any respondents who did not make it clear that they wanted themselves identified by name.

18 When asked this open-ended question, relatively few members could list one or more interest groups, from which it can be inferred that most members of the CBC are not seen by interest groups as being an effective lobbying tool, and thus have avoided these members' offices; or staff member may not have felt the need to relay lobbying efforts to the member. Congressional staff do serve as gatekeepers for their members. If a member represents a district that isn't too concerned with criminal justice issues, even if the discussion centers on racism in the system, staffers may not pass the information to their bosses. And since mandatory minimums for crack cocaine aren't often considered in the committee and on the House floor, the issue may not have merited a memo to the boss when an interest group contacted a congressional office. This is not to say that certain members of the CBC are not very familiar with many interest groups as each year during CBC week (the annual legislative weekend) members such as Bobby Scott, Maxine Waters, and John Conyers routinely host a session with the focus on this issue.

19 The CBC member who made this response is not from New York, but believes that Koch is in the forefront of advocating alternative sentences and helping those who have been sentenced under New York's notorious Rockefeller Drug Laws.

20 We're covered the term trustee and delegate in Chapter 2. We modified terms combined the terms "trustee," "delegate," "active participant," and passive participant," to create a category that reflects the subtext of this research that explores the dual role of

African Americans in Congress as African Americans and Democrats and how this duality impacts their political behavior.

21 www.thomas.loc.gov (107th Congress).
22 This provision will be discussed later in this book.
23 "Insights into the Inmate Population," *The Washington Post* (March 21,2003), sec. 1A.
24 Conyers as Chair of the Judiciary Committee, for example, and Rangel as Chair of the Ways and Means Committee.

ACTIVITY 1

Party, party, party...

A Chapter 3 Exercise

Instructions:

In the space above, explain why party classification has historically been a determining factor of behavior within the CBC. Please consider the section of the chapter dealing with ideology when preparing your response.

107th Congress

[Please tear out your completed response so you can turn it in to the instructor]

ACTIVITY 2

In the boxes, describe information from
CBC interviews covered in the chapter . . .

A Chapter 3 Exercise

CBC view on Democratic political behavior

CBC view on legislative process

CBC view on mandatory minimum interest groups

ACTIVITY 3

Applying a book concept to a real-life issue...

Ideology: CBC Self-Identification

Crime Ideology: CBC Self-Identification

Instructions:

Part 1: Within the *Ideology* box, please discuss what you think is important about how the CBC members identified themselves as covered in Table 2.1 in the chapter. Feel free to do outside research using the Internet.

Part 2: Within the *Crime Ideology* box, please discuss what you think is important about how the CBC members identified themselves as covered in Table 2.1 in the chapter. Feel free to do outside research using the Internet.

A Chapter 3 Exercise

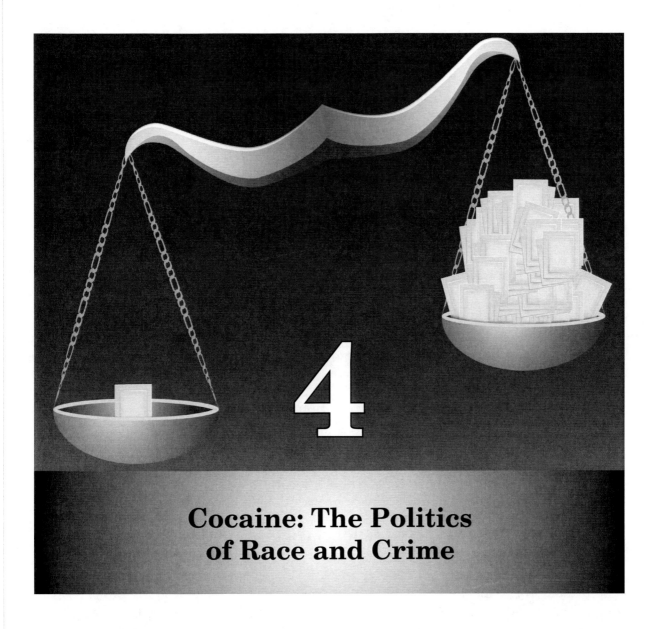

Cocaine: The Politics of Race and Crime

Chapter 4 Synopsis: The chapter examines how mandatory minimum laws for crack/powder cocaine made it onto the congressional agenda during the 1980s. It looks at committee hearings, congressional votes, agenda setting, and the congressional activity surrounding the law from 1984 until 2005.

During the year 1993, of those sentenced for crack cocaine, 88.3 percent were Black and 95.4 percent were non-White. Even though the [Sentencing] Commission has conceded that there was no intent by the Legislature that penalties fall disproportionately on one segment of the population, the impact of these penalties nonetheless remains. If the impact of the law is discriminatory, the problem is no less real regardless of the intent. This problem is particularly acute because the disparate impact arises from a penalty structure for two different forms of the same substance. It is a little like punishing vehicular homicide while under the influence of alcohol more severely if the defendant had become intoxicated by ingesting cheap wine rather than scotch whiskey. That suggestion is absurd on its face and ought be no less so when the abused substance is cocaine rather than alcohol (Vice Chairman of the United States Sentencing Commission, April 1997).[1]

We have provided the reader with an overview of mandatory minimum laws for crack cocaine, how they came about, a short history of racism in the criminal justice system, and a case study featuring CBC members serving in the 107th Congress. This chapter will go into deeper explanation as to why Congress considered mandatory minimum laws for crack cocaine and congressional activity surrounding the law during this 20-year history.

Disparate sentencing leads many to distrust the criminal justice system. A society with little confidence in its institutions may become apathetic in the operation of its government. In its second report to Congress urging an elimination of the crack versus powder disparity, the USSC wrote:

> One of the issues of greatest concern surrounding federal sentencing policy is the perception of disparate and unfair treatment for defendants convicted of either possession of or distribution of crack cocaine . . . . While there is not evidence of racial bias behind the promulgation of this federal sentencing law, nearly 90 percent of the offenders convicted in federal court for crack cocaine distribution are African American while the majority of crack cocaine users are white. Thus sentences appear to be harsher and more severe for racial minorities than others as a result of the law. The current penalty structure results in a perception of unfairness and inconsistency.[2]

In a concurring opinion in a 1997 report to Congress, Gelacak, the Vice Chairman of the Sentencing Commission, expressed his belief that if there is any law that should be changed immediately, it is the mandatory minimum for crack cocaine law as it currently exists. He believes that it is very discriminatory and is juxtaposed to the fairness in the judiciary system. He wrote:

> . . . Eliminating discrimination is a principle to which this nation has committed itself. As a signator of the United Nations International Convention on the Elimination of all Forms of Racial Discrimination, the United States pledged to "take effective measures to review governmental, national and local policies, and to amend, rescind, or nullify laws and regulations which have the effect of creating or perpetuating racial discrimination wherever it exists." Clearly the 100:1 powder/crack cocaine ratio would qualify as such a law.[3]

In essence, the Vice Chairman of the United States Sentencing Commission, who has studied this issue since the guidelines were in place, calls this policy racial discrimination, although that was not the intent of the law. Despite the special reports to Congress on the unfairness of the mandatory minimum penalty, there have only been a few congressional hearings on this issue. Surprisingly, the first occurred in 1993, the second in the year 2000, and a few more within the past few years.

Agenda Setting/the Emergence of Crack Cocaine

In a study such as this, it is important to thoroughly explore how an issue makes it onto the congressional agenda. Why did Congress single out crack cocaine to be punishable by a mandatory five years in prison without the possibility of parole? While we will not delve too deeply into to beginnings of the so-called "War on Drugs," it should be noted that this policy did come about as a result of the Reagan administration's drug war. The United States has been dealing with a drug war since the 1960s. Indeed, in 1956, Congress passed the Narcotic Control Act of 1956, which implemented mandatory minimum penalties for drug importation and distribution offenses.[4] These sentences, like those passed in 1986, provided for long, fixed sentences for first-time offenders, and even death for those convicted for a third time. In 1970, 14 years after the 1956 Act was enacted, Congress

> . . . . passed the Comprehensive Drug Abuse Prevention and Control of 1970 that repealed virtually all mandatory penalties for drug violations. While sponsors of the legislation indicated a particular concern that mandatory minimum sentences were exacerbating the "problem of alienation of youth from the general society," other factors contributed to the general concern. Some argued that mandatory penalties hampered "the process of rehabilitation of offenders" and infringed "on judicial function by not allowing the judge to use his discretion in individual cases." Others argued that mandatory minimum sentences reduced the deterrent effect of the drug laws in part because even prosecutors viewed them as overly severe . . . .[5]

Less than two decades after the repeal of mandatory minimum sentences, an environment returned to Congress that resulted in the legislative body reinstating draconian drug laws. In 1982, President Ronald Reagan declared a "War on Drugs," which placed a national focus on the issue of drug abuse, specifically cocaine.[6] During the 1980s, crack cocaine became a major problem in the inner cities. By 1985, crack had spread nationally. The nightly news reports of drive-by shootings and gang wars made the issue a national concern. Congressional hearings focused heavily on the crack cocaine epidemic. During the hearings and on the House floor, congressional statements indicated that members of Congress believed that crack cocaine was more dangerous than powder cocaine. Three and a half months after the death of Len Bias, the Anti-Drug Abuse Act of 1986 passed.[7]

As written by Edith Cooper:

> The general nature of the anti-drug abuse legislation seemed to be driven by awareness of the crack cocaine problem that had been heightened by the media

especially in 1986. One commentator observed that several investigators believed that the response by the media and politicians appeared to have been well out of proportion to the seriousness of the crack cocaine problem. The USSC study that stated that Congress's conclusions about the dangerousness of crack were based on the assumptions that it was more addictive than cocaine powder, there was a greater correlation between crack use and crime than with other drugs, crack use could lead to psychosis or death, young people were more prone to use crack, and its ease of manufacture, use, purity and potency would lead to widespread national use. Although scientific research results available in 1986 did indicate that cocaine-freebase smokers did tend to have an intense craving for the drug, there was not enough scientific research about crack use per se, nor accurate prevalence of data available, to confirm those beliefs.[8]

The agenda-setting stage of the public policy process is important to include in this book because it helps in the understanding of ways a single issue reaches the stage where public officials are seriously discussing it. In his book, *Agendas, Alternatives, and Public Policies*, John Kingdon discusses political and policy streams. Within these streams are members of the policy community, congressional staffers, specialists, and more importantly, ideas. Ideas are floating around waiting to become an agenda item. The policy entrepreneur is always waiting for a policy window to open whereby he or she can take one of the ideas floating in the stream and place on the agenda.[9] In this scenario, the Reagan administration, particularly his attorney general, could be considered as seeking to help further his war on drugs, and the Len Bias death, subsequent media attention, and gang violence in inner cities created an opening for a policy window.

In their book entitled *Agenda and Instability in American Politics*, Baumgartner and Jones discussed the ways in which an item makes it onto the congressional agenda. Two key points are important about their work: the increased focus by the media on an issue that brings about a congressional response and viewing issues from a broader context in order to understand why it makes an apparent sudden appearance on the agenda.[10] When crack was considered by the national public, it was viewed as a plague coming from within the inner cities. During the 1980s, when America focused on a conservative agenda and a belief that people in the inner cities had an opportunity to participate in the American Dream but failed and thus were reverting to criminal behavior, the need to pass stringent drug enforcement laws emerged. The rhetoric often used was that there was an inner-city pathology of violence.[11] The nightly news shows were full of tales of gang violence that frightened the American public.

Early Congressional Response

During the 1980s, the House Select Committee on Narcotics Abuse and Control (HSCNAC), chaired by Congressman Charles Rangel (D-NY), held a series of hearings about drug use and abuse around the country.[12] The purpose of the Committee was to provide oversight to and review the problems of narcotics, drug and polydrug abuse, and control. The committee held various hearings and conferences in order to pursue its mission. Committee reports accompanied the field hearings and conferences. One such report, entitled "A Survey of Members of Congress about Drug Abuse in Their Districts," was issued during the second session of the 98th Congress in 1984. According to the report, "over 96 percent of the respondents characterized drug abuse in their district as either severe or moderate with the reports being equally divided between the two positions. The five most prevalent drugs, in order of frequency of mention are marijuana, cocaine, stimulants, tranquilizers and hallucinogens, all of which were reported by more than half of the responding members."[13] What is interesting about the report is that the majority of members surveyed expressed concern that it was marijuana that was widely used among young adults and teens (cocaine was believed to be used mostly by adults 25 and older) and that it was heroin use and addiction that was deemed to be most costly and damaging to both the individual and to society. In the years prior to the report, deaths and hospital emergency visits attributed to heroin increased dramatically as did violent and property crimes.[14] While the report acknowledged that cocaine, since the late 1970s, was being made available more cheaply and thus becoming more accessible to adolescents, it was marijuana and heroin abuse that seemed to be the most concern to the 92 members of Congress who participated in the survey. The members represented districts in 32 states, including the District of Columbia. Despite these concerns, it would be crack cocaine that Congress chose to highlight during debate on legislation that passed within two years of when this report was issued. This may be due to the images of those perpetrating the crime. In this case, it is the African American male. As mentioned in Andrew Hacker's book on race relations in America, what most Americans regard as "black crime" has become a preoccupation of public and private life. Black men, and the offenses they commit, are viewed differently from other felons and felonies.[15] Singling out a drug because of its perceived use by a minority group is not new.

According to Mike Gray, since the early 1900s when the federal government began making domestic and international laws, racism played a key role in its rhetoric. During the early consideration of cocaine legislation in the early 1900s, a physician hired by the State Department to be the equivalent to what is now known as the drug czar persuaded Congress to issue laws by saying that "cocaine is often the direct incentive to the crime of rape by Negroes."[16] Southern legislatures were most likely to buy into this stereotype. According to Gray, they had heard that cocaine turned African Americans into zombies who could not be taken down by bullets.[17] While the language used at the time was overt, the language used by today's members of Congress are covert but essentially imply the same thing, that African Americans are responsible for the use and spread of drugs to the suburbs. Further, it can be argued, the nightly images of African American males involved in gang warfare over drugs contributed to unconscious racism by many members of Congress who may have stereotypes about African American males. Thus the mandatory minimum penalty for crack cocaine, particularly its vast difference in relation to that of powder cocaine, touches on underlying racism or unconscious racism.

On July 16, 1985 during the first session of the 99th Congress (the Congress that enacted mandatory minimum penalties for crack cocaine), the HSCNAC held a hearing entitled "Cocaine Abuse and the Federal Response." The purpose of the hearing was to focus on the medical and social impact on what was labeled as the "cocaine epidemic," as reports stated that 25 million Americans used cocaine. Chairman Rangel used his opening statement to criticize countries for exporting cocaine and the White House for reducing drug treatment funds. In an effort to dispel the belief that cocaine was a glamorous drug used by the wealthy he stated:

> The belief that cocaine is the toy of the wealthy and well-educated has been shattered. Many blue collar workers and young people are users today. Some of our witnesses today will elaborate on those facts. . . . The Committee has invited the three members of our first panel this morning, not to point a finger at an administration seemingly unable to shut off the source of supply of cocaine to this country or to seal our borders from its illegal importation, not to provide a platform for an expression of out witnesses' remorse. You, Mr. Keach, Mr. Eller, and Ms. Carrington, have been asked to appear before the Select Committee so that we may collectively and more successfully rebut the glamorous images and myths concerning cocaine. We are subjected, with almost daily regularity on television, in the movies, in the print media, to the impression that cocaine is somehow a safe, recreational drug. We wish to highlight for the public the dangers of cocaine use.[18]

Subsequent HSCNAC hearings, including a July 1986 hearing entitled "Trafficking and Abuse of 'Crack' in New York City" and a July 15, 1986 hearing entitled "The Crack Cocaine Crisis," continued to highlight the prevalence of crack.[19] By this time, crack had been around since the late 1970s, as has been mentioned, but the image was moving from cocaine users as consisting of the "glamorous set" to that of an inner-city gang member. This image led to the creation of mandatory minimum penalties for crack. There was a growing perception that crack cocaine was public enemy number one.

Len Bias

While Congress made an attempt to take power away from liberal judges they believed were too lenient by creating the USSC in 1984 for the purpose of establishing sentencing guidelines that judges had to use, it was the death of Len Bias from an apparent cocaine overdose that led to the most punitive anti-drug legislation passed by Congress. The death of Len Bias plays a significant role in the speed in which Congress crafted this legislation. His death in June 1986 (from a *powder*-cocaine overdose) became an instant headline, and Congress responded by crafting legislation without going through the normal committee process.[20] Early on, members of Congress assumed it was a *crack* cocaine overdose and responded accordingly. In describing what Len Bias' death meant to the movement to create harsh mandatory minimum penalties for drug use and abuse, Mike Gray writes:

On the night of June 18, 1986, Boston Celtics draft choice Len Bias—a dazzling young black athlete on the brink of fame and fortune—died of a heart failure from cocaine poisoning. This tragedy turned out to be larger than life because Bias was no ordinary hoop star. Unlike the dangerous and arrogant street punks now flavoring the nightly news, here was a clean-cut kid from a religious family in search of the American Dream. The fact that the dream was within his grasp when he was cut down made it all the more frustrating. If such a thing could happen to a Len Bias, it could happen to anybody. In the following month the networks aired seventy-four evening news segments about crack and cocaine, and any lingering doubts America had about the drug was evaporated.[21]

The intense news coverage of gang wars and crack babies, particularly following the death of Bias, prompted the American public to see the face of a drug user not as one associated with glamour or wealth, but rather one associated with inner city African Americans, who, it was believed, were destroying their communities and their babies, and if something was not done, the destruction would reach communities outside these communities, thus adhering to what Congressman Rangel hoped to accomplish. Marijuana and heroin, still popular drugs, were replaced with the image of crack use among African Americans. Given the failed presidential bid by Massachusetts Governor Michael Dukakis, whom Republicans painted as being soft on crime because he allowed an African American prisoner, Willie Horton, to have a temporary weekend pass known as a furlough, Democrats did not wish to be viewed as being soft on crime by letting this high-profile death go unpunished. The Democratic bill had many Republican amendments that made the bill heavily punitive, but Democrats contributed to harsh legislation with their rhetoric as well. This effort on the part of Democrats to make themselves look tough on crime resulted in a collusion with Republicans against the very people Democrats claim as their constituency, African Americans. Thus, crime and criminal justice issues are tools in the Democratic and Republican strategy to win votes.

The Politics of Race and Crime

In an article that discusses both the issue of racial bias within the criminal justice system and how political parties use the issue of race as a wedge issue, Marion Orr examines the support for anti-crime legislation by Democrats, Republicans, and the CBC since the 1970s. Specifically, he links tough crime policies with the desire to win votes of White conservatives. Crime and crime policy have traditionally been a subtheme in racial politics.[22] President Franklin Delano Roosevelt was lobbied by African American leaders to support federal anti-lynching laws but he refused to do so, fearing that such a law would alienate southern White voters. President Nixon, during the 1970s, used the "law and order" theme to energize a White backlash in opposition to Black political mobilization. And Presidents Ronald Reagan and George Bush exploited race and crime in order to win over White voters. At the same time, "in the 1980s and 1990s crime became a central concern of African American leaders as they resisted the increase in violent crime in inner-city communities."[23] Traditionally, Democrats have emphasized preventive measures as a means of deterring crime while Republicans have emphasized punitive measures. African American legislators seemed to be balancing the need to fight crime with the punitive measures offered by both parties. Crime legislation proposed during the 1980s was part of an overall conservative law and order effort to prove to the public that both Democrats and Republicans would not tolerate drug use and abuse. During the 1990s, while the punitive focus remained, a Democratic president balanced it with preventive programs. Grants were not simply going to beef up law enforcement and to build more prisons, but also to community development programs. Republicans did not support these measures, but there was an effort by Democrats to cater to them, nevertheless. The argument is that politics drove anti-crime policy, rather than a legitimate effort to fight crime. Winning votes were key to proving that they were not vulnerable and thus supported and initiated the same types of policies.

Marc Mauer, in *Race to Incarcerate*, discusses the changes in the political environment that resulted in policies that have increased the prison population. He notes:

[Former President] Carter cited the inequities in the criminal justice system that often penalize blacks and other minority groups more than whites. He said that as a young Governor of Georgia, he and contemporaries like Reubin Askew in Florida and Dale Bumpers in Arkansas had "an intense competition" over who had the smallest prison population. "Now it's totally opposite," Mr. Carter said. "Now the governors are bragging on how many prisons they've built and how many people they keep in jail and for how long."[24]

A challenge for politicians in the post-civil rights era is overcoming "the rise of a racially coded language that dislodged the need for overtly racist appeals. Coded messages depend on mobilizing the fears of white voters, yet thrive by detaching the problems that generate anxieties from the conditions that give rise to them."[25] Unfortunately, whether the language is covert or overt, it is not a new phenomenon. There have been many publications written about the racial disparities in the criminal justice system that have long existed. Some of those publications have already been mentioned in this study. The two systems of justice have long been an obstacle for African Americans to overcome. For example, after the Civil War, vagrancy laws were passed that essentially allowed for the arrest of African Americans who were without proper work permits. These laws resembled the Black Codes that were in place prior to the Civil War. The convict-lease system was also a measure intended to target African Americans.[26]

In *Long Memory*, Berry and Blassingame provide the following excerpt from *Time Magazine*:

Whites often assume that civil rights acts and court decisions made law the black man's redeemer. In practice, many blacks see the law as something different: a white weapon that white policemen, white judges and white juries use against black people. Indeed, blacks are clearly over-represented in crime and punishment . . .

Blacks are arrested three and four times more than whites, partly because police stop and search blacks more frequently than they do whites . . . . Most of the victims of black crimes are black. Example: Black women are 18 times more likely to be raped than white women, and usually by Black assailants. Once caught, black suspects are more likely than whites to be convicted than acquitted, and more likely to receive stiff sentences . . . According to many experts, one factor in this proportion is poverty: few defendants can afford skilled lawyers.[27]

Thus, dual treatment by the criminal justice system remains a concern with the CBC. Berry and Blassingame go on to write: "The criminal justice system punished and harassed black political prisoners whose crimes might have been ostensible against property but whose basic offense to the system was their race. Racism imprisoned small-time thieves, among whom blacks disproportionately represented but released white collar swindlers or political operatives with a reprimand."[28] The point made is that crimes that are likely to be committed by those near the poverty line (i.e., property crimes) are set up to be most harsh in nature, even though it is not an explicit policy dealing with race. White-collar crimes such as embezzlement that are likely to be committed by those who have wealth or in the position of achieving wealth do not receive the same harsh penalties. Thus, to paraphrase Berry and Blassingame, severe penalties for crimes against property have traditionally "been reserved for those offenses which black people were in the best position to commit more often."[29] It is within this context that the crafting of mandatory minimum penalties for crack cocaine can be considered.

Congress Reacts

Chapter 1 includes Congress' initial reaction to the death of Len Bias with the passage of HR 5484, the Anti-Drug Abuse Act of 1986, making the 100:1 disparity between powder and crack federal law. It was clear that crack had become the most dangerous drug in America in the minds of the media and Congress. In September 1986 when the Senate introduced The Comprehensive Narcotics Control Act of 1986. Senator James Sasser (D-TN) stated "[Crack] is as dangerous as any drug in the street and more addictive than almost any of them. Then we say that if you possess 50 grams you are a major trafficker — 10 years to life for the first offense. If you have even 5 grams in your possession, it's 5 to 25 years."[30] It took less than three months for Congress to pass this very harsh drug legislation. In the hysteria to fight drugs, particularly the "crack problem," Congress speedily passed a bill that days after passage many admitted that they did not know what the entire bill contained. The media, which had contributed to the euphoria, condemned Congress for passing such a large bill so quickly. On February 26, 1987, the House Select Committee on Narcotics and Abuse and Control held the first of several oversight hearings on the 1986 Anti-Drug Abuse Act. The hearing was entitled "Implementation of Provisions of the Anti-Drug Abuse Act of 1986." A review of the statements from Republicans such as Michael Oxley (R-OH) to Democrats such as Charles Rangel indicated that there was

(1) confusion about what the bill contained, (2) frustration of the speed by which the bill passed, and (3) lack of funds for prevention programs. Overall, there was much support for the legislation, but there was criticism along party lines over provisions of the bill. Congressman Oxley referred to the bill and the amendments on the floor as a bidding war in which many members had a sky is the limit type of attitude.[31] What this Select Committee hearing and others to be mentioned later in this book relay is that these hearings that are away from the House floor debate and constant media coverage detail a great concern over the lack of prevention, education, and treatment. Many of the hearings offer faces of drug victims that are as diverse as the country as opposed to that of simply a young black male. For sure, in several hearings there was a great concern about the drug plague in inner cities, but incarceration did not seem to be the priority among those who offered testimony. At this particular hearing, John P. Walters, Special Assistant to the Secretary of Education, made an exasperated statement in response to Congressman Rangel's consistent questions about what the president offered in terms of funding for drug education in schools. The issue was that there was not enough education funds allocated in the 1986 Act. Mr. Walters said:

> . . . Second, it does not cost a lot of money. And the discussions about funding levels and ongoing support I think divert us from the fact that what we need is a clear message. We need to supervise our children. The fact of the matter of the profile of the characteristic student user in this country is: a middle class kid, both parents in the family, a male, and white. It's not some poor inner city kid that has been abandoned by his folks. But a lot of news stories lead you to believe that . . .[32]

In spite of the large anti-drug bill and the uncertainty of all that it contained and whether it would fully achieve goals, Congress passed another bill in 1988, the year of a presidential election. The additional anti-drug bill in 1988 contained more punitive measures for dealing with drugs, while it did also have funding for prevention and education.

Anti-Drug Abuse Act of 1988

In 1988, Congress passed another omnibus anti-drug abuse bill. This $2.1-billion legislation contained harsh penalties for both drug users and dealers. This bill contained an amendment that established a mandatory minimum sentence for the mere possession of crack cocaine, making it the only federal mandatory minimum penalty for a first offence of simple possession of a controlled substance.[33] Congressman Clay Shaw (R-FL) introduced this amendment. He said the following during the debate on the House floor:

> We must not let the drug dealers outsmart us. As lawmakers, we must devise creative solutions to such changes in drug trafficking patterns. This is the purpose

of my amendment. The 1986 law provides tough penalties for 5 or more grams of crack only. My amendment would slap drug dealers with a stiff minimum mandatory prison of 5 to 20 years for the possession of a minimum of 5 grams on a first offense, for the possession of 3 grams on a second offense, and a possession of 1 gram on a third offense. Obviously this will not completely solve the crack problem but it will, at least, reduce the amount of crack on the streets.[34]

This amendment resulted in more prison construction and more African Americans being subjected to a five-year sentence for mere possession of crack. Congressman Rangel rose in opposition to this amendment. As floor manager for this bill, it is Congressman Rangel's duty to ensure that controversial legislation is debated within the time frame offered and to call for a recorded vote if he feels that his party needs to go on record via the vote about the issue. He said during the debate on the amendment:

Mr. Chairman, I admit that this is consistent with our get-tough or look-tough policy, and I really think this is an ideal amendment to vote for just prior to an election, but I know the gentleman believes that we have a get-tough Attorney General with a get-tough Justice Department that has really supported everything right down the line that has been presented to increase penalties . . . . But, Mr. Chairman, the gentleman has read the Attorney General's report on this provision, and they clearly indicate that they are in opposition to it, that this would permit some of the traffickers to manipulate drug statutes so as to minimize the penalties that are imposed in this.[35]

Interestingly, Rangel seemed convinced that this amendment would fail via voice vote. In a conversation on the House floor with Shaw, Rangel said that when the amendment fails via voice vote that he hoped Shaw would not ask his colleagues to vote on an amendment that simply sounds like Congress is getting tough on crime.[36] The Anti-Drug Abuse Act of 1988, which included Shaw's amendment, passed the House by a vote of 375–30.

Congress, in both this legislation and previous legislation, included funds for prison construction to take into account the number of individuals who would be arrested and convicted. Increased prison construction was part of the overall strategy. During consideration of the 1986 legislation, Congressman LaFalce (D-NY) said:

The resort to increase penalties to combat criminal activity has often been undermined by the paucity of available prison space. Needless to say, a long sentence is of little value if overcrowding of prison facilities influences prosecutors to arbitrarily drop or reduce charges or necessities the release of convicted felons. The legislation puts its money where its mouth is in this regard and appropriated several hundred millions for Federal prison construction.[37]

Like Congressman LaFalce, Democrats joined Republicans on the floor of the House and Senate in making strong statements in favor of tough on crime legislation. As has been mentioned, Democrats were readily contributors to the rhetoric and amendments that led to such a wide disparity between the treatment of crack versus powder cocaine.

The Anti-Drug Abuse Act of 1988 passed during an election year with many in Congress pressured to go on record as being tough on drugs. Like the first bill, Democratic members expressed concern over the legislation but voted for it nevertheless. An incumbent president was exiting and both Democrats and Republicans were hoping that the issue would help them win the presidency. Further, the attempt to polarize the public on crime continued throughout the 1988 presidential campaign with the use of the Willie Horton ad.[38] Although Democrats were in control of Congress, the Republicans were instrumental in passing amendments that would become the "meat" of the legislation. Additional evidence of this reality is the statement, "Republicans savored their success saying the amendments proved that the will of the majority was to have a tough, anti-crime, anti-drug user bill."[39] That there was not a single vote on the amendment that would make mere possession of only crack cocaine subjected to a mandatory minimum penalty serves as an indicator that the role of African American leadership on this issue was at least "questionable." A founding member of the CBC participated in the debate over this amendment and even taunted his Republican colleague by saying that he would embarrass himself if he called for a vote because surely the amendment on the face of it would fail. When the amendment passed by voice vote, it was the founding members of the CBC who did not call for a recorded vote, which at the very least would have put all members on record as supporting a particularly harsh amendment based on hysteria, and at the most, would have possibly allowed CBC members to provide unity and leadership that may have served to combat some of the strong language and political posturing of their colleagues. Members of the CBC listened intently to the congressional debates, and they understood that this issue was more political than sound policy, nonetheless, the CBC vote was divided on final passage of these pivotal anti-drug abuse bills.[40]

1990 Crime Bill

By 1990, Congressman Hughes, who chaired the House Judiciary's subcommittee on crime and who was instrumental in crafting key provisions of the anti-drug legislation in 1986 (before it went to the House floor) expressed concern about the mandatory minimum penalties contained in the 1986 and 1988 anti-drug bills. According to Eric Sterling, Hughes felt that the political will to soften the penalties did not exist among Democrats nor Republicans so instead, Hughes requested that the USSC review and issue a report about the impact of mandatory minimum penalties in general.[41] He offered this as part of the 1990 crime bill. In 1991, the USSC issued its report, which "concluded that the most efficient and effective way for Congress to direct sentencing policy is through the established process of sentencing guidelines, rather than through mandatory minimum penalties. The Commission reasoned that Congress could thereby achieve the objectives of mandatory minimum penalties . . . without compromising other important legislative goals."[42]

1994 Crime Bill

By 1994, mandatory minimums for crack cocaine had been law for eight years. The Omnibus Violent Crime Control and Law Enforcement Act of 1994, heretofore to be referred to as the crime bill, would be the fourth major crime bill passed by Congress since the sentencing reform legislation of 1984. The year 1994 was different in many ways. The previous year saw the inauguration of a Democratic president. Both chambers of Congress and the presidency were controlled by Democrats. In addition, 1993 saw an increase in women members of Congress and a substantial increase in CBC membership. However, the political environment was the same in many ways. President Clinton campaigned for the presidency as a moderate Democrat who wanted to demonstrate that a Democratic president could be tough on crime. As has been the case with crime legislation throughout the 1980s, this bill became a game of one-upmanship between Democrats and Republicans. In 1993, Clinton vowed to sign a major crime bill by the end of the year. During his campaign, he vowed to do something about the gridlock in Congress surrounding crime. In an address to the American people in early 1993, President Clinton said "The American people have been waiting long enough . . . They want more police on the street and fewer guns."[43] In writing about the politics surrounding the crime bill, Eric Sterling states that "the political value of longer sentencing fully blossomed in 1993 with Washington State initiative (passed on November 2, 1993)—a mandate of life imprisonment without parole after three convictions for serious felonies. The next day, the United States Senate began consideration of an omnibus anti-crime bill, without a day of hearings."[44]

In terms of heightened awareness of the issue of mandatory minimum penalties for crack cocaine, members of the CBC and various civil rights groups held a hearing in 1993 about how this issue was impacting the African American community. There was a new demand by these members that mandatory minimum penalties be eliminated or at the very least substantially reduced. President Clinton prided himself on being a New Democrat. With this description comes a development of coalitions of Democrats that abandon, or at least tone down, traditional liberal claims that prevention is the key to fighting crime in favor of law-and-order rhetoric, which includes standing by law enforcement and supporting initiatives that would benefit them.

The issue of crime remained a politically salient issue, one in which President Clinton believed Democrats in Congress could use in order to win over Reagan Democrats. Indeed, Clinton and a Democratically controlled Congress passed a crime bill that had fewer preventive measures than CBC members and progressive members advocated. This bill included two provisions specifically related to mandatory minimums for crack cocaine.

One was safety valve legislation, which allows some judicial discretion in sentencing for crack and powder cocaine cases. To quality, the defendant must meet five stringent and subjective conditions. As a result, very few of those serving a sentence for crack cocaine benefit from the safety valve legislation. Among the conditions are (1) a maximum of one criminal history point, (2) no involvement of a weapon, (3) the person must not have been an organizer or leader, (4) the person must not have been engaged in a criminal enterprise, and (5) the person has to provide all information about the offense to the government in a timely manner.[45] There have been criticisms that judges and prosecutors refused to believe that the individual was providing all information, thus a person meeting all of the conditions but the latter would not be able to escape a mandatory minimum sentence. According to the USSC, powder cocaine offenders more frequently qualify for the sentencing reduction under the safety valve legislation than crack cocaine offenders. In 2000, nearly 38 percent of powder offenders received a reduction compared to approximately 15 percent of crack cocaine offenders. Thus, the inherent race and class bias of mandatory minimum penalties exists even under measures designed to help some offenders avoid a five-year-plus sentence. Nevertheless, given the environment that seemingly mandates a politician to be tough on crime, the best opponents of mandatory minimum legislation could get passed as a part of the Omnibus Crime Bill was the safety valve legislation. Although passage of this is recognition that current penalties were harsh, the efforts to make the safety valve retroactive failed. Congress also, as part of the crime bill, directed the Sentencing Commission to issue another report on mandatory minimum penalties, with a specific focus on powder and crack cocaine. "Specifically, Congress directed the Sentencing Commission to report on the current federal structure of differing penalties for powder cocaine and crack cocaine offenses and to provide recommendations for retention or modification of these differences."[46] The Crime bill passed by a vote of 235–195 with 24 CBC members voting for the bill and 12 against.

The 1995 United States Sentencing Commission Report

The last vote taken by the House of Representatives on mandatory minimum penalties for crack occurred in October 1995. The aforementioned amendment in the crime bill called for this report. The environment in Congress was fairly conservative as Republicans had taken control of the House at the start of the 104th Congress (1995–1996). In addition, several senators switched from the Democratic party. They did so with the stated belief that President Clinton and Democrats were for liberal big-government programs, thus getting away from the values of the American people. Although Clinton's 1992 presidential campaign strategy as a moderate Democrat helped to put a Democrat in office, his policies, to some key voters, belied modernism. As Gary Jacobson mentions in an article on the 1994 elections, President Clinton began to alienate Reagan Democrats, southerners, and the largely male Perot constituency with his focus on racial and gender diversity in administration appointments. Jacobson states that "Exit polls revealed only 40 percent of southerners approved of Clinton's performance, compared to 51 percent in the northeast and 45 percent elsewhere. Among white southern men, Clinton's approval stood at a dismal 27 percent."[47]

Also, the language about devolution, i.e., returning power to the states, was similar in many ways to that of Nixon's Silent Majority language. Thus Democrats and Republicans continued their battle to prove to White conservative voters that one party was more conservative than the other. It should be noted that the American public was highly charged along racial lines following the verdict in the O.J. Simpson case, where polls and newspaper/magazine articles showed a divide among African Americans and Whites on this issue. The Million Man March, called by controversial figure Minister Louis Farakhan, furthered created an environment of heightened racial tension.[48]

It is within this context that Congress considered a report from the USSC. In February 1995, the USSC issued a report to Congress. It was in October 1995, several days after the Million Man March, that Congress voted on and overwhelmingly rejected the USSC's recommendations, the first time in the history of the USSC that Congress had done so. The recommendation by the USSC would:

> . . . make the starting point for determining sentences for crack offenders the same by adopting a 1-to-1 quantity ratio at the powder cocaine level and would have prvovided enhancements for violence and other harms disproportionately associated with crack cocaine.[49]

The USSC also recommended removing a mandatory minimum penalty for simple possession of crack cocaine. In essence, under the USSC recommendation, it would take the same level of crack as it takes for powder to receive a mandatory minimum. The USSC concluded in its report that the laws were unjust, disproportionately affected African Americans, and could not be justified. Within Congress, Democrats and Republicans overwhelmingly rejected the report by a vote of 332–83. It is interesting to note that the bill passed via voice vote (meaning they, too, rejected the report) in the Senate on September 29. The sole African American in the Senate, Senator Carol Moseley Braun, may have been able to put her Democratic colleagues on record by requesting a recorded vote. Many bills pass Congress via a voice vote. Generally those bills are noncontroversial. At times, even with the noncontroversial bills, a member of Congress will call for a vote so that his or her colleagues will have an opportunity to go on record as saying they voted for the bill. This also works with a popular bill among one party and the public that the opposite party will allow to pass without a vote to avoid controversy. To put the member of the opposing party on record of supporting the legislation introduced, a roll-call vote will be called. Essentially, regardless of the level of support for a bill, members often use roll-call votes as a political tool. If the legislation is about reciting a prayer on school grounds and Democrats oppose it, but would allow for it to pass via voice vote, a Republican member will call for a roll-call vote. If Democrats oppose the bill, the vote will be used in an ad that states, "my Democratic colleague voted against allowing your child to pray in school." The importance of Braun, the sole African American in the Senate at the time, cannot be underestimated. A call for a roll-call vote, although symbolic, would have allowed the CBC to understand which members in other body would be supportive in crafting a House-Senate resolution on this issue. Further, it may have been a signal to the participants in the Million Man March that someone in the Senate was fighting on their behalf. Among the CBC members in the House who voted, the vote was unanimously in favor of the report. President Clinton signed into law the legislation, thus rejecting the Commission's proposed guideline changes.[50] After the vote took place, Attorney General Reno reiterated her 1993 position that the disparities should be reduced. However, she came under criticism for not entering into the debate while the legislation was considered.[51] The USSC, as has been mentioned, was directed as a result of an amendment offered by Senator Kennedy (D-MA) to present an additional recommendation on limiting the disparity between crack and powder cocaine.[52]

By the time this vote was taken, Congress was fully aware of the impact these laws have had on the African American community. The USSC's report contained this information and groups such as Families Against Mandatory Minimums (FAMM), the American Civil Liberties Union (ACLU), the National Association for the Advancement of Colored People (NAACP), and the Leadership Conference on Civil Rights (LCCR) were all vocal on this issue. On this point, law professor David Cole provides some understanding about what "the numbers" actually showed. He writes:

> In 1992, the United States Public Health Service estimated, based on self-report surveys, that 76 percent of illicit drug users were white, 14 percent black, 8 percent Hispanic, figures which roughly match each group's share of the general population. Yet, African Americans make up 35 percent of all drug arrests, 55 percent of all drug convictions, and 74 percent of all sentences for drug offenses.[53]

It has already been mentioned that the vote took place just days after the Million Man March was held on the ground of the United States Capitol. In part, this March was a recognition that conservative politics of the 1980s and 1990s were detrimental to the needs of African Americans. Democrats and Republicans during this era were competing for White voters in order to maintain power positions in Congress and the presidency. In the waning months before the 1996 presidential election, Democrats in Congress and in the presidency ignored the evidence that these laws were discriminatory, ignored traditional and nontraditional civil rights groups on this issue, and ignored the CBC so that they could appeal to southern voters and the "soccer mom" voters that they were as tough on crime as Republicans.

The USSC would present two more reports on this issue between 1996 and 2002, one in 1997 and another in May 2002.[54] Congress acted on neither the 1997 nor the May 2002 report. Thus the 100-1 disparity for the treatment of crack cocaine versus powder cocaine would continue to be the law of the land. Further, although white Americans continue to use crack cocaine more frequently than African Americans, it is African Americans that overwhelmingly receive a mandatory penalty of five years plus for crack violations. Despite a change in the presidency from a Republican during the 1980s to a Democrat during the 1990s, there had been little effort on the part of Democrats in Congress and in the presidency to address this issue during this time period, in spite of the USSC's reports. Indeed, in 1997 the CBC criticized President Clinton for not going far enough on the issue of mandatory minimums for crack cocaine.

In the final analysis, at the fifteenth anniversary mark of the passage of these laws, there continued to be no indication that this law will be changed or softened. Democrats continue to persuade African Americans that they are the party that best addresses their interests and the CBC continues to advocate the notion that a Democratically controlled Congress and the presidency will result in progressive legislation. After two decades of a policy that, in part, based on their near unanimous vote on the 1995 recommendation by the USSC, is an indication that CBC members believe is unfair and unjust, there is little indication to believe that they can persuade their colleagues to overturn this regressive legislation. The fear of losing House and Senate seats seems to be stronger than their commitment to address the USSC's data and analysis on the impact of mandatory minimums has had on the African American community.

A practice in American political campaigns is to compete for votes. At various stages of the party system, different groups (i.e., ethnicity, gender, age) have been attracted to a particular party for various reasons. At times, a party is able to attract previously alienated groups from said party. The issues of race and crime have been issues used to compete for votes.

Party Competition/Party Politics

A strong two-party system has consistently existed in the United States since the birth of the Republican party in the mid-1800s. Since that time, African Americans have had a strong allegiance to either the Republican or the Democratic party. African Americans supported the Republican party for the presidency of Abraham Lincoln until 1936 when they began to support Franklin D. Roosevelt.[55] From 1860 until 1932, the Republican party, with key exceptions, remained the party that worked to include African Americans and the Democratic party, particularly in the South, practiced White domination and African American exclusion. Even as President F.D. Roosevelt attracted millions of African Americans known as Roosevelt Democrats, the Republican party continued to champion civil rights legislation. For many Americans, both African American and non-African Americans, President F.D. Roosevelt provided economic opportunities that were needed after the Great Depression. By the 1960s, however, race would become an important factor in changing voter allegiance. Southern whites began to leave the Democratic party in 1964 due, in large part, to the last year of John F. Kennedy's presidency, in which he openly championed civil rights and sent troops to Mississippi, Alabama to protect civil rights protestors and to pursue the right of African Americans to attend the University of Alabama and the University of Mississippi.

President Lyndon Johnson continued to carry out civil rights measures. In signing the Civil Rights Act of 1964, a bill that arguably made the federal government more active on behalf of African Americans, President Johnson remarked that he had just turned the South over to Republicans for a long time to come.[56] Indeed, President Johnson was the last Democrat to win by the White vote.[57] Barry Goldwater, sensing that Democrats were losing their base in the South, campaigned to attract the southern White vote. He was successful in winning five Deep South states—this was an accomplishment for a Republican to pick up victories in the solid Democratic South. This competition for southern White votes that successfully began in the 1960s continues today.[58]

We argue that party competition for White swing votes placed African American interests at risk. Democrats did not want to be considered the party that is soft on crime, because this would further jeopardize their efforts to win back the Reagan

Democrats. The result was that Democrats began to focus less on preventive measures and more on punitive measures, which is why they have overwhelmingly supported mandatory minimum sentences and tough crime legislation since the 1980s. Democrats in Congress refused to support efforts to reduce or eliminate mandatory minimums. Paul Frymer argues that the Democratic party has taken the African American vote for granted. He calls this theory "electoral capture," and it is the based on the idea that when a group, such as African Americans, demonstrates loyalty to a party, they are less likely to leave the party because in many cases, the opposing party is not advocating the interests of the group. He writes:

> The opposing party does not want the group's vote, so the group cannot threaten its own party's leaders with defection. The party leadership, then can make the group for granted because it recognizes that, short of abstention of an independent (and usually electoral suicidal) third party, had nowhere else to go. Placed in this position by the party system, a captured group will often find its interests neglected by their own party leaders. These leaders, in turn, offer attention and benefits to groups of "swing" voters who are allegedly capable of determining election results.[59]

He goes on to make a statement that helps to characterize the voting behavior and rhetoric of Democratic members of Congress on mandatory minimum laws for crack cocaine and on the issue of crime in general. He writes:

> As long as the party closest to African American voters fears the opposition will make attacks on racial grounds, it will compensate by distancing itself from black interests, ironically leading situations where it, and not the opposition party, launches high profile attacks o black interests. When dealing with African American voters, party leaders must engage in the very unique calculation of weighing the potential advantage of bringing in black voters against the potential loss of white voters. Few other interest groups—whether demographic or occupational-carry such a burden.[60]

There is much research that would support his argument. In their book, *Prejudice, Politics, and the American Dilemma*, Sniderman, Tetlock, and Carmines contend that even in the current era race is as much as an American dilemma as it was when Gunner Myrdal wrote about it more than a half century ago. It has become more complicated in that the government has implemented programs such as Affirmative Acton to help African Americans who have been wronged; however, today, racial cleavages remain very strong. They argue that politics reinforces these cleavages. Politically salient issues such as welfare and crime have been used by Democrats to demonstrate how close they are to the Republican idea of being tough on criminals. As Frymer, the Edsalls, and others would argue, in recent decades, as competition for White swing voters has grown stronger, both political parties behave similarly on crime in order to please certain voters. Sniderman, Tetlock, and Carmines tell us that "Candidates competing for popular support strive to turn the issues of the day to their advantage, and issues such as race are no exception, whether invoked indirectly, or directly, as in the anti-affirmative action ads of the Jesse Helms campaign."[61]

President Clinton's rise to the presidency of the United States is an example of a Democrat actively seeking White voters. In 1992, President Clinton was determined that he would not let the right beat him on crime. Running as a moderate Democrat, early in his campaign he displayed his will to support the death penalty by returning to Arkansas to oversee the execution of a mentally impaired African American male (see "Bill Clinton's Death Penalty Waffle," by Alexander Nguyen, The American Prospect, December 19, 2001). On the issue of mandatory minimums, his Attorney General (Janet Reno) expressed concern over these policies and initiated a study on it. The study found that over a third of those convicted of drug offenses were low-level drug offenders with limited criminal histories, no violence, and a minimal role in the drug trade.[62] According to Mauer,

> The report had been completed in August 1993, but was not released until February 1994. Had this study been issued in a timely manner, it could have played an important role in the national debate on the crime bill. Instead, the White House clearly made efforts to dilute any impact it may have had. According to *The New York Times*, Attorney General Reno "soon learned the White House game plan: never expose Clinton's right flank on crime."[63]

This helps to explain President Clinton's limited efforts to support less harsh mandatory minimum laws for crack cocaine throughout his two-term presidency. Ronald Reagan helped to set the ideological battle on the issue of crime, the Democrats, in seeking to maintain congressional seats and the presidency, began to mimic Republicans on this issue and the Congressional Black Caucus was caught between the need to protect its national constituency and the party in which the bulk of its members identify. It is, in part, the competition for white southern votes that led to the passage of tough criminal justice penalties such as the one that is the subject of this book.

These laws were made as a result of mass hysteria by the media and Congress on the issue of crack. There was little or no basis for the law other than Congress wanting to appear to get tough on crack dealers. Years later, after evidence has been presented that the laws are ineffective and discriminatory, the same Congress (many of whom remained in Congress throughout today) has been extremely slow to react to reports stating that the laws are ineffective and actually hamper crime fighting efforts.

A point also to be made is that in 1986, during the height of the media campaign on crack and violence in the inner cities, there were 19,257 homicides, 3.9 percent were drug related. In 1988, there were 17,971 homicides of which 5.6 percent were drug related. In 1993, there were 23,180 homicides of which 5.5 percent were drug related.[64] The point is that while the perception was that most homicides were drug related and thus more must be done in terms of imprisonment, these statistics show that the assumption was false. It also indicates that while the jail population increased as a result of mandatory minimums for crack cocaine, the homicide rate increased throughout the late 1980s and 1990s. While African American faces continued to fill the prisons, the homicide rate did not decrease nor did the continued flow of drugs into the community. Crack cocaine cannot be made without powder cocaine, and legislation allowing those with 499 grams of powder cocaine to go unpunished, in terms of receiving a mandatory minimum sentence, was ineffective. As a Rand report tells us, a cocaine wholesaler can have 454 grams of powder cocaine and not be subjected to a mandatory minimum sentence. If he sells his 454 grams to eight lower-level dealers, those individuals could each have 56 grams of powder cocaine and still not be subjected to a mandatory minimum. These eight lower-level dealers can then each sell to eight street-level dealers who turn the powder into crack cocaine. These 64 street-level dealers who have turned the original 454 grams of powder into crack cocaine would be subjected to the federal mandatory minimum laws.[65] It cannot be emphasized enough that crack cocaine cannot be made without powder cocaine, yet suppliers of 454 grams of powder cocaine, even if caught, would not have gotten a mandatory minimum sentence, where as the 64 street-level dealers who ultimately receive the powder cocaine would each be subjected to five years in prison for having a portion of the original 454 grams of powder!

The street level dealers, at least those that are targeted, are often young, poor, African American, or Hispanic. These are the groups most targeted by the police, which is evident when one considers that over 80 percent of those in prison for drug charges are African Americans and Hispanics, while surveys demonstrate that they are no more likely to use or sell drugs than White Americans.

Indeed, there have been court cases challenging the constitutionality of providing two separate penalties for the abuse of the same drug. John Hope Franklin and Genna Rae McNeil, in *African Americans and the Living Constitution*, chronicle the challenges African Americans have had in obtaining their full rights as citizens based on principles and rights outlined by the United States Constitution. Charles Ogletree, a contributor to the book, chronicles the disparate treatment of African Americans in the criminal justice system with regard to the issue of crack versus powder cocaine. For example, in Minnesota, five African Americans convicted of possession of crack cocaine challenged the Minnesota criminal statute that allowed judges to sentence more harshly those convicted of crack as opposed to those convicted of powder, citing that the separate sentencing had a disproportionate impact on African Americans. Evidence was presented by the defendants that bolstered their claim. In Minnesota, over 90 percent of those charged with possession of crack were African American while over 80 percent of those charged with the possession of powder were White.[66] The Minnesota Supreme Court upheld the lower court ruling that the "penalties for crack cocaine, in contrast to powdered cocaine, had a disproportionate and unconstitutional impact on African Americans."[67]

There continues to be debate as to whether mandatory minimum penalties violate the equal protection clause of the Fifth and Fourteenth Amendments and also whether the crack cocaine laws violate the Eighth Amendment. The fact that there is a mandatory minimum for simple possession of crack cocaine and not simple possession of powder cocaine has raised concerns and has been challenged.[68]

Conclusion

Whether intended or unintended, the mass incarceration of African Americans has occurred as a result of mandatory minimum penalties for cocaine. A policy window, as discussed by John Kingdon's work on agenda-setting, has opened to correct the unintended consequences, yet, with the exception of a safety valve legislation, there has not been a major overhaul of the mandatory minimums for crack cocaine legislation. The conservative movement of the 1980s that led to these tough crime policies was virtually institutionalized in Congress as a result of the 1994 Congressional elections (the 104th Congress) when the Republicans gained control of the House of Representatives for the first time in 40 years and issued a Contract with America that did not have the interests of African Americans in mind. A golden opportunity was lost, and the CBC would continue to face an uphill battle to overturn legislation harmful to African Americans and the disadvantaged. The purpose of this chapter was to discuss why mandatory minimums for crack cocaine are an issue that impacts African Americans, how the legislation reached the congressional agenda, the attitudes expressed by members in committee hearings and on the floor that led to the laws, and the portrayal of violence in the inner cities to justify the wide disparity in the treatment of the same drug. This chapter demonstrated that Congress quickly passed a bill without the legislation going through a normal committee process with both Democratic and Republican politicians attempting to demonstrate how tough they were on crime. It was an effort to appeal to voters during an election year. After the 1986 legislation became law, the USSC issued several reports criticizing mandatory minimum penalties in general, and specifically mandatory penalties for crack versus those for powder cocaine. Despite this information, the very Congress, Democrats and Republicans, that rushed to put the legislation on the congressional agenda has refused to put it back on the agenda to address the disparity. Indeed, there have been relatively few hearings over the course of the past two decades on the issue.

Historically, politicians have used the issue of race and crime to justify harsh laws that penalize African Americans. While past laws were specific in naming African Americans as the group that would bear the brunt of the penalties, modern-day politicians in both parties circumvent the issue of race and instead make the argument that the policy is race neutral and the fact that African Americans suffer disproportionately from the penalties is merely a coincidence. The very fact that politicians in considering harsh penalties stated that crack was cheaper and easily accessible to poor communities is an indication that they knew who would be arrested and convicted of these crimes. Thus, they did not have to say that this legislation targets African Americans. The Democrats have largely abandoned a discussion of poverty, lack of education and work opportunities, inadequate housing, and particularly the historical treatment of local law enforcement officials toward African Americans as all contributing to the incarceration of this group, in favor of espousing rhetoric that more individual responsibility is needed and more law enforcement officers are needed to fight crime. This issue speaks to a historical double-edged sword in the African American community:

one that acknowledges that more law enforcement officers on the street level contributes to what many label as the criminal injustice system.

Further, the result of targeting money for increased law enforcement and prisons for drug offenders, resources allocated to law enforcement to investigate, arrest, and convict those who commit white-collar crimes are often less than that invested in those convicted of drug crimes. Congress seems to prefer to devote more money to building prisons to accommodate the perceived increase of those convicted as a result of the 1986 and 1988 anti-drug bills. This further demonstrates a double standard within the American criminal justice system. An article in *Fortune* magazine highlighted the number of white-collar crimes that have occurred during the 1980s and 1990s and the economic damage these crimes have caused. The Enron and Anderson Consulting Companies' alleged crimes have been in the public eye, but many such crimes have occurred, if on a smaller scale. Despite the millions of dollars lost from fraud and other crimes and the number of victims of these crimes, "the white-collar inmate population has actually shrunk in proportional terms from 2.8% of the total in 1985 to 0.6% today. Much of that is due to mandatory minimum drug-sentencing laws."[69] This creates the perception that politicians will use get tough on crime and "throw them in jail and throw away the key" language when it comes to crime among those in the inner cities. As mandatory minimum penalties for drugs and other such laws demonstrate, when the laws appear to target those in the inner cities, politicians are quick to talk about the need to fight crime. This is a pattern in the United States system of criminal justice that African American officials continue to battle.

Keyterms

Endnotes

1 "Special Report to the Congress: Cocaine and Federal Sentencing Policy" (as directed by section two of Public Law 104-38, The United States Sentencing Commission, Concurring Opinion of Vice Chairman Michael S. Gelacak, April 1997.
2 *Special Report to the Congress: Cocaine and Federal Sentencing Policy* (Washington, DC: The United States Sentencing Commission, April 1997), p. 8.
3 Ibid., Concurring Opinion of Vice Chair Michael S. Gelacak, p. 3.
4 United States Sentencing Commission's Report to Congress on Mandatory Minimum Penalties, 1991, p. 6.
5 Ibid., p. 7.

6 Cooper, Edith Fairman "The Emergence of Crack Cocaine Abuse in the United States: A Public Health Perspective." *CRS Report for Congress* (Washington, DC: Library of Congress, p. 50.

7 Ibid., p. 47.

8 Ibid., p. 50.

9 Kingdon, John, *Agendas, Alternatives, and Public Policies*, 2nd edition (New York: Harper Collins College Publishers, 1995).

10 Baumgartner, Frank, and Bryan Jones, *Agendas and Instability in American Politics* (Chicago: University of Chicago Press, 1993).

11 A discussion of the images of those using drugs can be found in Clarence Lusane's *Pipe Dream Blues: Racism & The War on Drugs*, Boston, MA, South End Press, 1991, chapter 2. In addition, Dan Baum's book entitled *Smoke and Mirrors: The War on Drugs and the Politics of Failure,* Chapter 15, entitled "Sarejevo on the Potomac, 1986," Boston, Little, Brown and Company, 1996 also discusses the rhetoric and the images of crack houses that the media and politicians focused on during the passage of these laws.

12 The House Select Committee on Narcotics Abuse and Control was abolished in 1993 purportedly as a money-saving mechanism.

13 "A Survey of Members of Congress About Drug Abuse in Their Districts: A Report of the Select Committee on Narcotics Abuse and Control," Ninety-Eighth Congress, Second Session (Washington, DC: U.S. Government Printing Office, 1985).

14 Ibid., pp. 7–8 .

15 Hacker, Andrew *Two Nations: Black and White, Separate, Hostile, Unequal* (New York: Ballantine Books, 1992), p. 180.

16 Gray, Mike *Drug Crazy: How We Got Into This Mess and How We Can Get Out* (New York: Routledge, 1998), p. 46.

17 Ibid.

18 "Cocaine Abuse and the Federal Response," Hearing before the Select Committee on Narcotics Abuse and Control, House of Representatives Ninety-Ninth Congress, First Session, Tuesday, July 16, 1985, pp. 61–63.

19 In October 1986, the CBC also held a joint hearing with the House Select Committee on Narcotics Abuse and Control to examine federal response to drug trafficking and abuse. This hearing will be discussed in a upcoming chapter.

20 Maur, Marc *Race to Incarcerate, The Sentencing Project* (New York: The New Press, 1999), p. 62.

21 Gray, pp. 107–108.

22 Orr, p. 226.

23 Ibid.

24 Mauer, p. 56.

25 David Calverson, "The Welfare Queen and Willie Horton," in Mann, Coramae Richey, et al. *Images of Color, Images of Crime*. 3rd edition. Cary, NC, Roxbury Press, 2007, p. 243.

26 A discussion of vagrancy laws, Black Codes, and the convict lease system can be found in Eric Foner's book *Reconstruction in America, 1860–1880,* New York, Harper & Row Publishers, 1988. Some argue that laws have been passed such as the ones mentioned above for the purpose of controlling the African American population. In the minds of some, the mandatory minimum penalties for crack cocaine are an extension of those laws. While watching a documentary on MSNBC entitled *Locked UP*, one of the inmates proclaimed with frustration that police officers are modern-day slave catchers. They target Blacks and then lock them away in prison. This was a modern-day Black American's

perception of a slavery-era phenomenon. See also Douglas A. Blackmon's book entitled *Slavery By Another Name: The Reenslavement of Black Americans from the Civil War to World War II*, New York: Anchor Books, 2009.

27 Berry, Mary Frances and John Blassingame, *Long Memory* (Oxford: Oxford Press, 1983), p. 228.

28 Ibid.

29 Ibid., p. 229.

30 United States Sentencing Commission, May 2002,p. 9.

31 "Implementation of Provisions of the Anti-Drug Abuse Act of 1986: Hearing Before the Select Committee on Abuse and Control," House of Representatives, One Hundredth Congress, First Session, February 26, 1987 (Washington, DC: United States Government Printing Office, 1987), p. 4.

32 Ibid., p. 34.

33 United States Sentencing Commission, May 2002, p. 11.

34 Congressional Record, September 16, 1988, p. 24274.

35 Ibid., p. 24275.

36 Ibid.

37 Congressional Record, September 11, 1986, p. 22993.

38 This controversial campaign ad depicted an African American who was furloughed from prison by the Democratic presidential candidate. Horton committed violent crimes against a young White couple while on furlough.

39 "House-Passed GOP Bill has Clear GOP Imprint." *Congressional Quarterly* (September 24, 1988), 46, Issue 39, p. 2661.

40 The following year, during the Congressional Black Caucus Annual Legislative Weekend, the House Select Committee on Narcotics Abuse and Control held a hearing entitled "The Federal Drug Strategy: What Does It Mean for Black America?" Members of the CBC and other interested groups gave testimony about the impact of drugs in African American communities and ways the federal government has achieved and failed in fighting the war on drugs. This report will be analyzed in detail in an upcoming chapter that specifically analyzes the CBC's response to mandatory minimums for crack cocaine.

41 Interview with Eric Sterling, Chief Legal Counsel to Congressman Hughes at the time this legislation was debated in Congress, June 2002.

42 "Special Report to Congress: Cocaine and Federal Sentencing Policy," United States Sentencing Commission, February 1995.

43 "Senate Ok's Omnibus Anti-Crime Bill," *CQ Almanac* (1993), p. 294.

44 Sterling, Eric, "The Sentencing Boomerang: Drug Prohibition, Politics, and Reform," *Villanova Law Review* (1995), p. 412.

45 United States Sentencing Commission, May 2002, p. 60.

46 "Special Report to Congress: Cocaine and Federal Sentencing Policy," United States Sentencing Commission, (February 2005), Executive Summary.

47 Gary C. Jacobson, "The 1994 House Elections in Perspective," *Political Science Quarterly* (Summer 1996), 111(2), 207.

48 Among the articles reviewed by the researchers on the topic includes "A Controversial March Puts Black Leaders on the Spot" (*U.S. News and World Report*, October 23, 1995), which highlighted unfavorable comments toward Farrakhan, including a comment by Republican CBC member Gary Franks who called the Nation of Islam the Black equivalent of the Ku Klux Klan. "They are organizations that hide behind a veiled shield of doing what's good for their race, while increasing the racial divide via their hatred for

others"; an article by *Newsweek* reporter Joe Klein, "Can Powell Reach Them?" (October 30, 1995), which discusses the level of support among the Black middle class for Louis Farrakhan; another article in the same magazine by Ellis Cose, which also looks at Farrakhan's appeal among the Black middle class; and an article by Adolph Reed in the Progressive that criticizes Black leaders on their response to the O.J. Simpson verdict, the Million Man March, and the Reagan Administration ("Black Politics Gone Haywire," December 20, 1995).

49 United States Sentencing Commission," A Special Report to Congress: Cocaine and Federal Sentencing Policy (as directed by section two of Public Law 104-38)," (Washington, DC: United States Government Printing Office, April 1997).

50 Ibid.

51 Michael Isikoff, "Crack, Coke, and Race: Are the Differences in Cocaine Sentencing Fair?" *Newsweek*, (November 6, 1995), 77.

52 *The 51st Annual CQ Almanac, 1995, 104th Congress, 1st Session* (Washington, DC, Congressional Quarterly, Inc., 1995), pp. 6–26.

53 Cole, David. *No Equal Justice: Race and Class in the American Criminal Justice System* (New York: The New Press, 1999), p. 144.

54 In 2007, Congress would finally allow USSC recommendations become law. This will be discussed in the chapter covering the 20th year anniversary of mandatory minimum laws for crack cocaine.

55 Theodore Reuter, *The Politics of Race, African Americans and the Political System*, p. 240.

56 Edsall, Thomas, and Martha Edsall, *Chain Reaction: The Impact of Race, Rights, and Taxes on American Politics* (New York: W.W. Norton and Company, 1992), p. 37.

57 Dr. Lorenzo Morris, a panel discussion held by the Congressional Black Associates entitled "Why Americans Don't Vote: Apathy or Alienation," October 2000. Also, see a chapter entitled "Race and the Two Party System" in *The Social and Political Implications of the 1984 Jesse Jackson Presidential Campaign*, Santa Barbara, CA, Praegar Publishers, 1990, edited by Dr. Lorenzo Morris. In the chapter an analysis of voting trends of both African Americans and Whites is offered. (See also Sabato, Larry J, The Year of Obama: How Barack Obama won the White House (New York: Pearson Education, Inc., 2010) for a discussion of demographics and the election of President Obama. Obama received 43% of the White vote in his historic 2008 election.)

58 Scholars Earl and Merle Black in their book entitled *Politics and Society in the South* and in their (2002) book about the rise of Southern Republicans give a very detailed and chronological account of the movement of southern White voters from the Democratic party to the Republican party.

59 Paul Frymer, *Uneasy Alliances, Race and Party Competition in America* (Princeton, NJ: Princeton University Press, 1999), p. 8.

60 Ibid.

61 Paul Sniderman, Philip Tetlock, and Edward Carmines, *Prejudice, Politics, and the American Dilemma* (Stanford, CA: Stanford University Press, 1993), p. 25.

62 Mauer, p. 75.

63 Ibid.

64 Dorsey, Tina L.; and Middleton, Priscilla. *Drugs and Crime Facts—NCJ 165148*. U.S. Department of Justice Office of Justice Programs. Washington, D.C. (Undated), p. 2.

65 Caulkins, Jonathan P., Peter C. Rydell, William Schwabe, and James Chiesa, "Mandatory Minimum Drug Sentences: Throwing Away the Key or the Taxpayers' Money" (Santa Monica, CA: Rand Drug Policy Research Center, 1997), p. 20.

66 Ogletree, Charles, "Blind Justice? Race, the Constitution, and the Justice System," in John Hope Franklin and Genna Rae Mcneil (eds.), *African Americans and the Living Constitution* (Washington and London: The Smithsonian Press, 1995), p. 242.
67 Ibid.
68 Doyle, Charles, "Federal Mandatory Minimum Sentencing Statutes: A List of Citations with Captions, Introductory Comments, and Bibliography," *CRS Report of Congress* (Washington, DC: The Library of Congress), pp. 22–23.
69 Clifton Leaf, "It's Time to Stop Coddling White-Collar Crooks: Send Them to Jail," Fortune (March 25, 2002), 145(6), 64.

ACTIVITY 1

How much did "race" impact what was done to address "crime"?

A Chapter 4 Exercise

Instructions:

In the space above, explain what the book talks about regarding the emergence of crack cocaine and the increasing role taken by legislators. Please consider the sources cited in the book dealing with putting drug legislation on the political agenda when preparing your response.

Crime
in
America

[Please tear out your completed response so you can turn it in to the instructor]

ACTIVITY 2

In the boxes, describe from the increasing public
attention on drug crime . . .

A Chapter 4 Exercise

Early Congressional Response

Len Bias

Anti-drug Abuse Act of 1988

ACTIVITY 3

Applying a book concept to a real-life issue...

1990 Crime Bill   1994 Crime Bill

Instructions:

Part 1: Within the 1990 *Crime Bill* box, please discuss what you think is important about how that bill sought to address the emerging drug problem. Feel free to do outside research using the Internet.

Part 2: Within the 1994 *Crime Bill* box, please discuss what you think is important about how that bill sought to address the emerging drug problem. Feel free to do outside research using the Internet.

A Chapter 4 Exercise

[Please tear out your completed response so you can turn it in to the instructor]

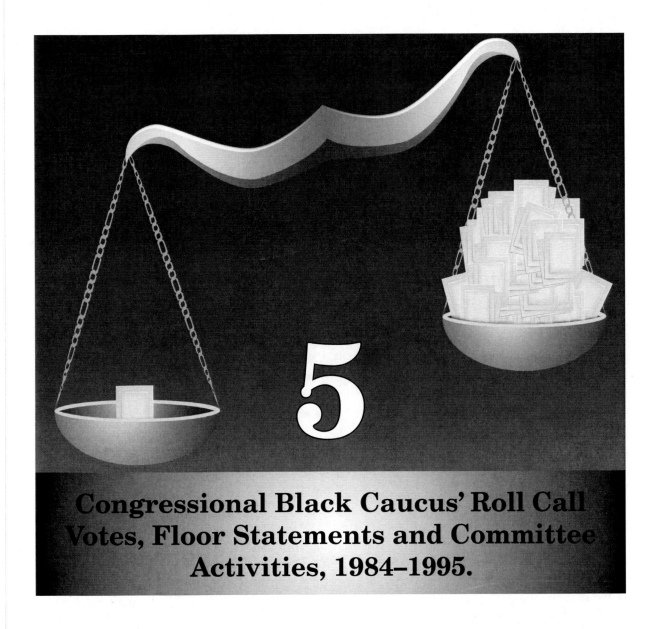

5

Congressional Black Caucus' Roll Call Votes, Floor Statements and Committee Activities, 1984–1995.

Chapter 5 Synopsis: This chapter examines the impact of mandatory minimum penalties for crack/powder cocaine on the African American community. It explores incarceration rates among African American men, women, and juveniles during the time frame of 1984–1995. In addition, it explores laws Congress passed since 1986 that have consequences for those convicted under these laws, i.e., limiting access to student loans, housing, welfare benefits, changes in the foster care system that makes it easier for parents to lose custody of children, and so on.

The rich get richer and the poor get prison. (Congressman Donald Payne-see footnote 42)

As we have shown, both Democrats and Republicans introduced and voted for tough crime policies throughout the 1980s and 1990s. As a group that consists primarily of Democrats with a mission of advocating progressive legislation, individual members of the CBC will take cues from sources outside the leadership of the organization in determining their vote preferences. This chapter directly assesses the response of the CBC to legislation containing mandatory minimum penalties for crack cocaine by way of exploring CBC members' voting records on several key bills mentioned in a previous chapter, as well as floor and committee statements.

CBC and Democratic Political Behavior on Crime Legislation, 1984–1995

The first bill that served as a precursor to the 1986 anti-crime legislation was the Comprehensive Crime Control Act of 1984, which provided for a major overhaul of federal sentencing procedures, allowed pretrial detention of certain defendants, prohibited tampering with computers, and increased penalties for major drug offenses. Of particular interest as it relates to this research is that the measure established sentencing guidelines for judges to use in imposing sentences. As reported by *Time Magazine*, the measure was intended to eliminate disparities in punishment for the same crimes, to dismantle the present parole system, and to establish a seven-member commission (the United States Sentencing Commission) to set sentencing guidelines.[1] Before the measure passed, there was political bickering between Democrats and Republicans about which party was preventing substantial crime legislation from passing. House Republicans, in an effort to pass the measure, introduced a motion to recommit the 1985 fiscal continuing resolution bill (a continuing resolution bill allows for the government to continue functioning while Congress passes appropriations bills for the upcoming year) back to the House Appropriations Committee with the instructions that the crime legislation should be attached. The House Appropriations Committee acted as instructed immediately and the measure was sent back to the House floor for a vote. It passed by a "key vote of 243–166 (R-153–3; D 89–163)."[2] This vote is also significant in that a Republican in a Congress where Democrats hold the majority introduced this motion to "recommit." A motion to "recommit" means that the legislation is to be sent back to the committee in which it originated for further changes. In each of the bills below, the significance of the CBC vote will be measured by (1) the CBC member's vote with the Democratic Party (this variable is for the purpose of exploring whether CBC members voted with their party on these crime measures), (2) the CBC member's vote with the Chair of the CBC (the CBC has a whip position to persuade CBC members to vote a certain way on measures; as the Chair is the head of the organization, a vote in opposition to his or her vote is a sign of Caucus disunity), (3) whether those with leadership positions within the Democratic party voted with the party (this is to determine whether

CBC members in key leadership positions are more likely to support the party position), (4) the CBC member's vote with the ADA and with the NAACP, where a scorecard is issued (these organizations opposed anti-crime measures in Congress and are considered progressive civil rights and civil liberties organizations; it is expected that a group such as the CBC would vote in accordance to these organizations' wishes), (5) whether those with 55 percent or more African Americans in their congressional districts were more likely to vote with the Democratic party (because the legislation considered was known to disproportionately impact the African American community as statements from CBC members on the floor and in committee hearings indicate, it is expected that those with more than half of their constituents consisting of African Americans will oppose measures that will disproportionately affect their constituents), (6) whether seniority influenced the vote with the party (the longer a member is in office, the more likely he or she is to become institutionalized and thus support the needs of the party above the needs of the CBC), and (7) whether the CBC member's region determined his or her likelihood of voting with the party position (urban members, for example, may feel a greater need to support the party position on crime than rural members who may not have the level of drug-related crimes in their areas).

The Appropriations Committee immediately acted on the measure and attached the crime legislation as instructed. The House approved the measure on the same day by a vote of 316–91 (with 151 Republicans voting for and 48 against with 209 Democrats voting for and 43 against. The vote of the CBC was divided. The CBC unity on this vote is 26 percent. In comparison, the unity of the Democratic party for this vote is 66 percent. The percentage of members who voted with the Chair of the CBC is equivalent to the Democratic unity vote. Of the five CBC members who held leadership positions in the Democratic Caucus, all but one voted with the party, thus one can infer that leadership in the party influences one's vote. Those with 55 percent or more of African Americans in their congressional districts were just as likely to vote with the party as those with less than 55 percent of African Americans in their congressional districts (six members with 55 percent or more of African Americans in their districts voted with the party and six members with fewer than 55 percent of African American in their districts voted with the party). However, those with fewer than 55 percent of African Americans in their congressional districts were more likely to oppose the party position.[3] Those serving less than three terms voted with the party position in stronger numbers than those serving more than three terms, although those serving three terms or more are almost evenly divided in their vote on this bill (five in favor of the party position and five against). Only three members serving fewer than three terms deviated from the party position. Region did not prove to be significant in the way members voting on this legislation. Members overwhelmingly represented districts in the Midwest. The votes of these members were almost divided among those who supported the legislation and those that did not, the case is the same for the West. There was only one member from the South (and the vote was with the party), and the sole member from the Southwest did not declare a position. Of those members in the Northeast, four members voted in favor of the party's position and only one opposed the party's position. Of the seven founding members still in Congress, four voted against the party's position and three voted with the party. As the review of the variables indicates, there was not unity among CBC members on the vote. A number of variables can be used to explain the vote. The CBC was less united on this resolution. The week following this resolution, House Democrats "countered by consolidating the various separate anti-crime bills into a single measure that the House passed under the suspension of the rules, 406–16."[4] On the floor of the House, Democrats praised the measure as a step forward in fighting crime. Hughes, Chair of the House Subcommittee on Crime, who was instrumental in crafting the 1986 legislation that contained mandatory minimum for crack cocaine, said of it:

> . . . This bill, which was developed in our Criminal Justice Subcommittee, not the Subcommittee on Crime, which I chair, is not everything I want in the way of sentencing reform, but it contains most of the measures that reform advocates have been pushing for, without success for years. It provides mandatory sentencing guidelines, eliminates parole, and provides tough penalties for violent career criminals. Other important measures in this package, the work product of not only the Crime subcommittee, but of the arts (sic) subcommittee under the leadership of the gentleman from Wisconsin (Mr. Kastenmeir) and the Criminal Justice Subcommittee under the leadership of the gentleman from Michigan (Mr. Conyers) include: An Anti-Insanity Defense Act: The Comprehensive Drug Penalty Act, which includes forfeiture and new much tougher penalties for drug traffickers . . .[5]

One of the key points in this citation is that it demonstrates the role of Democrats in both supporting and crafting tough anti-crime legislation. Congressman Conyers, it should be noted, would vote against this legislation even though he is given credit for helping to craft it. This speaks to the complexity of Democrats and CBC members working together on legislation. Democrats largely had as their purpose to prove that they could be tough on crime, while CBC members such as Conyers had as their purpose to ensure that the rights of African Americans and the poor were protected during the process.

Congressman Clay was among the CBC members who responded on the floor of the House when this legislation was debated. He asked for a clarification of the types of "criminals" who would be subjected to the prevention that allowed judges to detain defendants before their trial if they determined that the defendant was a flight risk.[6] Congressman Conyers' objections were along the same lines. He argued, "when we authorized preventive detention in an unconstitutional way to permit the Federal courts to lock up a person without parole without finding guilt based on the judge's guess about the person's future behavior, I think we have a constitutional problem. So I am swallowing hard about this measure."[7] There was not a concern voiced on the floor of the House of Representatives by CBC members during debate on this bill about enhanced sentencing guidelines. As was mentioned, there were only 16 members of Congress who voted against the legislation. The CBC vote was divided, with eight members voting against the measure and 11 voting for the measure.[8] The CBC had a 16 percent cohesion rate on this legislation.

On October 11, the Senate voted to retain the anti-crime provisions placed in the continuing resolution that was sent to the president and signed into law. This 1984 legislation was a precursor to the anti-crime euphoria that would drive Congress to pass the Anti-Drug Abuse Act of 1986. Polling data indicated that crime was a major concern among African Americans. According to data from the National Opinion Research Center, "nearly 75 percent of Blacks surveyed . . . wanted stiffer penalties from criminals and more money allocated to fight the rising crime rate."[9]

Prior to the last vote on anti-crime legislation by the House of Representatives for the 98th Congress, the House Select Committee on Narcotics Abuse and Control held a hearing entitled "Drugs—The Effects on the Black Community." The hearing took place on September 28, 1984, during the Annual Congressional Black Caucus weekend. It is important to analyze CBC participation and statements during these hearings because it demonstrates the level of individual participation, interest, and knowledge on this subject. A group that is united on this issue would attend hearings and/or issue statements in an effort to make it known to their colleagues, constituents, and interest groups that this is something that is a priority for them. Also significant is that a founder of the CBC as well as it current chair (at the time) was the chairperson of hearings dealing specifically with narcotics issues. His participation coupled with his influence to persuade his CBC colleagues to participate is significant in measuring CBC interest on this issue. There were just two CBC members recorded as being present during this hearing.[10] They were Congressman Rangel, who, as mentioned, chaired the committee, and Congressman Walter Fauntroy. Rangel said it was important to the CBC for this hearing to take place to discuss the question "as to the impact on drug addiction and drugs in general, and its effects on the black community."[11] It is interesting to note that the focus on the forum was not on legislation passed by Congress during the previous months. Only panelist Charlene Jarvis, Washington, DC City Council Member, mentioned her opposition to the recently passed legislation. She said that the legislation that contains mandatory minimum penalties on drug activities would compound the problems the District and the nation faced. Those problems, according to Jarvis, included overcrowded prisons and even higher costs of incarcerating those who are drug users and sellers.[12] Most of the discussion from the participants mentioned the importance of stopping the flow of drugs from entering the country and about how additive drugs are, so addictive that people will forgo basic needs in order to get their next high. From the tone of the panelists, drug addiction should be treated more as a health program than a law enforcement issue.

Congressman Rangel was a strong proponent of tougher drug laws during this debate because he believed drugs have had a devastating impact on the African American community. Given his view on the drug problem, one can surmise that drug abuse was a permanent threat that needed politicians from both sides of the aisle to address. He both criticizes the Reagan administration and politicians who ignore the issue, while pushing aside Councilwoman Jarvis' concern that tougher sentencing laws are creating unintended consequences. In addition, his comments are further indication that a founding member of the CBC believed that the way drug issues are debated in this country depends on the prevailing perception of who is using the drugs. This is important to keep in mind for the assessment of the 1986 anti-drug act and the perception of the areas and people using and abusing crack cocaine. A founding member of the CBC with the understanding of how issues are exploited during political campaigns would recognize that political rhetoric about the urban poor does not include the need to seriously address poverty, unemployment, and other structural issues, but does include discussion about the need to incarcerate people. Thus Congressman Rangel and other CBC members should be wary about the type of legislation he and the CBC support. His statement is crucial to understanding some of the ideas that may influence the debate among CBC members. Rangel's statement:

> This Administration looks upon the problem as a local problem, No.1, they put out a report just yesterday . . . where they believe the answer to the problem that we are facing is one of education and prevention, which wouldn't be too bad, if they thought the Federal Government would be involved in preparing programs or resources in order to show our youngsters how dangerous it was to abuse drugs.

> But they believe that this should be a local and State initiative which private sector people, comic books, or whatever they do, to assist in this, in having the First Lady from time to time appear on situation comedies when it gets to our international effort.

> And certainly, I am not trying to single out Jamaica because we have many friends and constituents from Jamaica, but if we can't deal with a small country that is so dependent on us in terms of economic exchanges in trade to deal with their crop, because of the political relationship between Jamaica and the United States, then it seems to me, as other panelists have said, that we are not even showing the heads of these foreign countries that we mean business.

> Now, Councilwoman Jarvis has pointed out, as you find more white Americans being afflicted with this *disease* (emphasis added), you will see changes in the attitude in terms of the Federal Government, but we do have a pretty hard-hitting community . . .

> And so, there has to be an outrage felt and I do not sense that outrage. It bothered me that with all of the candidates that were running for President, how difficult it was to get any of the candidates to focus on this issue, any of them.

> It just seems as though narcotics and the narcotic addiction is not a sophisticated thing for people to talk about, and especially not diplomats, and so it is not a question of leaving depressed—as someone has said—we got a committee that has been exposed to the effects of the addiction.[13]

Congressman Rangel's belief that drug dealers should be punished regardless of the circumstances and that African Americans are at fault for selling drugs to one another serves as a contrast to other CBC members who look at race and racism as the blame and thus oppose mass incarceration.[14] Those two divergent views lead to one explanation as to why the CBC has at times been disunited on anti-drug legislation. This dichotomy in thinking (i.e., drug abuse is an addiction and disease, but if people use drugs, they must be blamed for damaging the community) may be seen as an omen as to how CBC members as a whole voted for, supported, or remained silent on the passage of mandatory minimum laws for crack cocaine. Congressman Fauntroy is the only CBC member who is recorded as saying anything during the hearing. Other CBC members who served on the HSCNAC during that year included Congresswoman Cardiss Collins (D-IL) and Congressman Ed Towns (D-NY). This can be seen as an earlier indication that the CBC did not present a united front in opposing mandatory minimum penalties for crack cocaine.

CBC and Democratic Political Behavior of Crime Legislation, 1986–1988

In July 1986, the HSCNAC held two separate hearings during the same week on the issue of cocaine. Both hearings occurred after the death of Len Bias. This is important because, as mentioned, it was the death of Len Bias that served as a catalyst for passing the Anti-Drug Abuse Act of 1986. His death became the focus of both the media and the Democratic and Republican leadership.[15] What is most significant about these hearings as they relate to this research is the lack of presence by CBC members. After the death of Len Bias, Speaker Tip O'Neill ordered every congressional committee to draft an anti-drug bill. It was an election year and Democrats wanted to prove that they were as tough on drugs as their Republican colleagues. The CBC has had as its strategy to place its members on key committees so as to have a greater impact on legislation. Thus, it can be argued that a Caucus that is concerned about the way African Americans are portrayed during this debate and the potential impact would attend the HSCNAC hearings. However, the opposite is true, and while members are permitted to submit prepared remarks to any committee hearing, CBC members who do not serve on the HSCNAC did not submit statements declaring a position on issues addressed. There is also a lack of prepared statements entered into the record by CBC members who do not serve on the HSCNAC.[16] As mentioned, this speaks to the lack of an organized effort on behalf of the CBC to have substantial input on an issue affecting the African American community. As stated earlier, the images of urban African Americans helped to shape the emergence of crack cocaine legislation via passage of tough drug sentencing laws.

In addition to the absence of CBC members, for the most part, testimony and questioning of the invited guests treated the spread of drugs in a nonracial manner. The hearings focused on how addictive crack was, how it had become a national security issue, how the administration was not doing more to help local law enforcement, and how the administration failed to stop drugs from coming into the country. Testimony of the witnesses created a sense of urgency that something needed to be done immediately.

Congressman Conyers and Congressman Rangel's attitude toward the courts and criminal justice system provides insight into the political behavior of the CBC. Both Conyers and Rangel come from states that have enacted tough drug sentencing laws since the 1970s (the Michigan "650 Life," which mandated life in prison for even certain first-time drug convicts and the Rockefeller laws in New York, both of which resulted in nonviolent drug offenders receiving life in prison). Congressman Conyers chaired the Subcommittee on Criminal Justice of the House Judiciary Committee throughout most of the 1980s. Based on transcripts from the Subcommittee of Criminal Justice and House Judiciary Committee, Conyers is on record on several occasions as opposing the sentencing guidelines because they only serve to give prosecutors more discretion. Conyers did not believe that stopping the spread of drugs would be resolved by more arrests and more prison construction. He also mentioned that harsher drug penalties will have a negative effect on African Americans.[17] Congressman Rangel, on the other hand, advocated for more prisons and prosecutions. This may be a reason for the lack of a unified message among the CBC.

In addition, Conyers often expressed concern about the already overcrowded prison conditions and about how the 1984 law to establish the sentencing commission and to abolish parole and the 1986 anti-drug act would only worsen the situation. Conyers visited prisons in Michigan and saw the overcrowding first hand.[18] Congressman Rangel seemed to have a single-minded focus on crack and the damage the drug was having on the community. His focus was such that when he held a hearing on the spread of heroin, a Republican member of the House Select Committee remarked that it is about time that he focused on another drug. As mentioned in a previous chapter, Congressman Rangel wanted crack to become a household issue. He was frustrated that power cocaine use was considered glamorous and he wanted to change that image. He succeeded in doing so; crack would be far from being viewed as a glamour drug.

There was a legitimate disagreement among CBC members and hearing participants as to whether poverty and other conditions led to drug use in the African American community and whether incarceration or treatment is the preferred treatment. For example, in 1989 Jesse Jackson voiced criticism of President Bush's drug strategy stating that "it was under financed, failed to take the views of the affected communities into account and ignored the underlying poverty that contributes to drug use."[19] Congressman Rangel, on the other hand, stated on more than one occasion during the HSCNAC that poverty did not lead to drug use, and he had a strong law and order approach to dealing with crack. In other hearings, he said poverty may contribute to drug use, so even he was not clear on this issue. Congressman Rangel was criticized by some CBC members such as Congressman Mfume for allowing Republicans to have so much time during committee hearings.[20] This is important to note because, again, it underlines the internal discussions by the CBC members as a unified drug strategy. The vote analysis thus far and the vote analysis of other legislation considered in the research demonstrated that senior members, even founding members, could not come to agreement as measured by the roll-call votes. Because of Congressman Rangel's position as both a founding member of the CBC and the Chair of the HSCNAC that had as its purpose to study the issues of narcotics, his views and influence were crucial. Also significant is that there was testimony in Congressman Conyer's Subcommittee on Criminal Justice and Congressman Rangel's Committee that these laws would and were having a disproportionate impact on African Americans and systemic racism remained a problem in this country. A unified vote against such measures, even if only for symbolic purposes, would be characteristic of a body formed to promote the interests of African Americans and to combat harmful legislation. Instead, what is shown is that CBC members do not necessarily follow the cues of the chair of the CBC nor the founding members of the group. Region, seniority, and the percentage of African Americans located in a congressional district also influence the vote.

There were members who consistently mentioned the twin problems of dealing with drugs. Congressman Harold Ford, Sr. (D-TN) eloquently made this point during a hearing when he said:

> Materialism has replaced our long-standing traditions of preserving the family, pursuing higher education for the sake of learning; and focusing our overall spiritual needs as a primary salvation for our communities. The selling of drugs by young people is motivated by having the signs of material success that otherwise were denied—designer clothing, jewelry, expensive cars are being advertised as the indications of success. Those are accessible to our youth who sell drugs because of the money that is involved in that profit that is the drugs itself. However, the drug trade ultimately brings into communities further economic distress and results in addicted mothers, cocaine babies, AIDS victims, and homicide in drug-related crimes. It does not bring the hopes of changing our lives in the long run, in striving to obtain those values traditionally associated with communities in which we live.[21]

As mentioned, it was the Anti-Drug Abuse Act of 1986 that contained the mandatory minimum penalties for crack and powder cocaine. The fact that CBC members supported this legislation thwarted subsequent cries of racism. As legal scholar and professor Randall Kennedy observes:

> The absence of any charge by black members of Congress that the crack-cocaine differential was racially unfair speaks volumes; after all, several of these representatives had long histories of distinguished opposition to any public policy that smacked of racial injustice.[22]

Kennedy goes on to write "that several of these representatives demanded a crackdown on crack is also important. It suggests that the initiative for what became known as the crack-powder distinction originated to some extent within the ranks of African American congressional officials."[23] Therein rests a central research question. African American leaders in Congress during the 1980s were calling for efforts to address drug-related crimes in inner cities. Does the call by African American leaders to get help in fighting crime mean that "help" should be primarily defined by more punitive measures, rather than assistance with many socioeconomic issues thrust upon the African American community over a span of centuries? These harsh cocaine penalties were driven by a law-and-order president and a desire on behalf of Democrats to write a tough crime bill in an effort to win votes during the congressional election year.[24]

CBC members often have a choice between accepting legislation even if they oppose provisions in it or outright rejecting legislation. Critics argue that this type of compromise explains why electoral politics does not and cannot create leaders and cannot have the result of African American leaders in Congress adequately protecting the interests of African Americans. Support for regressive legislation, even if it is an amendment within a larger bill, allows conservatives to argue that the legislation cannot be as bad as people say, after all, the vast majority of Democrats and African Americans in Congress supported it. The Anti-Drug Abuse Act of 1986 passed by a vote of 378–16, with Republicans voting in a cohesive bloc.[25] At this time, there were 21 members of the CBC. Of the 16 members of Congress who voted against the bill in 1986, seven were CBC members. CBC unity on this vote was just 26 percent, while the unity score for the Democratic party on this issue was 86 percent. The Chair of the CBC at the time, the late Rep. Mickey Leland (D-TX), voted with the Democratic party position. The vote was nearly split in terms of members voting with the chair and those voting opposite the chair (9–8). Of the founding members of the CBC still in Congress at the time this vote was taken, four voted opposite of the CBC chair and three voted with the chair. Each CBC member who held a leadership position with the party at the time the vote was taken voted with the party. Neither the NAACP nor the ADA scored this vote. There is no noticeable difference between the way members with more than 55 percent of African Americans in their districts voted compared to those with less than 55 percent of African Americans. Further, of those with 55 percent or more of African Americans in their district, the vote was evenly split. Of those with less than 55 percent of African Americans in their congressional districts, seven voted with the party position and three voted in opposition. Seniority seems to be a determinant of one's voting choice. Of those serving three terms or more, eight voted with the party and five against. The vote difference is less noticeable among those serving fewer than three terms, with three voting with the party and two voting in opposite of the party position. CBC members representing congressional districts in the Midwest voted against the position of the party (6–2) more so than any other region. The northeast delegation (those that voted) were 100 percent in favor of the party position. The western delegation favored the party position by a 3–1 margin. The south and southwest members, although numbering just two members at the time this vote was taken, voted in favor of the party's position.

There are several reasons why members choose to not support legislation, but given the historic treatment of African Americans by the criminal justice system and given the CBC's commitment to support progressive legislation, one would expect that the CBC would have been united in opposition to legislation that did not receive the normal committee debate/review process, legislation that was debated during a presidential year, and legislation that came about as a result of hysteria about crime in inner cities.

On September 25, 1987, the HSCNAC held another hearing during CBC week.[26] The only CBC member recorded attending is Congressman Rangel, who chaired the Committee. The hearing focused on the devastating impact AIDS was having on the African American community. Michael Quinlan, the Director of the Federal Bureau of Prisons, testified that "the two most compelling problems facing the Bureau of Prisons in the next several years are the impact of population increases on an already strained system and the large potential for increase of the HIV infection. We have tried to meet this challenge by a comprehensive proposal that monitors the incidence and its spread."[27] He also testified that "Blacks and Hispanics comprise 51 percent of the current Bureau of Prison population. Of the federal inmates who have been identified as having some state of the disease, 78 percent are black or Hispanic. . . Among federal inmates, we find that minorities comprise 82 percent of AIDS patients, 83 percent of the intermediate state patients, and 74 percent of those who test positive for the disease but have no symptoms."[28] The importance of this testimony is that the director of the BOP was sounding the alarm about the impact of policies that will lead to more pressures on the system. It has been mentioned in a previous chapter that the CBC is concerned about those policies that disproportionately impact poor and disadvantaged communities. Testimony that three-fourths of those in the prison population suffering from HIV/AIDS are African Americans and Hispanics is important for a body such as the CBC to consider. Yet, in spite of this testimony, there was not a sense of urgency to reduce harsh penalties on minor drug offenders.

During the 1980s, drugs and AIDS were major issues that policymakers considered. Legislation passed that increased the prison population among African Americans would necessarily create an imprisoned population of those with HIV/AIDS as Quinlan's testimony indicates. This is a dual concern of the African American community, which makes the political behavior of their congressional leaders, as measured by roll-call votes, attendance at the HSCNAC hearings, and/or statements for the record, necessary to mention. Quinlan is a political actor alerting the HSCNAC of the potential consequences of its actions in supporting legislation that will lead to a substantial increase in the prison population. The rate of HIV and drug abuse was high both within and outside the prison system. One can argue that harsh legislation helped states shift the burden of dealing with the rise of AIDS and drug abuse to the federal prison system to make up for the lack of federal resources that were given to state and local governments to handle these dual problems. The most powerful testimony given during this hearing came from former Congressman George Hansen.[29] He exposed federal and state prison officials for their treatment of prisoners with HIV/AIDS and how they fail to prevent the spread of AIDS to the general population. He expressed his dismay that prison officials do not have the will to deal with HIV. He said that prison officials engaged in both inhumane and discriminatory practices toward inmates. Hansen told Rangel that alternative sentencing is needed. "Unload the jails. Send people home. Limit the expense and liability to the taxpayer. If people are trustworthy enough to report voluntarily and go to these so-called honor camps, these level one camps, why keep them there at $20,000 to $30,000 a year at taxpayers' expense when they could be home, in 'house arrest' or some other type of acceptable punishment program?"[30]

The new sentencing guidelines, coupled with the mandatory minimum penalty of crack cocaine that fell outside of the jurisdiction of the sentencing guidelines, were of a great concern to those fearing a substantial increase in the prison population. On October 6, a bill, sponsored by Conyers, that would delay the implementation of the sentencing guidelines failed by a vote of 181–231 in a Democratic Congress. This is further indication that many Democrats in Congress were unwilling to be seen as being lenient with criminals.[31]

CBC and Democratic Political Behavior on Crime Legislation, 1989–1992

In 1989, the HSCNAC held another hearing during CBC Week entitled "Drug Legalization—Catastrophe for Black Americans." Once again, no CBC members were listed as present and no statements were issued save for the chair of the committee. The attendance by CBC members to these hearings is important because it helps to understand the extent to which CBC members used the House Select Committee on Narcotics to advance their collective beliefs and behavior on drug legislation. That CBC members were largely absent from these hearings, even the one that took place during the annual legislative conference, helps to explain the lack of unity on crack legislation in particular and crime legislation in general.

Within a month after the hearing on drug legalization, Congress passed another anti-drug abuse bill that continued to increase the prison incarceration rate among African Americans. Although CBC members were, by the time of the 1989 hearings, aware of the impact the anti-drug legislation of 1986 and 1988 had on the African American community, one of the founding members of the CBC did not use his hearings to form a unified strategy among CBC members to oppose tough sentencing penalties, which is an indication that the CBC did not have the necessary clout or will to persuade their Democratic colleagues to oppose harmful anti-crime legislation. By the end of 1989, the prison population reached an all-time high. In the first months of 1989, the prison population increased by a record of 46,004 inmates, making the total population 673, 565.[32] "The rise not only broke the record for half year increases but was higher than any annual increase in the 64 years the Government has kept such records."[33] The Attorney General used this information to garner support and passage of the president's crime bill, which included funding to construct 24,000 new federal prison beds. It was estimated that 1,800 prison beds would be needed per week to keep up with the increased prison population.[34] To return to Quinlan and Hansen's testimony, this increased population level further puts those incarcerated at greater risk of contracting AIDS, which contributes to an additional health crisis among African Americans. The increased inmate population was attributed to harsh drug laws and increased sentencing. In writing about the increased prison incarceration level, Zachary Dowdy tells us that "one of the effects of this boom has been the shifting of federal funds from minority and poor communities that export prisoners to poor white towns, which started 'hosting' prisons in the 1990s as a means of escaping economic despair. In fact, new studies are showing that in a society that ratcheted up its criminal penalties to control crime and place offenders out of sight and out of mind, the prison industry has begun to affect the political landscape."[35] In an article he wrote about the crisis in urban America, Ron Walters discusses how policies passed during the 1980s enhanced the social problems in inner cities. Essentially, he stated that during this time period, both Congress and the Reagan administration, with the conservative, anti-big government rhetoric, supported a transfer of hundreds of billions of dollars in funding from social programs, including those dealing with employment training and supporting inner city social infrastructure needs. The language against cities took on a de facto anti-Hispanic and anti-Black tone.[36] The issues mentioned by Walters coupled with anti-drug legislation were salient issues used to win votes as some of the previous literature indicated.

The CBC would have its challenges crafting a unified drug message even after President Reagan successfully completed two terms and was succeeded by Republican George Herbert Walker Bush, who also wanted to make his mark on the War on Drugs. Democrats criticized the president's drug policy, but that criticism mainly came from how to fund his $7.9-billion proposal. Democrats were criticized, however, by the late Ron Brown (African American), then the Chairman of the Democratic Party, about the response to the president's plan. According to *The New York Times*, Brown essentially derided Democrats for bungling their response to what Bush had proposed as his drug control strategy. While Brown was also critical of Bush's plan, he believed that Democrats let the message get away from them by focusing on increased taxes. His point was that Democrats responding to Bush's proposal by calling for an increased taxes to fund proposals would lead to a collective sigh by the American people: "The tax and spend Democrats; there they go again." Among the public comments in expressing opposition over Brown's statements by CBC members came from Congressman Rangel and Congressman Gray.[37] Gray proclaimed that the chair will come to understand that every Democrat has the right to his opinion, and Rangel stated, in part, that new resources, presumably from taxes, were needed to deal with the drug crises. These comments demonstrate the divergent views among African American Democrats in power about the role of the party and the difficulty of Democrats to find a voice that would resonate among the American people that they were better on drug policy, thus making at least the drug issue one of the strategies to win votes rather than one that addresses the impact the laws have had on African Americans. Two prominent African American congressmen voiced public disagreement with their party's chairman. Further, Democrats in Congress, notably Senators Byrd and Biden, introduced and supported legislation that called for across-the-board spending cuts of just under 6 percent and an additional 53 percent of the drug budget going to law enforcement.[38]

On September 15, 1989, during the Annual Legislative Conference, the HSCNAC held a hearing entitled "The Federal Drug Strategy: What Does It Mean for Black America?" This hearing took place just days after the report about the increase in prison population came out. Remarkably, neither the statistics about the increased prison population reported earlier during the year nor mandatory minimum penalties were a focal point of this committee. There was criticism of President Bush's plan, such as the statement above made by Rev. Jesse Jackson, but the CBC members who participated did not focus on the disparity between crack and powder.

The September 15th hearing was attended by CBC members Rangel and Mfume, who at this time served on the HSCNAC. Each of the CBC members and the African Americans who testified discussed the devastation drugs have had on the African American community and how the war on drugs seem to be failing as addiction continues to rise. However, the crack-cocaine disparity was not a focal point nor was it addressed by the CBC members in attendance. This hearing takes place three years after Congress passed the crack-powder cocaine penalties. Ironically, Congressman Rangel declared that "Congress has been very, very silent in this war against drugs."[39] This "silence," as the CBC would realize by 1993, resulted in a substantial increase of nonviolent drug offenders, mostly African Americans and Hispanics, serving long prison terms for nonviolent offenses. Randolph N. Stone, a public defender in Cook County, IL, did mention in his opening statement that the jails were filling up in Chicago not because of increased drug use, but because of mandatory penalties.[40] In an exchange following his comments, Chairman Rangel said he agrees with Stone but goes on to say that some bums deserve to be in prison. He also reiterates what Dick Gregory stated in his testimony in that we have to take the streets back from dope pushers. Thus, on the one hand, there is Stone as the voice that is saying that incarceration is doing just as much damage to the community as drugs, and on the other hand Rangel, Jackson, and Gregory supporting the mindset expressed by Drug Czar William Bennett in his statement that not incarcerating people costs more than the $20,000 to $30,000 it takes to incarcerate individuals. Bennett's exact statement was that "If more jails are needed, more prisons are needed, build them. And you're right. They're expensive . . . But it costs a lot of money to keep a drug dealer out of jail."[41] This prevailing viewpoint goes to the comments made by Randall Kennedy that African American members of Congress supported or at the very least gave aid and comfort to those advocating a law-and-order approach. It would not be until 1993 when the CBC would finally hold hearings solely to discuss the negative impact of mass incarceration on the African American community as a result of the War on Drugs.

The HSCNAC held more hearings on the impact of drugs in the American community until it was abolished in 1993, but the hearings were not focused on the sentencing disparities between crack and powder cocaine. In some of these hearings there was the occasional question by a CBC member about the impact of these laws. In a hearing about the role of the Justice Department in fighting the war on drugs, Congressman Donald Payne voiced frustration over priorities and the lack of a comprehensive approach to dealing with crime. Congressman Payne advocated full implementation of the Weed and Seed program whereby the tools to fight crime would be provided for local law enforcement and at the same time, alternative programs for the youth would be implemented. In questioning Attorney General Thornburgh during this hearing, entitled "The Justice Department's Role in the War on Drugs," Congressman Payne also voiced dismay that billions of dollars were going to build more military planes, yet we still have one in four children living in poverty. He made an interesting comment that demonstrates the mindset of at least one CBC member, and that is that in this country, the "rich get richer and the poor get prisons."[42] Thornburgh's response was similar to what others who appeared before the Committee during the 1980s articulated. He testified that fighting crime is a civil rights issue because if there is violence, then people do not feel safe and secure in their homes. He (Thornburgh) went on to say that it was his belief that:

> The only way to deal with those people (drug abusers) is to get them off the street and to prison. I hope that when they are in prison, they have the opportunity to rehabilitate themselves if the kinds of education programs that Director Quinlan has instituted in our Federal prisons are carried out there and by our State and local counterparts, but the threat to the community from the violent criminal, and that's the criminal I'm talking about, had got to be dealt with in terms of tough law enforcement, and I don't apologize for that.[43]

Congressman Payne's response was in agreement with tough law enforcement, but he stated that tough law enforcement would not work if education and other programs did not follow. Thornburgh was suggesting that people should be arrested and then use programs established in prison to rehabilitate them. With the growing prison population by 1991, it was already known that even in prison, there would be very limited opportunities for prisoners to get assistance, and this does not touch on the point of nonviolent offenses being subjected to long prison terms. The manipulation seems to be the equating of violent offenders with drug offenders to justify widespread incarceration. During this hearing, there was also an exchange between Congressman Mfume and Thornburgh that addresses the impact of mandatory minimum laws on juveniles and prison overcrowding that can be found in Appendix 5.

The exchanges among CBC members such as Payne and Mfume demonstrate a growing concern among by CBC members about the mass incarceration of African American adults and juveniles and concern about a strong law and order approach absent of any other ways to treat the drug and crime policy. The HSCNAC would be abolished in 1993 with no hearings specifically addressing the crack/cocaine disparity. Also, as has been mentioned, there were so few CBC members who attended these hearings, even those held during CBC week. A House Select Committee has no power and no authority to propose legislation. House Select Committees are generally established to address a particular problem faced by the nation. The House Select Committee on Narcotics, given that it was chaired by a CBC member during the height of the War on Drugs, is a committee that could have been part of the CBC's overall strategy to influence their colleagues and the public about drugs and anti-drug legislation. However, less than a fifth of the CBC members throughout the hearings specifically mentioned in this research attended the hearings or issued public statements to be included in the official record. These hearings, as measured by so few attendees, is one demonstration that there was not a strategy on behalf of CBC members to highlight the anti-drug legislation of 1986 and 1988, which helps to understand why the roll-call votes by the CBC on anti-crime legislation were not unified. It should be understood that the House Select Committee was composed of both Republican and Democratic members. However, since a CBC founding member headed it, the expectation would be that once the figures began to surface about the growing number of African American men and women entering prison, CBC members would use this committee to put sentencing disparity on the congressional agenda.

Although Democrats were instrumental in writing and passing the tough criminal justice sentencing policies of the 1980s, they failed to win the 1988 presidency. With drugs among the very top issues concerning the American public, Democrats further demonstrated that they could be just as tough on drug use and just as instrumental in addressing this issue as Republicans, however, Republican Presidents were given credit for maintaining a sound drug policy. In a 1989 *New York Times* CBS poll 69 percent of the respondents approved of President Bush's drug plan. Further, less than half (44 percent) of the respondents agreed with the question that President Bush's plan devoted too much to law enforcement and not enough on problems such as unemployment and poverty. Also, "the proportion of Americans who cited drugs as the nation's most important problem has nearly tripled since the end of July, to 64 percent from 22 percent. The rise came after weeks of sustained coverage of the worsening crack epidemic and the turmoil caused by cocaine barons in Colombia and after Mr. Bush's address to the nation Tuesday when he outlined his anti-drug policy. The percentage was the highest recorded for any single issue since the Times/CBS News poll began in 1976 and is one of the highest registered by any major national survey."[44] Also of particular interest is that 69 percent of the respondents agreed that occasional cocaine use should be prosecuted and punished while only 43 percent agreed that occasional use of marijuana should be prosecuted and punished.[45] President Bush's drug plan, like the legislation passed in 1986 and 1988, called for stiffer penalties on first-time drug offenders and for drug users. It is interesting to note that according to this poll, 84 percent of the respondents believed that first-time offenders should be given treatment. Democrats struggled to find a voice on this issue, which is a reason the chairman of the party (Ron Brown) criticized their response.

CBC and Democratic Political Behavior, 1993–1995 (103rd and 104th Congresses)

CHANGING ATTITUDES

The year 1993 was historic in that a Democratic president was inaugurated for the first time in 12 years. It also saw a substantial increase in CBC numbers—an increase of 16, which brought the total to number to 40. After the 1990 census, majority-minority districts were created in an effort to increase the number of African Americans and other ethnic groups in Congress. With increased membership comes increased challenges on the unity of the CBC. The members were diverse in terms of age and region represented, and several CBC members during the 103rd Congress were placed in significant leadership and/or committee positions. This increased membership also coincided with a Democratic president, thus, theoretically, the mostly Democratic CBC membership would be able to persuade their colleagues to overturn mandatory minimum penalties for crack cocaine.

President Clinton made crime a major issue during his presidential campaign. As was mentioned, he vowed that he would push through a major crime bill in Congress. Given the new diversity of the CBC and the individual member's role in the

Democratic leadership, the issue of supporting crime legislation that would provide for more law enforcement as the president wanted, yet also provide for adequate funding for programs such as Weed and Seed, Midnight Basketball, alternative sentencing, etc., would pose a challenge to CBC unity. It became increasingly difficult to ignore the societal harms of drug addiction and abuse and how incarceration was not solving the problem. As Congressman Rangel, who had supported tough-on-crime policies, stated in a 1992 HSCNAC report "we must admit that whatever we are doing is not working. In the decade that just passed, our nation doubled its prison population, created mandatory sentencing for dozens of drug offenses, expanded capital punishment, greatly extended the powers of the police and prosecutors—all while the crime rate doubled and the consumption of legal drugs skyrocketed."[46]

The Sentencing Commission's 1991 Report

As was mentioned, the USSC submitted a report to Congress in 1991 in response to a directive from Congress. According to the report, "there are over 60 criminal statutes that contain mandatory minimums applicable to federal offenses in the federal code today. Only four of these statutes, however, frequently result in drug convictions: the four relate to drug and weapons offenses."[47] The report also confirms "the disparate application of mandatory minimum sentences in cases in which available data suggest that a mandatory minimum is applicable appears to be related to the race of the defendant, where whites are more likely than non-whites to be sentenced below the applicable mandatory minimum."[48] As is reported in a *Washington Post* editorial critical of the current crack/powder penalties, while three times as many Americans use powder cocaine than crack cocaine, it is the latter that receive far more prosecutions. And a representative sample of crack possession cases, according to the USSC, showed that all of the defendants were black.[49] Further, there was growing concern that many violent criminals such as rapists and murderers were being released early because cells were being filled by drug offenders. According to a *Newsweek* article, "the number of adults in state and federal prisons more than tripled between 1986 and 1991; nearly one in every three new state prisoners is a drug offender, up from one in 25 in 1960."[50]

President Clinton's Attorney General Janet Reno announced during the first year of his presidency that she would conduct a sweeping review of mandatory drug sentences "to determine if packing prisons with small-time offenders—say sentencing a 19 year old courier to five years for transporting as little as five grams—makes sense or justice."[51] Reno was very sympathetic to the belief that treatment was more effective than incarceration, which is a reason she established a Drug Court program in Florida in an effort to give people a second chance.

Congressional Hearings

During the spring and summer of 1993, two key hearings were conducted by separate U.S. House Judiciary Subcommittees. One hearing focused on the growth in the prison population and one specifically devoted to the issue of federal mandatory minimum sentencing. Democrats were still in control of Congress, thus they chaired these committees and, unlike the HSCNAC, were able to report legislation for consideration on the House floor. Although CBC members began to recognize the disparity between crack and powder sentences as evidence in some of the comments made in the more recent HSCNAC hearings, there continued to be few CBC members attending these hearings or submitting statements for the record.

On May 12 and July 29, 1993, "The Federal Prison Population: Present and Future Trends" hearing was held. The hearing was chaired by Congressman Williams Hughes. The only CBC member in attendance was Congressman Conyers, who served on the subcommittee, and there were no other CBC statements recorded. This hearing featured the current (at the time) director of Bureau of Prisons and the former director. Both expressed great concern over the rise in the prison population and contributed it to mandatory minimum drug penalties. They also expressed the desire to see more alternative sentencing of nonviolent offenders. Kathleen Hawk mentioned the reduction of good time and the elimination of parole have contributed to offenders serving much longer prison sentences, which was contrary to what occurred prior to these laws where many of the same offenders would have been given parole and recommended that good-time behavior be restored and shorter sentences be given out.[52] She also stated that "In 1980, about 25 percent of our sentenced inmates were drug offenders. Currently, over 60 percent are with us for drug convictions, and, by 1997, we are projecting that 72 percent of our inmate population will be drug offenders."[53] This is crucial, considering the USSC's report stating that African Americans were bearing the brunt of these mandatory sentences with the overwhelming number receiving mandatory minimum sentences for crack cocaine being African Americans.[54] Congressman Conyers, in his statement, continued to express the alarm over the increased number of African Americans under the criminal justice system and said:

... hardly a day goes by in my office when I don't receive letters from inmates from all over the country asking me to help reform the mandatory minimums. They don't understand why in many instances they are serving longer terms than more violent inmates. They don't understand how they can be rehabilitated when conditions are so crowded and often understaffed. They also don't understand why the prison population is so overwhelmingly Black and Hispanic when the drug trade in all its dimensions is a multi-racial enterprise. They all end with a plea to help—not so much for themselves but for others.[55]

This hearing was fairly cordial and much more sympathetic to the cost of mandatory minimums to both taxpayers in terms of increased budgets for prisons to house nonviolent offenders and for the nonviolent offenders themselves. This is in great contrast to the hearing held on July 28, 1993, which dealt specifically with federal mandatory minimum sentencing. The hearing, chaired by Congressman Schumer (D-NY) featured a variety of individuals from judges, prosecutors, family members of those sentenced who were in the process of being sentenced, and from one individual who'd been sentenced for 10 years under the conspiracy provisions of the law. Congressman

Schumer was very unsympathetic to the stories of nonviolent offenders serving long prison terms and said that individuals such as some who gave testimony about their horrible experiences were exceptions to the rule.[56] Schumer, a prominent Democrat, expressed the belief that the vast majority of those serving mandatory minimum sentences are career criminals with long records of previous convictions. Thus his stated position was that he would support a safety valve whereby certain nonviolent, first-time offenders would have a chance to avoid a mandatory minimum penalty, but that he would not support eliminating mandatory minimum penalties. Further, he was fairly hostile in his questioning of Julie Stewart, the president and founder of FAMM. He virtually accused her of overstating the number of nonviolent offenders receiving mandatory prison sentencing. In fact, Stewart remarked in her testimony before the July 29th hearing on prison trends that "I testified before the Crime and Criminal Justice Subcommittee on the issue of mandatory minimum sentencing. It was a very sobering experience, because I felt that many of the members of the subcommittee had closed minds coming into the meeting and I was very disappointed by that. I am delighted to see that the people who were here earlier do seem to have some interest in this issue and want to see us move along the spectrum to find a solution to the prison overcrowding problem. So I am very appreciative that this experience will be more pleasant than yesterday's."[57]

During his questioning of the witnesses, Conyers made the following comment about the political nature of mandatory minimum penalties:

Also, it is very political to be tough on crime. I know this does not come carefully to your attention, but politicians love to brag about how much tougher they are on crime by inference, although he may be saying he is tough on crime, too, so we can get into the usual bidding war.

'I voted for 15 mandatory, new mandatory death penalties in the crime bill.'

'Oh, is that all? I voted for 20.'

'Well, I voted for 10 others in another bill that weren't in there so I am tougher on crime than you.'

In the meantime, crime keeps going up, Michigan went bankrupt with a good Governor because we built so many state prisons that we couldn't even open them up after we had built them because we had no money to staff them. It took another 12 to 16 months to open up the prisons that we busted ourselves in tax effort trying to do.[58]

This continues to demonstrate how a politically salient issue such as crime can create dissent among CBC members. They are attempting to appeal to both their constituents and to their party members.

The contrast to the hearings chaired by Congress Schumer and Congressman Hughes, both Democrats, the statements made by Congressman Schumer and Congressman Conyers above demonstrate the challenges for both Democrats and CBC members to be united in overturning mandatory minimum penalties, or, at the very least, eliminating the 100–1 disparity. For a Democratic president to support overturning tough crime penalties, he would need the support of Democrats on the House Judiciary Committee. A conflict between the president and a major Committee chairperson such as Congressman Schumer would lead to the type of divisiveness the Democratic party wants to avoid. The objective of the lead Democrat, President Clinton, was to continue to portray the party as one that is tough on crime. Thus, the advocacy of the CBC to eliminate mandatory minimums became secondary and the Caucus was unable to persuade the president and their Democratic colleagues to seriously address mandatory minimum penalties for crack cocaine. The issues as articulated by Conyers and others involve the politics of crime, the issue of prison overcrowding and the necessary funding and mechanisms to reduce overcrowding, unintended consequences of the 1986 and 1988 laws, and the disproportionate number of African Americans serving long prison terms for drug offenses. These were the issues considered as President Clinton attempted to pass another comprehensive crime bill. Further, there seemed to be a misunderstanding of what the public prefers. Opinion polls already mentioned seemed to indicate that while the public is concerned about crime, it is not supportive of focusing on mass incarceration. In her written testimony, Stewart cites public attitudes listed in the Bureau of Justice Statistics Sourcebook 1991 that 61 percent of those polled preferred attacking social problems, while 32 percent wanted more prisons and law enforcement; on the question of how more money should be spent in an effort to fight illegal drugs, 40 percent stated that they preferred to teach the young, 28 percent said to work with foreign governments, 19 percent said to arrest sellers, 4 percent to help overcome addiction, and 4 percent to arrest users.[59]

Civil Rights Forum

In August 1993, following these two hearings, a forum, sponsored by the ACLU and the Coalition for Equitable Sentencing, was held in the Rayburn House Office Building. The forum, entitled "Racial Bias in Cocaine Laws," was designed to alert the public and politicians about the racial bias in mandatory minimum sentences and in an effort to influence the debate surrounding the crime bill. Co-sponsors of the forum included the Congressional Black Caucus Foundation, the Committee Against Discriminatory Crack Law, the Southern Christian Leadership Conference, and the Criminal Justice Foundation.[60] Following this forum, Congressman Rangel, who had been vocal about tougher drug sentencing laws and who supported legislation during the 1980s that included mandatory minimums for crack, introduced legislation to eliminate the disparity in sentencing between crack and powder cocaine. Nkechi Taifa, then Legislative Counsel for the American Civil Liberties Union, organized the forum. She first heard about mandatory minimum penalties for crack cocaine in 1993 after she was asked to testify before the USSC on this issue.[61] She discovered that there was little political activity on Capitol Hill surrounding mandatory minimum penalties. Further, she had a difficult time convincing civil rights groups to join her in co-sponsoring the forum because it was not an issue they wanted to deal with.[62] After C-SPAN stated its intentions to cover the forum and after media reports, organizations began to sponsor the forum and CBC members began to participate. The ACLU drafted a bill that would eliminate mandatory minimum penalties for crack cocaine and then targeted a member whom they felt had the most influence. Since Congressman Rangel was a strong advocate for tougher drug sentencing laws, they approached his office to introduce the legislation. The ACLU believed that for a member who had previously supported tough drug legislation to introduce a bill to overturn mandatory minimum penalties for crack would encourage others to co-sponsor the legislation. The ACLU took advantage of the gathering of civil rights groups at the forum and the media attention to get a bill introduced.[63] Unfortunately, any opportunity for the CBC members who came in during the 103rd Congress to use the House Select Committee on Narcotics Abuse and Control to voice opposition to mandatory minimum laws ended in January 1993 by a vote of 237–180. The vote to reauthorize the committee came about, according to Congressman Rangel, as a result of "a fight over committee budgets, and influx of new members and committee jurisdiction."[64] The CBC's vote was united in keeping the HSCNAC; House Democrats were not united in its vote. The Democrats were still in the majority during the 103rd Congress. Congressman Rangel's legislation had no co-sponsors; however, six days after he introduced his legislation, Congressman Craig Washington introduced a bill designed to prevent crime and to reform the criminal justice system to make it (the system) fairer. His bill, introduced on October 19, 1993, contained 30 co-sponsors, including the following CBC members: Congresspersons Clay, Dellums, Hastings, Lewis, Holmes-Norton, Rangel, Stokes, Tucker, Watt, Brown, Conyers, Jefferson, Mfume, Payne, Reynolds, Rush, Scott, Thompson, Waters, and Wynn.[65] Nkechi Taifa said in a statement before Congress about Congressmen Rangel and Washington's legislation that:

> In the 103rd Congress, Representative Rangel (D-NY) introduced H.R. 3277 to eliminate the disparity and make sentences of those convicted of crack cocaine offenses equivalent to the current sentences for powder cocaine. This legislation was later incorporated into "The Crime Prevention and Criminal Justice Reform Act" introduced in the 103rd Congress, and was offered by Representative William Hughes (D-NJ) as an amendment to "The Violent Crime Control and Law Enforcement Act" (H.R. 3355). The original Hughes Amendment, however, was replaced with a provision adopted unanimously by the U.S. House of Representatives and later signed by President Clinton as part of the 1994 Crime Bill. The provision directed the Sentencing Commission to study the issue and submit a report to Congress on the differing penalty levels between powder and crack cocaine by the end of the year. Congressman Rangel reintroduced the "Crack-Cocaine Equitable Sentencing Act" as H.R. 1264 in the 104th Congress.[66]

It is important to note that his reintroduced legislation had just 12 co-sponsors, seven of which were CBC members.[67] Craig Washington was defeated during the 1994 congressional elections. Nevertheless, since the passage in 1986 of legislation continuing mandatory minimum penalties for crack and powder cocaine, there is noticeable CBC legislative activity to address mandatory minimums and the disparities that exist between the sentencing of crack and powder cocaine offenders.

The 1994 Crime Bill

In August 1993, President Clinton announced the elements of a crime bill that he hoped to be introduced by Democrats. According to *Congressional Quarterly*, his fall campaign to pass a crime bill was "an attempt to make good on his promise to deliver what divided government could not."[68]

By 1994 President Clinton and a Democratically controlled Congress passed a crime bill that had fewer prevention measures than CBC members such as Congressman Washington advocated. It is important to note that Washington introduced an alternative crime bill that would eliminate all mandatory minimums. His legislation also called for the use of $3 billion included in the crime legislation proposed by the Senate for the purpose of new prison construction to instead be used to expand drug treatment for prisoners and to fund programs such as Head Start and midnight sports leagues in troubled neighborhoods.[69]

Congressman Washington's legislation did influence the inclusion of more preventive measures in the crime bill voted on by the House of Representatives, but in a compromise with conservatives, the final version of the bill reduced the funding for many prevention-related programs, a watered-down attempt to address the number of first-time nonviolent offenders who receive a mandatory minimum penalty (this is a safety valve provision). There were actually three votes on the bill: first rule vote, second rule vote, and the final passage vote. The first rule to bring up the 1994 crime bill failed by a vote of 210–225. This vote had 11 CBC members voting against the rule (including the only Republican member of the CBC), and 27 members in favor. After this vote on the first rule failed, negotiations took place and a second rule was developed. Some of the concessions included a reduction in funding for prevention programs. CBC members who voted "no" on this second rule were Earl Hilliard, William Clay, Bobby Scott, Maxine Waters, and Mel Watt; CBC members counted as "not voting" were Mel Reynolds, Walter Tucker, and Washington. A table is not constructed for the vote on the second rule since it had little significance. The first rule vote and final passage are most significant to tell the story of this vote in relation to African American support for a Democratic president's moderate crime legislation. The final passage of the conference report for the 1994 Crime Bill, which was signed into law, passed by a vote of 235–195 in the House. There were 24 CBC members who voted in favor of the legislation, and 12 members who voted against it (2 are counted as "not voting"). The CBC unity score on the first rule was just 42 percent. The Democratic party unity on this vote was 53 percent, or just over half the party voting with leadership. The chair of the CBC is among the 27 members who voted with the party's position on the first rule.

The NAACP did not issue a score card for the first rule, nor did the ADA. However, the ADA used a Liberal Quotient in which their legislative committee chooses 20 votes it considers the most important for the session. Each member receives five points when he or she votes with the ADA. Most of the CBC members received a score of 80 or above, which makes them a fairly liberal block of legislators. However, six CBC members received a rating of below 80. This is significant in that a body with approximately 40 members will have difficulty offering its vote as leverage when a significant number of members (almost 1 in 6) may not vote on progressive legislation. Members with less than 55 percent of African Americans in their congressional districts were as likely to vote with the chair of the CBC and with the party as they were to oppose the chair and the party. However, those with over 55 percent of African Americans in their congressional districts were much more likely to support the party position than not (19–6). Members with less seniority (fewer than three terms) were more likely to support the party position than they were to oppose it (17–7). Those with seniority were almost evenly divided on their vote (8–6). At this point, there were more (CBC) members serving fewer than three terms in Congress than there were members serving more than three terms. The majority of the CBC members during the 103rd Congress hailed from the South, which is a noticeable shift from previous Congresses. Southern members voted with the party's position by a vote of 2–1. The next dominant region in terms of number of members is the Northeast. These members voted for the party's position by a vote of 7–3. There is no vast difference in the way members in the West and Southwest split their vote on this issue. Of the founding members still in Congress, all but one voted in opposition to the party's position. Six members holding such positions voted with the party, whereas three voted in opposition to the party position.

In addition to a call by CBC members for more preventive measures, CBC members such as Conyers and Rangel urged President Clinton to be cognizant of the racial disparity in the allocation of the death penalty and urged the president not to support efforts to limit the number of appeals death row inmates can have. CBC Chair Kweisi Mfume was initially very critical of the president's abandonment of this issue. He accused the president of not negotiating in good faith with the Caucus and inferred that many of the 38-member caucus would join other opponents of the bill in opposing the bill when it reached the House floor for a final vote.[70] Indeed, 10 CBC members voted against the rule to bring this bill to the floor. As reported by Clarence Lusane, after CBC Chairman Mfume threatened that he and other members of the CBC would vote against final passage of the crime bill if the racial justice provision is eliminated from the bill, President Clinton assured the CBC that he would issue an executive order on this issue. In return for the elimination provision from the bill for the sake of appealing to conservatives, Clinton assured the CBC that he would issue an executive order and make public statements about the need to ensure that the death penalty is administered fairly. The executive order would, of course, focus on the administration of the death penalty at the federal level. This was apparently enough to get Mfume on board to support the bill. But, as Lusane writes,

> This divided the caucus along the lines of those who opposed the bill because of the added death penalty provisions and other punitive measures, and those who supported the bill that the President needed politically.[71]

Essentially, rather than working with these members to make the bill more effective, Clinton sought the passage of the legislation by appealing to conservatives and offering a symbolic promise to the CBC. Congressman Conyers stated during the previous year that "without the Congressional Black Caucus signing off on this legislation it is not going anywhere, period."[72] Without full Caucus support, even up to the eleventh hour, the bill went far and became law. The elimination of mandatory minimums and/or the elimination of the disparities between the treatment of crack versus powder offenders would have to be considered in future Congresses. CBC unity on this vote is just 28 percent; Democratic unity on this vote is also a low 49 percent. More rank-and-file CBC members voted with the chair of the CBC than voted in opposition to his vote. Twenty-two CBC members voted with Congressman Mfume, who supported the party position in the Democratic caucus, five voted with the Democratic leadership and four voted in opposition. The NAACP also opposed the final passage of this legislation. However, more than half of the CBC members, including the chair, voted in opposition on the NAACP's scorecard. Only 13 CBC members voted with the NAACP. The overall CBC score from the ADA is very high with all but five scoring above 80. Of the five who scored below 80, two are southern members and one is a Republican. CBC members with more than 55 percent African Americans in their congressional districts favored the party position by a vote of 17–8, while those with fewer than 55 percent of African Americans in their districts split their vote with half voting with the party's position and half voting against the party. Those with little seniority were much more likely to support the legislation than those with three or more terms. Senior members split their vote on this legislation. Thus, there is no indication that newer CBC members took their voting cues from senior members of Congress. In fact, each of the founding members still in Congress voted against the party on this vote, yet new members of Congress opted to vote with the party, along with the chair as mentioned. (Note, include as an endnote- the full set of interviews and charts were part of dissertation research entitled "The Response of the Congressional Black Caucus to the Mandatory Minimum Laws for Crack Cocaine).

1995 United States Sentencing Commission's Recommendations

In 1995, Congress had an opportunity to eliminate the disparity between powder and crack cocaine during a rare Floor vote on the issue. The CBC nearly unanimously voted (all CBC members who voted supported the USSC's recommendations, with the exception of Gary Franks, the sole Republican member of the CBC) to overturn the penalties as they currently existed. The purpose of the vote was to accept a recommendation by the USSC that would:

> . . . [make] the starting point for determining sentences for powder and crack offenders the same by adopting a 1-to-1 quantity at the powder cocaine level and would have provided enhancements for violence and other harms disproportionately associated with crack cocaine.[73]

The USSC also recommended removing a mandatory minimum for simple possession of crack cocaine. Under the USSC's recommendation, it would take the same level of crack as it takes for powder to receive a mandatory minimum sentence. The USSC concluded in its report that the laws were unjust, disproportionately affected African Americans, and could not be justified. Within Congress, Democrats and Republicans overwhelmingly rejected this recommendation. President Clinton signed into law the legislation, rejecting the Commission's proposed guideline changes.[74]

Prior to this vote, Congress held a congressional hearing, entitled "Cocaine and Federal Sentencing Policy," in which it considered the USSC's report. The hearing featured members of the USSC, judges, academics, and others in the law enforcement community. The hearing, chaired by Congressman McCollum (R-FL), was attended by CBC members Bobby Scott, Mel Watt, and Sheila Jackson Lee, each of whom served on the Subcommittee on Crime, the subcommittee that these hearings were held. In addition, Congressman Rangel attended the committee hearing and entered a statement supporting the USSC's recommendation. Congressman Conyers also attended the meeting. It is interesting to note that the other Democrats on this particular committee (Congressman Charles Schumer and Congresswoman Zoe Lofgren) were not in attendance, nor were Democrats from the full committee, other than Congressman Conyers. Further, Congressman Stupak (D-MI) submitted a statement stating his opposition to USSC's recommended changes. In his statement he included the following:

> I, along with Congressman McCollum, will be sponsoring legislation to prevent the Sentencing Commission from lowering the minimum sentence for trafficking in crack cocaine. Without Congressional action, the Sentencing Commission's recommendations will become law by November 1, 1995. I strongly oppose these recommendations, and that is why I, along with Congressman McCollum, will draft and introduce legislation.[75]

Like those who opposed the USSC's recommendations, he reiterated that crack was more potent than powder and that it had a devastating impact on communities. For the most part, CBC members gave testimony about the disparity in sentencing. Dr. Arthur Curry, who had testified during the 1993 hearings about his son's case, testified at this hearing as well. His son was caught up in a five-year FBI sting involving suspects. His son had no arrest record, was at best a minor player, and by the prosecutor's admission was only involved during the last six months of the FBI sting, but received a 19-year prison sentence on a conspiracy charge.[76] These were the types of cases the CBC had been attempting to portray. Curry's son was one of the individuals whose sentence was commuted by President Clinton as he was leaving office.[77] Congressman Scott, for example, stated that "we have an anomaly that the way these mandatory minimums work, somebody with a little bit of crack will get more than a higher-up from which the crack is made. Shouldn't we punish the people higher up more seriously than the people lower down?"[78] To counter the insistence by Republican members that this law does not have a racial intent, CBC members discussed neighborhoods that are targeted and racial profiling that results in African Americans being arrested.

The full House of Representatives debated and voted on the Sentencing Commission's recommendations on October 18, 1995. This was a very heated debate that came down to two questions: Is there racism in the criminal justice system? and (2)

Even if crack is more addictive than powder, can it still be justified that it takes 100 times as much powder to receive the same penalty of one distributing or possessing crack?

More than one member made reference to the Million Man March that took place just days prior to this vote. Congresswoman Meek (D-FL) stated:

The facts have been revealed to us. The figures have been revealed to us. So what more do we need? What we see here is a study of what keeps this country in turmoil is when we do not look at the facts and the impact of the facts on the people we all represent.

Mr. Speaker, I think each of us saw the 1 million black men who were here the day before yesterday. They were crying out for fairness. That s all they are asking for. Fairness. So, that if someone used crack, they will get a sentencing. That there will not be a disparity just because one is convicted of crack cocaine and the other one is using cocaine.

. . . . Mr. Speaker, I want this particular rule or resolution killed, because it needs to be. I do not think it is bipartisan. It is just a matter of saying we want to be fair. We want to treat all Americans the same. We should not have a different yardstick; one for crack cocaine and one for cocaine. One yardstick for all with liberty and justice for all. That is all we ask.[79]

Congressman Conyers also recognized the significance of the Million Man March. He stated:

Mr. Speaker, 48 hours ago this nation, perhaps the world, was galvanized by the resolve that has never happened before publicly in our community. A million African American males came together to pledge to restore to fight for family values, to build up their neighborhoods, to fight crime, to root out evil and wrongdoing. Now, 2 days later, we come here to reexamine whether we will deal with this moment of fairness in terms of crack and powder disparity in sentencing.

Please listen to the members of the Congressional Black Caucus and their friends that bring us not expert testimony, but they live in, represent, have grown up with, are part of the communities that are being wracked by this unfair sentencing.[80]

Congressman Barney Franks (D-MA) also made reference to the Million Man March, but the significance is that he equated the plea of the CBC as an equivalent to a protest march. He said:

. . . So when, and I have to say this to the overwhelmingly white majority of which I am a part of in the House, when our African-American colleagues come here in large numbers and plead with us to allow a nonpartisan body of experts to change this racially disparate policy. It is a march to this floor of our African-American colleagues who are pleading with us to alleviate the most racially unfair policy in America, and, please, even if my colleagues disagree, do not tell them "Oh, this is in the interest of your community, this is what the people you represent really want." I believe that we do not stay in this place very long if we do not reflect the people who sent us here, and when we have this extraordinary expression from the wide spectrum of opinion we often get within the Congressional Black Caucus saying we are doing a terrible disservice to this nation and to these young people when we perpetuate this racially disparate situation, then it seems to me people ought to listen to them.

We have talked about the racial problems reflected in the verdict of O.J. Simpson. Many Members here, and let us be honest, many Members here were disappointed that a march led by Louis Farrakhan got such enthusiasm. I ask, "why do you think this is happening? Why do you have this great disparity?" It is partly because of the kinds of policies we have here. Can we really be so sure about maintaining this disparity in sentencing in the face of the Sentencing Commission's argument, even if my colleagues think that maybe they can make some technical justification because of the chemistry of the powder versus the chemistry of crack? Is it worth perpetuating the anger, and the anguish, and the sense of manifest unfairness that it brings? I do not see how anyone in good faith can argue that we, as a Nation, are well served by maintaining this.

Mr. Speaker, no one is talking about letting people walk. No one is talking about letting people off the hook. We are asking for recognition of a grave racial injustice.[81]

On the issue of the rationality of treating two versions of the same drug regardless of the racial disparity in sentencing it creates, Congressman Chaka Fatah said the following:

Mr. Speaker, it is idiotic for us to have a disparity in these ratios for powder cocaine or crack. In fact, I would say to the gentleman from Florida [Mr. Shaw] and the gentleman from Florida [Mr. McCollum], one has to have powder in order to make crack cocaine. The reality is that people who have powder cocaine are directly responsible for the creation of the crack cocaine. So, if one wanted to root out the evil and punish it, one would create the disparity in reverse.[82]

Or consider this statement from Congresswoman Eva Clayton (D-NC) during the debate:

Mrs. CLAYTON. Mr. Chairman, I rise in opposition to this bill and in support of the Conyers substitute. The distinguished jurist, Judge Learned Hand on one occasion stated, "If we are to keep our democracy, there must be one commandment, Thou shalt not ration justice." Indeed, this Nation is the leading democracy in the world because we labor to ensure that our citizens are governed by one standard of justice—equal under law, according to the inscription above the U.S. Supreme

Court Building. It troubles me that this bill seeks to disapprove the proposed sentencing guidelines regarding crack cocaine. The question is why? Do the recommendations of the Sentencing Commission create a dual standard of justice? The answer is "no." In fact, the recommendation of the Sentencing Commission is to create a single standard for all cocaine offenses—whether the offense involves powder or crack cocaine . That, it seems to me, meets the mandate of equal justice. Do the recommendations of the Sentencing Commission call for a change in sentencing for cocaine offenses? Again, the answer is "no." The recommendations simply provide for cocaine offenses involving crack to be equal to those involving powder cocaine—the penalty for both will be the same, and the penalty for powder cocaine remains unchanged. Mr. Chairman, let us not forget that the 1994 crime bill directed the Sentencing Commission to examine the disparity between sentencing for crack cocaine and powder cocaine offenses. The Commission followed that directive, and made 27 recommendations on May 1, 1995, including recommendations to equalize the penalties for crack and powder cocaine. The Commission did what Congress told them to do. Now—because the Commission did not do what some would have preferred that they do—we are faced with an effort to undo what they did. The Sentencing Commission is composed of judges and lawyers and others, expert in the field of sentencing. They conducted their business within the administrative authority given them by an act of Congress. No proponent of this bill has argued that the Commission acted without authority. They stayed within the banks of the law that created them. Why then do some now seek to negate the legitimate actions of the Sentencing Commission? Why are some willing to accept a dual standard of justice in our law enforcement system? Why are some willing to allow minority citizens, low income citizens, to bear a stricter sentencing burden than non-minorities bear—for the same offense? Why are some willing to overlook the fact that African-Americans account for almost 90 percent of those convicted of Federal crack cocaine charges? Those are the questions, Mr. Chairman, and they are compelling. I hope we will get some honest answers. Then, let us reject this ill-advised, constitutionally awkward legislation.[83]

The above was just a sample of the debate. A wide range of CBC members came to the floor to make a case to their Democratic and Republican colleagues to adopt the USSC's recommendations. Almost all of the CBC members referred to the Million Man March. While the March may not have influenced the timing of the vote or directly influenced CBC members, it did enter into the political debate surrounding a contentious issue that impacted the demographics of those attending the March. Congressman Conyers also introduced a substitute resolution that also overwhelmingly failed that would at the very least eliminate the mandatory minimum for the mere possession of five grams of crack.

The bill passed by a vote of 332–83 meaning that the USSC's recommendations were overwhelmingly rejected. It is important to note that in spite of the pleas by CBC members and on the floor of the House of Representatives, Richard Gephardt, the Minority Leader of House Democrats, rejected the recommendations. As was mentioned, this vote took place just two days after the Million Man March. This March, which was held on the grounds of the United States Capitol, consisted of hundreds of thousands of

African American men, many potentially affected by these laws. Hanes Walton suggests that when African Americans "suffer serious and significant reversals in their legal and economic rights, nationalist leadership has always made a bid for mainstream leadership roles and positions. The era of the Reagan-Bush-Clinton presidencies (i.e., 1980–1996) was just such a period. Fringe leaders like Minister Farrakhan and deposed NAACP Executive Secretary Reverend Benjamin Chavis made a grab for a mainstream leadership position within the Million Man March."[84] The significance of this March as demonstrated by Walton, concerns recognition that conservative politics of the 1980s and 1990s were detrimental to the needs of African Americans. While Democrats and Republicans during this era were competing for White voters in order to maintain power positions in Congress, members of the CBC remained critical of those policies, but split their vote, until 1995, on anti-crime legislation passed by the United States House of Representatives. Further, despite the mobilization of these men and unison of the CBC, the majority or Democrats in the House, Senate, and the president refused to listen as measured by their recorded vote and, in the case of the president (Bill Clinton), refusing to veto the bill that stopped the USSC's recommendation from moving forward. As was mentioned, the CBC unanimously supported the USSC's recommendation and opposed the legislation that would stop the recommendation from taking effect.

Analyses of the Key Years of 1993–1995

The years 1993–1995 were optimal years for overturning mandatory minimum penalties for crack cocaine and/or eliminating the disparities. The Congressional hearings on prison overcrowding and specifically on crack and powder cocaine featured testimony on the impact of African American incarceration rates and prison overcrowding as a result of nonviolent drug offenders sentenced to fixed and long prison terms. The vote in 1995 was the last vote taken on the floor of the House of Representatives on mandatory minimums for crack cocaine for another 15 years. That vote was a clear signal that the Democratic president and Democrats in Congress were more interested in obtaining conservative, White voters than they were in reducing the impact a law was having on the African American public. As was mentioned, hearings in 1993, reports from the USSC, Attorney General Reno's belief that the law should be examined, and advocacy to overturn such legislation by the American Civil Liberties Union, the National Association for the Advancement of Colored People, and the hundreds of thousands of African American men participating in the Million Man March could not persuade Congress to do what was right. At the request of Congress during the 1995 vote, the Sentencing Commission issued another report to Congress that again recommended that the disparity between crack and powder be substantially reduced. In its report, the USSC wrote:

> The Commission has accumulated a vast array of information about both powder and crack cocaine and about the changing markets for these drugs. Based on this work, the Commission is unanimous in reiterating its original core finding, outlined in its February 1995 report to Congress that, although research and public

policy may support somewhat higher penalties for crack than for powder, a 100–1 quantity ratio cannot be justified. The Commission is firmly and unanimously in agreement that the current penalty differential for federal powder and crack cocaine cases should be reduced by changing the quantity levels that trigger mandatory minimum penalties for both powder and crack cocaine. Therefore, for powder cocaine, the Commission recommends that Congress reduce the current 500-gram trigger for the five-year mandatory minimum sentence to a level between 125–375 grams, and for crack cocaine, that Congress increase the current five-gram trigger between 25 and 75 grams.[85]

It would be 2010 when Congress would finally raise the threshold that would trigger a mandatory minimum penalty for crack cocaine.

CBC and Democratic Behavior on Crime Legislation, 1997–2000 (105th–106th Congress)

In 1997, the CBC criticized President Clinton for not going far enough on the issue of mandatory minimums for crack cocaine. Congresswoman Waters, chair of the CBC at the time, sent a letter to President Clinton on behalf of the CBC criticizing him for (1) supporting recommendations that did not go far enough in eliminating the disparity of mandatory minimums from crack and powder and (2) claiming he had consulted with the CBC on the sentencing recommendations. Waters points to a contradiction with the second statement about having consulted with the CBC saying:

If the White House had consulted us, as they claim, considered our views and then rejected them, that would be one thing. . . . We wouldn't be happy with their conclusions, but we could live with that. But to claim consultation when there was none, is unacceptable.[87]

It is important to note that after the USSC issued its report to Congress in 1997, President Clinton asked Attorney General Reno and General McCaffrey (his Drug Czar) to study the report. They both sent the president a letter supporting the USSC's recommendation and again stated that the current 100–1 disparity had no justification and is racially discriminatory.[88] According to *The New York Times*, both Reno and McCaffrey wrote a letter that stated, in part, "We cannot turn a blind eye," they added, "to the corrosive effect this has had on respect for the law in certain communities and on the effective administration of justice."[89]

McCaffrey recommended a complete elimination of the 100:1 disparity because crack and powder are the same pharmacologically and in their addictiveness. More from the letter, "From a drug-abuse perspective, 1 to 1 made more sense to me."[90] The article concluded with a comment by General McCaffrey stating that he wants the Senate and the House to listen to rational arguments about changing the law.[91] In actuality, it was President Clinton who did not have the political will to listen to his

Attorney General, his Drug Czar, and members of the CBC and pushed for the USSC's 1997 recommendations to Congress to be considered.

Throughout the 105th and 106th Congresses (the Congresses immediately following the 1995 vote), members of the CBC continued to introduce bills to either eliminate mandatory minimums or to eliminate the disparity in sentencing between crack and powder cocaine. No single bill was co-sponsored by all CBC members or made it out of the committee.[92]

SECOND HEARING

The second hearing devoted specifically to mandatory sentencing laws occurred on May 11, 2000—it was entitled "Drug Mandatory Minimums: Are They Working?" According to a FAMM newsletter, it was convened by John Mica, chair of the Criminal Justice, Drug Policy and Human Resources subcommittee of the House Committee on Government Reform and Oversight. Once again, CBC members expressed opposition to mandatory minimum penalties for crack cocaine. In addition, John Steer, a member of the USSC, reiterated the statistics about African Americans serving longer sentences than Whites "since the percent of mandatory minimum cases in which the defendant was White decreased from 30 percent to approximately 23 percent. The percentage of cases in which the defendant was Hispanic increased from 33 percent to almost 39 percent. During this five-year period, Hispanics subjected to mandatory minimums displaced White defendants on an almost one-to-one basis.[93] This latter is a reason why it will be difficult for the CBC to build a coalition to bring powder penalties down to the level equal to crack cocaine penalties. Any effort to equalize the penalty for powder and crack cocaine by lowering powder cocaine penalties to the level of the current crack penalties as opposed to raising crack to the current level of powder penalties will not receive support from the Hispanic community because it would subject their constituencies to increased incarceration. In 2002, the Mexican American Legal Defense and Education Fund reported to the USSC that while the current penalties are very unfair, they would not support lowering the threshold for the amount of powder cocaine that would trigger a mandatory minimum penalty "because this would exacerbate racial disparity and have a negative impact on the Latino community."[94]

According to the FAMM gram, on July 25, 2000, the House Judiciary Committee amended HR 2987—the Club Drug Anti-Proliferation Act of 2000. The significance for mentioning this bill is the amendments offered by CBC members. For example, Congressman Conyers, Congressman Scott, and Congresswoman Waters offered an amendment that would repeal all drug mandatory sentencing statutes in federal law. The amendment failed by a vote of 18–8. All Republicans on the Committee voted against the amendment, and four Democrats joined them. Those Democrats that voted against the bill were Congressman Marty Meehan (D-MA), Congresswoman Zoe Lofgren (D-CA), Congressman Anthony Weiner (D-NY), and Congressman Steven Rothman (D-NJ).[95] Those who voted for the amendment included CBC members Sheila Jackson Lee, Waters, Watt, and Scott; in other words, all CBC members on the committee. The Democrats who opposed it are representatives from diverse parts of the country. This contributes to the difficulty of uniting their Democratic colleagues on the issue of mandatory minimums. It is possible that should these amendments had made it to the House floor, Democrats from these states would have objected to them in the same manner as the 1995 recommendations were objected to.

Another amendment offered during the July 2000 hearing included an amendment offered by Congressman Conyers that would allow judges to impose non-prison sentences on certain nonviolent drug offenses. "By unanimous consent, Chairman Hyde modified the Conyers amendment to insert after "drug-related offense," "involving a simple possession offense quantity of drugs as defined in title 21 United States Code." The Conyers amendment, as modified, was agreed to by voice vote.[96]

Another amendment offered by CBC members Scott and Conyers that passed during the committee mark-up was a report that requires the attorney general to study the racial impact of mandatory minimum laws.[97] It, too, passed via voice vote. The racial impact of mandatory minimums had been studied several times by July 2000 and was even mentioned in the May hearing. In addition, in late December, the GAO completed a study requested by Congresswoman Eleanor Holmes Norton about the rise in the female prison population and the challenges faced. The use and abuse of drugs played a key role in the incarceration of these women.[98] Even as late as 2000, there was reluctance by members of Congress to overturn penalties, but there was a recognition that they were not the best solution in sentencing.

By the conclusion of the 106th Congress, efforts on behalf of several CBC members to address this issue failed to garner another vote on the floor of the House of Representatives. While Democrats remained supportive of tough crime penalties and opposed to eliminating or reducing the disparity between the sentencing for crack and powder cocaine, the CBC's voting behavior demonstrates a change since the law has been in place. However, as the interview data presented in an earlier chapter demonstrates, members of the CBC are not likely to pressure their Democratic colleagues to publicly address this issue. Politics plays a major role in this decision. If Democrats appear to be soft on crime, then they risk losing any opportunity to regain the majority in the House and Senate because Republicans will use the issue against them. Thus, the CBC, because of its ties to the Democratic party, diverse constituencies, and individualistic attitudes among members, continue to be unable and/or unwilling to significantly address this issue. The next chapter will present a final analysis of CBC legislative behavior on mandatory sentences for crack cocaine.

Keyterms

Endnotes

1 Stengel, Richard. "More Muscle for Crime Fighters: A New Federal Code Tilts Toward the Government," *Time* (October 29, 1984), 74.

2 Congress and the Nation, p. 698.

3 Five members with fewer than 55 percent of African Americans opposed the party position and only two members with more than 55 percent of African Americans opposed the party position on this vote.

4 Congress and the Nation, p. 698.

5 *The Congressional Record*, October 2, 1984, p. 28592.

6 *Congress and the Nation,* p. 699 and the *Congressional Record*, October 2, 1984, p. 28595.

7 *Congressional Record*, October 1984, p. 28601.

8 Of those CBC members who voted, Congress members Clay, Collin, Crockett, Dellums, Leland, Mitchell, Savage, and Towns voted no; Congress members Conyers, Dixon, Ford Sr., Gray, Hawkins, Hall, Hayes, Owens, Rangel, Stokes, and Wheat voted yes.

9 "Poll: Blacks Want Stiffer Penalties for Criminals." *Jet Magazine* (June 4, 1984), p. 4.

10 For the purposes of this work, a CBC member is designated as "present" only when the official record so affirms.

11 House Select Committee on Narcotics Abuse and Control, Friday, September 28, 1984, p. 1.

12 Ibid., p. 40.

13 Ibid., p. 50.

14 Rangel said to one panelist that in the Black community, "We don't have people from Peru, or Mexico, or Thailand in our community selling drugs. We find agents from our family selling drugs to members of the family." In an exchange with a Howard University student who speculated that drugs were dumped on the Black community by the White community, Congressman Rangel disregarded the young man's comments and stated that even if he were correct, if people were not succumbing to the temptation of drugs and alcohol, it would not matter what was being placed in the community.

15 The first hearing, which took place on July 15th, is entitled "The Crack Cocaine Crisis" and it was a joint hearing with the Select Committee on Children, Youth and Families. The second hearing took place on July 18th and it is entitled "Trafficking and Abuse of 'Crack' in New York."

16 In the joint hearing that took place on July 15th, CBC members recorded as being present other than Congressman Rangel, who chairs the committee, was Walter Fauntroy, who also served on the Committee. CBC member Congressman Alan Wheat served on the Select Committee on Children, Youth, and Families; however, he was not recorded as being present nor did he submit a statement for the record. Other CBC members on the Committee but who were not recorded as being present included Congressman Towns and Congresswoman Collins. In the hearing that took place on July 18th (which took place in New York City), CBC members present were Congressman Conyers, Towns, and Rangel.

17 "Sentencing Revision Act of 1984." Hearings before the House Judiciary Committee, February 22, 1984, pp. 77–80.

18 "Sentencing Guidelines," Hearings before the Subcommittee of Criminal Justice of the Committee on the Judiciary, House of Representatives, One Hundredth Congress, first session on Sentencing Guidelines, May 12, June 11, 16, July 15, 22, 23, and 29, 1987.

19 Johnston, David, "Bush's Drug Strategy Is Criticized as Failing to Seek Views of Cities," *New York Times* (September 6, 1989), A8.

20 "Drugs and Cities: The Federal Response." House Select Committee on Narcotics Abuse and Control, June 30, 1993, p. 19 (this is an exchange between Rangel and Mfume).

21 "Drugs and Crime," Public Hearing before the Select Committee on Narcotics Abuse and Control, House of Representatives, One Hundred First Congress, First Session, May 12th, 1989. Note: This hearing was held in Congressman Ford's congressional district.

22 Kennedy, 1997, p. 372.

23 Ibid.

24 Interview with Eric Sterling, Chief Counsel of Congressman Hughes during the time when these laws were written; the interview took place on June 30, 2002.

25 "CQ House Votes." *Congressional Quarterly* (October 25, 1986), pp. 274–275.

26 The title of the hearing was "Intravenous Drug Use and AIDS: The Impact of the Black Community."

27 "Intravenous Drug Use and AIDS: The Impact on the Black Community." House Select Committee on Narcotics Control and Abuse, September 25, 1987, p. 20.

28 Ibid., p. 19.

29 Congressman Hansen spent seven terms in the United States House of Representatives. He was incarcerated at the same time he was allowed to appear at the hearing. He served his prison sentence during the years 1986 and 1987 and was asked to testify to give his personal account.

30 "Intravenous Drug Use and AIDS," pp. 24–25.

31 The Democratic vote was 162–181, CBC members who voted overwhelmingly supported the legislation.
32 "U.S. Prison Population Sets Record for a Year, in Six Months," *The New York Times* (Monday, September 11, 1989).
33 Ibid.
34 Ibid.
35 Dowdy, Zachery. "Crime and Punishment: How the U.S. Prison System Makes Minority Communities Pay." *The New Crises* (July/August 2002), . 34.
36 Walters, Ronald. "Targeting Resources to Central Cities: A Strategy for Redeveloping the Black Community." *The Black Scholar: The Urban Crisis* (1993), 3.
37 See Appendix 3 for comments.
38 Oreskes, p. A1.
39 "The Federal Drug Strategy: What Does It Mean for Black America?" House Select Committee on Narcotics Control and Abuse, September 15, 1989, p. 22.
40 See Appendix 4 for his opening statement.
41 House Select Committee on Narcotics Control and Abuse, September 15, 1989, p. 7.
42 "The Justice Department's Role in the War on Drugs." House Select Committee on Narcotics Abuse and Control, July 25, 1991, p. 45.
43 Ibid., p. 46.
44 Berke, Richard, "Poll Finds Most in the U.S. Back Bush Strategy on Drugs," *The New York Times*(Tuesday, September 12, 1989).
45 Ibid.
46 "On the Edge of the American Dream: A Social and Economic Profile in 1992," a report by the Chairman, Select Committee on Narcotics Control and Abuse, One Hundred and Second Congress, Second Session, March 1992.
47 "Special Report to Congress: Mandatory Minimum Penalties in the Federal Criminal Justice System," United States Sentencing Commission, August 1991, p. ii.
48 Ibid.
49 "Same Drug, Different Penalties." *The Washington Post* (August 4, 1993), A16.
50 Beck, Katel, et al. "Kicking the Prison Habit: Drug Criminals Fill the Cells: Is there a Better Way?" *Newsweek* (June 14, 1993): 32–33.
51 Staff Reporter. "Retrieving the Jailer's Keys: Attorney General Reno Launches a Review of Mandatory Minimum Sentences." *Time Magazine*, 141(20), May 17, 1993, p. 21.
52 "Federal Prison Population: Present and Future Trends." Hearings before the Subcommittee on Intellectual Property and Judicial Administration of the Committee on the Judiciary in the House of Representatives, One Hundred and Third Congress, First Session, May 12 and July 29, 1993, p. 28.
53 Ibid., p. 8.
54 In this hearing, there was a general consensus among both Democrats and Republicans that incarcerating non-violent offenders put undue pressure on the Bureau of Prisons and on taxpayer dollars. Congressman McCollum (R-FL) was sympathetic to the idea of lowering the sentences for nonviolent criminals although, as was mentioned, he was instrumental in defeating the USSC's 1995 recommendations to eliminate the crack-powder sentencing disparities.
55 "Federal Prison Population: Present and Future Trends." Hearings before the Subcommittee on Intellectual Property and Judicial Administration of the Committee on the Judiciary in the House of Representatives, One Hundred and Third Congress, First Session, May 12 and July 29, 1993, p. 233.

56 Schumer's statement can be found in Appendix 6.

57 "Federal Mandatory Minimum Sentencing." Hearing before the Subcommittee on Crime and Criminal Justice for the Committee on the Judiciary, House of Representatives, One Hundred and Third Congress, First session, July 29, 1993.

58 "Federal Mandatory Minimum Sentencing." Hearing before the Subcommittee on Crime and Criminal Justice for the Committee on the Judiciary, House of Representatives, One Hundred and Third Congress, First session, July 29, 1993, p. 36–37.

59 "Federal Prison Population: Present and Future Trends," p. 242.

60 "Cocaine and Federal Sentencing Policy." Hearing before the Subcommittee on Crime of the Committee on the Judiciary, House of Representatives, One Hundred and Fourth Congress, First Session, June 29, 1995, pp. 156–157.

61 Personal interview with Nkechi Taifa, July 30, 2003 in the offices of the Open Society Institute in Washington, DC.

62 Ibid.

63 Ibid.

64 Sirica, Jack. "House Axes Narcotics Committee." *NewsDay*, Long Island, New York. January 27, 1993, p. 28.

65 This information comes from a legislative search conducted using www.thomas.gov. This bill number is HR 3315 and the Congress is the 103rd.

66 "Cocaine and Federal Sentencing Policy," p. 165.

67 This come from a search of the bill via www.thomas.gov.

68 Idelson, Holly, "Democrats' New Proposal Seeks Consensus by Compromise," *Congressional Quarterly*, (August 14, 1993), 2228.

69 Ibid.

70 Mathis, Nancy, "Black Caucus, Clinton at Odds Over the Crime Bill," *Houston Chronicle,* Washington Bureau, (July 15, 1994), A1.

71 "Unity and Struggle: The Political Behavior of African American Members of Congress," *The Black Scholar, San Francisco, 24*(4) (Fall 1994), 16–28.

72 Idelson, p. 2229.

73 "Special Report to the Congress: Cocaine and Federal Sentencing Policy" (as directed by section two of Public Law 104–38), United States Sentencing Commission, April 1997, p. 1.

74 Ibid.

75 "Cocaine and Federal Sentencing Policy." Hearing before the Committee on Crime of the Committee of the Judiciary, House of Representatives, One Hundred Fourth Congress, First Session, June 29, 1995.

76 Ibid., p. 106–107

77 "Rep. Maxine Waters Unveils Bill to Eliminate Mandatory Sentences for Low-Level Drug Offenders," Press Release, *Families Against Mandatory Minimums*, May 23, 2003.

78 "Cocaine and Federal Sentencing Policy," p. 144.

79 "Disapproval of Certain Sentencing Guideline Amendments (House of Representatives-October 18, 1995)" accessed courtesy of the *Congressional Record* on 5/30/2003. This section of the Congressional Record is 98 pages; pp. 22–23 of 98 (accessed online).

80 Ibid., p. 22 of 98.

81 Ibid., p. 27 of 98.

82 Ibid., p. 21 of 98 .

83 "Disapproval of Certain Sentencing Guideline Amendments (House of Representatives-October 18, 1995)". This statement was accessed online via www.thomas.gov on May 24, 2008. The online length of the entire debate can be found on pages H10255–H10284.

84 Walton, Jr., Hanes. "Public Responses to the Million Man March," *The Black Scholar* (Fall 1995).

85 "Special Report to Congress: Cocaine and Federal Sentencing Policy" (as directed by section two of Public Law 104–38), United States Sentencing Commission, April 1997, p. 2.

86 In an upcoming chapter of this book, we will present a discussion of the USSC recommendation made in April-May 2007. Congress had until November 2007 to approve the recommendations, providing an opportunity for many crack offenders to have sentence reductions, but not those who receive a five-year penalty.

87 "Congressional Black Caucus Blasts President's Crack/Powder Cocaine Sentencing Recommendations: CBC Denies 'Consultation' with White House." Press Release, Office of Congresswoman Maxine Waters, July 22, 1998, p. 1.

88 Wren, Christopher, "Reno and Top Drug Official Urge Smaller Gap in Cocaine Sentences," *The New York Times*(July 22, 1998), 1.

89 Ibid., p. A12.

90 Ibid.2

91 Ibid.

92 The 105th Congress, according to the Library of Congress' website that allows access to bill information (www.thomas.loc.gov), lists 11 bills relating to mandatory minimums for drugs and/or crack cocaine, none of which made it out of committee. Three were introduced by CBC members, and for the 106th Congress there were fewer than 10 bills introduced regarding mandatory minimums for drug penalties and/or crack cocaine (four were introduced by CBC members).

93 "Historic Hearing on Mandatory Sentencing: Drug Mandatory Minimums, Are They Working." *Families Against Mandatory Minimums' FAMMGRAM* (Fall 2000), pp. 4–5.

94 "Report to the Congress: Cocaine and Federal Sentencing Policy," United States Sentencing Commission, May 2002, Appendix D-3.

95 "Federal Legislation Watch: Drug Bills Spark Sentencing Debate." *FAMMGRAM*, Fall 2000, p. 16.

96 House Rpt. 106-878-Part 1- Methamphetamine and Club Drug Anti-Proliferation Act of 2000, from www.thomas.gov (click on committee reports), accessed on May 24, 2008. Note, the bill did not pass during this Congress.

97 Ibid.

98 The report entitled "Women in Prison: Issues and Challenges Confronting the US Correctional Systems," was issued to Eleanor Holmes Norton by the GAO in December 1999. It can be read in its entirety at www.gao.gov (insert "Women in Prison, in the search engine—)

ACTIVITY 1
Votes, Statements, and Committees...

A Chapter 5 Exercise

Instructions:

In the space above, explain what the book talks about regarding the role of the CBC on the crime legislation between 1984 - 1995. Please consider the role of various committees mentioned in the chapter when preparing your response.

1984–1995

[Please tear out your completed response so you can turn it in to the instructor]

ACTIVITY 2

In the boxes, describe book details on the crime legislation
of the following years . . .

A Chapter 5 Exercise

1986–1988

1989–1992

1993–1995

[Please tear out your completed response so you can turn it in to the instructor]

ACTIVITY 3

Applying a book concept to a real-life issue...

The Sentencing Commission 1991 Report

Congressional Hearings of 1993

Instructions:

Within the two boxes above, please discuss these two events and what you consider important about each one.

A Chapter 5 Exercise

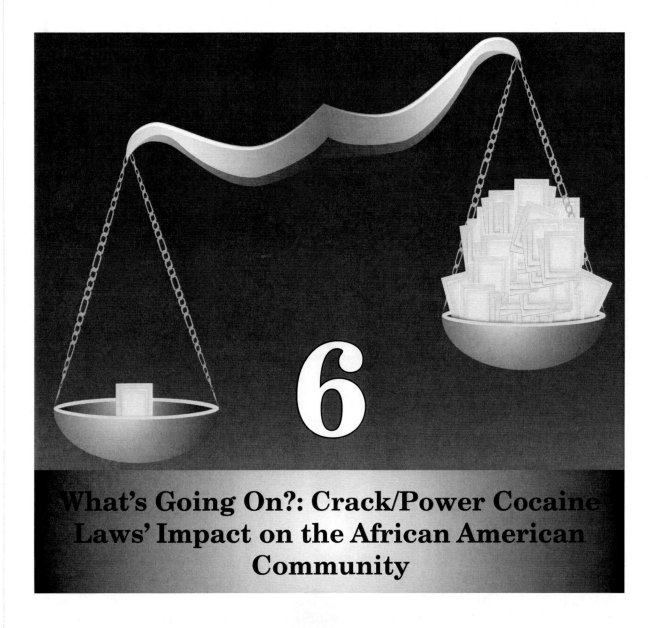

What's Going On?: Crack/Power Cocaine Laws' Impact on the African American Community

Chapter 6: This chapter looks at mandatory minimum laws on the eve of its 20th year anniversary. How has it impacted crime rates, the selling and distribution of drugs? How does the U.S. penal institution look 20 years after a law that greatly enhanced the prison population?

Why are they working to reduce Meth sentencing but aren't even talking about insiders here for crack? That's not fair and on top of that, crack folks didn't hear about any kind of treatment programs until after the Meth folks were getting treatment. . . . Now, they've even introduced legislation to give "good time" to those convicted of Meth, but make no mention of those convicted of other drugs. . . . Why?[1]

Even at the turn of the 21st century, the impact of mandatory minimum drug laws had almost 20 years to brew. The quote above made by an inmate within an Arkansas prison, questioned the logic and priorities of all making decisions related to fairness in drug sentencing and societal views regarding the incarceration of prisoners even though methamphetamine and crack cocaine have both been called "epidemics" by those in power. Harris and Miller[2] assert that African American families have been harmed by these laws in many ways as families struggle to deal with the disparity in incarceration compared to drug laws for different drugs. Not only do the inmates suffer, but their families and extended families as well. As Angeli put it:

> The impact of the "100-to-1" disparity is felt almost exclusively by black defendants. In 1993, for example, blacks accounted for 88.3% of federal crack distribution convictions; 4.1% were white. [I]in contrast, whites accounted for 32% of those sentenced for powder cocaine distribution; 27.4% were black. Since the average sentence for trafficking in crack is more than five years longer than the average powder sentence, federal cocaine laws clearly have a large disproportionate impact on black defendants.[3]

The importance of this direct incarceration impact is the fact that "impact" transcends into an almost "norm" in the minds of some about African American males.[4] Part of this mindset is that sentencing disparities are almost unknown to many Americans and therefore, they make assessments about criminality simply based on the number of people either arrested or incarcerated, not the realities, i.e. nuances, associated with some drug crimes being treated differently by society than other drug crimes. Therefore, a negative label, or "otherness,"[5] is attached to being a convict, both during and after release from prison.[6] The authors of this manuscript participate in community reentry programs, and it is common for many "insiders" to believe it is not to their advantage to state their conviction on any job application, for fear of not being able to gain employment. This is especially troubling if the crime has no relevance to the type of job being applied for.

Historically, the legacy of slavery is an appropriate filter of grasping the impact on African Americans; this is due to the reality of how political realities supported economic disenfranchisement. Stereotypes and myths exist with respect to African Americans based on the legacy of slavery in the United States and in other parts of the world. "Internal inferiorization," that is, the learned misperception of self leading to self-hatred, results from the perpetuation of a societal system that either values or devalues humans.[7] In this case, being of African descent is historically devalued within American society more so than being from other areas of the world, which had psychological impact in terms of the value of African American life in American society.The criminal justice system supported this disenfranchisement. As Williams[8] explains:

When one takes an objective perspective of the history of the African American male; i.e. hangings, murder, beatings, and Jim Crow laws, it is no wonder that this group continues to try to exist in social, political, and economic systems that have been far from user-friendly.

So in essence, incorporating an understanding of cumulative disadvantage over time is important in properly addressing realities such as this sentencing disparity.[9] With respect to the crack versus powder disparity, many African American males are pulled from the work force and feel this label of being a convict might exclude them from any legitimate opportunity in the future, regardless of whether it is related to their crime. As a result, an enormous segment of the young Black male population has been removed from both the job market and the Black community at large by the disability and stigma of conviction. The effects are devastating, both on an individual level and on the African American community as a whole.

The reality of the increase of African Americans in prison resulting from the mandatory minimum laws has been exacerbated by the actions of policymakers. The office of the U.S. president is the highest policymaking position in the country. Any statements, actions, or appointees tend to reflect the interests of this position. The Justice Policy Institute, among others, has expressed concern about the growing prison population under President Bill Clinton's administration. An analysis of the Justice Police Institute demonstrates the line Clinton walked, the need, in his view, to support tough-on-crime policies, while personally abhorring mandatory minimum sentences and wanting prison policies to be reexamined. In essence, based on comments made as he was leaving office and control of criminal justice policies to others, President Clinton contradicted:

. . . the last eight years of his stance on crime control in one sentence. President Clinton devoted two consecutive campaigns to "getting tough on crime," signing into law a bill that included the largest increase in crime control funding ever, and promoting measures that revoked sentencing discretion from federal judges. [10]

Clearly, being "soft on crime" has been a designation politicians in recent decades have fought to deflect. In fact, many Democratic candidates and office holders have enacted harsh public policy in order to avoid the appearance of being considered soft on crime. With respect to politics and voting, racial stereotypes still represent a tool that is used often to aid in appeal to White voters. The civil rights movement was marked by African Americans being able to, for the first time, choose the name that they would prefer to be called by, and that was the term "Black." This psychological victory within society was connected incidentally to the use of racial stereotypes in the post–civil rights era. A tool used often by politicians in the current post–civil rights era is to use racially coded language (often simply referred to as coding) that has been used to enhance fear of White voters toward political victories by fellow politicians. In essence, racial stereotypes have served presidential candidates and national agendas. The fear created among White voters has produced very few responses toward underlying problems that actually drive those fears. This chapter to some degree is important, then, to help understand some of the background behind this coded language and how detrimental it has been in dealing with drug issues. Former President Ronald Reagan made many statements that helped to foster and continue fears of White voters primarily to elections, and this has been well documented. Reagan himself described welfare as an abuse of Great Society programs and by the recipients of that public assistance, insisting that welfare undermined the values and well-being of American families. Implicit with these explanations was the connection to drug use by African Americans and how this should be of concern to (in particular) White Americans. These alleged welfare abuse stories came to play a significant part in Reagan's messages when he would run for various offices, not just for president, but before then as well. Like President George Bush, who was attempting to continue Ronald Reagan's legacy when he was running for office, intensified his own campaign by exploiting those fears about crime in young White males. This exploitation involved using the Willie Horton story as an attempt to proclaim that if support for Democrats happened, there would be rampant Black criminality that would continue to destroy society. This exploitation involved the use of public television commercials that associated the Dukakis campaign with Willie Horton, who was a Black felon. The importance of the Willie Horton story was that the specific incident with a Black male that committed a series of rapes against randomly selected White people who fit an upscale, suburban type of profile and played into a stereotype on Black criminality. As the campaign progressed, many White voters saw Dukakis as being incapable of protecting White citizens against rampant Black criminality. During the same time period (the 1980s), there were an increasing number of Black conservatives who made public statements in support of these moves by Republicans. These statements were obviously useful in helping conservatives to deflect any charges of racism, for (their belief was that) if there was racism, there certainly would have been no Blacks who would speak out in support of these actions.

Another important dimension in understanding the racial nature of creating these blocks of White voters in terms of using fear to impact them was a public concern with the crack vs. powder cocaine epidemic. The growing concern that attention placed on this drug epidemic mixed with the recent books of the time alleging that race was connected to intelligence and prepensely to commit crime, by the fact that there were many television commercials produced by the Bush campaign that stated that Dukakis was "soft on crime." One of these television commercials even depicted prisoners walking through a revolving door. Afterward, continuing in the same tone, Bush vetoed the Civil Rights Act of 1990, claiming that even though he cares about civil rights, he would not support quotas; this was his rationale for vetoing the Civil Rights Act. Again, this very statement was never properly explained even when asked by reporters and others directly of the president and did not provide any type of statement regarding how to correct the legacy of lack of access and poor distribution of resources, which, in essence, mandated some type of redistribution formula. What is most amazing to people today, in the 21st century, is that looking back, the use of race for political gain was very blatant.

Certain attention on impact must address the difference with respect to how the drugs methamphetamine and crack cocaine have been addressed even though they have both been ranked as epidemic in American society. Figure 6.1, from a recent study on methamphetamine and crack cocaine, provides some understanding of similarities and differences with respect to efforts to address both drugs.[11] What this study indicates is that during a 20-year period, essentially since the birth of the federal mandatory minimum for crack cocaine, politicians and print media ranked crack cocaine and methamphetamine as the same in terms of a societal problem; they used the word "epidemic." However, 37 policy differences, mostly centered around precursor chemical control and sentencing guidelines/conflicts resulted in efforts to address methamphetamine and crack cocaine being unequal during the same time in which they were considered epidemic by print media and politicians. An interesting nuance to this reality is that 28 similarities were found that mostly centered around crack cocaine and methamphetamine abuse being either regional or local issues. This implies that there is no justifiable reason for the increased efforts to reduce sentencing guidelines for methamphetamine at many levels (e.g., state, local), while efforts to do the same for crack cocaine have largely been ignored with the exception of the U.S. Supreme Court in 2007.[12]

The connection of health issues to incarceration is of concern to both scholars and practitioners. In terms of the health impact, AIDS and the connection of AIDS to African American men incarcerated has been devastating.[14] The Prison Rape Elimination Act (PREA) is an example of how policymakers have used their authority to positively address one of the health issues associated with incarceration. According to one state corrections official:

PREA has made corrections agencies take a closer look at our operations and helped us realize that we can do better at preventing and addressing the multitude of issues associated with prison sexual assault and custodial sexual misconduct.[15]

For women, the impact of mandatory minimums has been devastating and has added certain nuances to be considered. From three strikes, to crack versus powder, to the Rockefeller laws, women have felt an impact that has negatively impacted women individually, but the criminal justice system in attempting to respond to this reality. To be sure, African American women in the years following the 1986 drug law are more than twice as likely as Latino females and five times as likely as White females to be in prison. According to a recent article in the *Washington Post,* 36 of 1,000 African American women can expect to go to prison compared to 5 out of 1,000 White women. Further, two-thirds of these women have at least one minor child:[16]

Some twenty-five years ago, it was almost unheard of to find a woman in state or federal prison. Before the "war on drugs" approximately two-thirds of all women sentenced in federal court were given probation, and women comprised less than five percent of all prisoners.[17]

By 1998, almost a million women were incarcerated.[18] There are no shortages of data that clearly demonstrate the disproportionate impact mandatory minimum laws have had on the African American community beyond the incarceration figures. Since

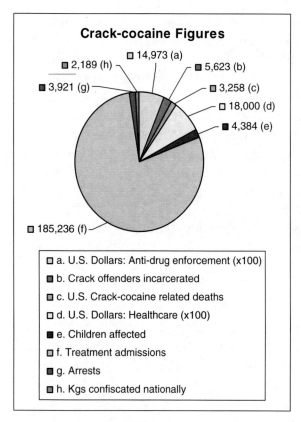

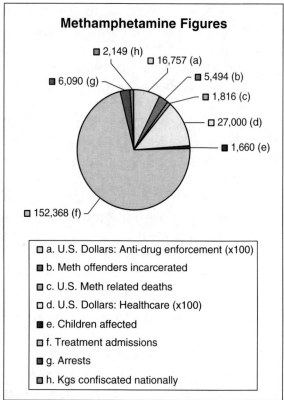

Figure 6.1:   Side-by-Side Comparison of Methamphetamine and Crack Cocaine[13]
Source: Johnston, Sara-Michelle; Montague, David; Stanberry, Artemesia; Byrne, Jaime. *Methamphetamine and Crack Policies: Different Treatment for Different Drugs?* [Working Paper] (2008).

federal mandatory minimum laws are classified as felonies, they impact the right to vote, an estimated 13 percent of African American males are now disenfranchised.[19] Because the laws require a minimum of five years in prison without the possibility of parole, it removes a family member—including a mother or father—from the home for a substantial period of time. Mandatory minimum laws also remove many young men and women from the community. These young people could possibly become better citizens with the proper amount of educational investment. The psychological impact of having a large segment of communities entering the prison system also aggravates problems facing African Americans, and it contributes to the development of African American females who have to spend their formidable years without their mothers.

In addition, during the 1990s, Congress passed legislation that (1) prohibits those with drug convictions from receiving welfare benefits unless they meet certain conditions established by states, (2) prohibits the receiving of federal student loans unless certain conditions are met and (3) prohibits eligibility to reside in public housing.[20] When a female leaves prison, she is left without the safety of public housing, particularly if her conviction is related to drugs. In most cases, it is only drug convictions that receive the treatment mentioned above. With the enactment of mandatory minimums for crack cocaine, it has been African Americans that have made up the bulk of these convictions. Very few communities can survive under the conditions described. It is imperative that African American leadership make drug reform and prison incarceration a top agenda item as it affects everything from education to labor.

Perhaps one of the more harsh policies resulting from the drug war is the stripping of parental rights. If African American women are portrayed as bad mothers or mothers who have children just for a check from the government, it makes it easier to design policies to remove parental rights. It should go without saying that these laws are not specifically targeted toward African Americans, at least it is not spoken. However, by the 1990s, it is evident which group of Americans is disproportionately impacted by the "war on drugs" and thus is more likely to bear the brunt of the laws passed during the 1990s that impact those convicted of drugs. For example:

> The Adoption and Safe Families Act of 1997 prohibits individuals with certain criminal convictions from being approved as foster or adoptive parents. It also accelerates the termination of parental rights for children who have been in foster care for fifteen of the most recent twenty-two months.[21]

As mentioned, a mandatory minimum penalty requires even a first-time nonviolent offender to serve five years in prison. Thus, it is quite easy for mothers to lose something that is most basic to them, the right to be mothers. We have discussed the 100:1 disparity in drug sentencing laws and the fact that African Americans are arrested for drug use and abuse in far disproportionate numbers than their actual drug use. The discriminatory nature of the laws have negatively impacted African American men and women, and subsequent policies passed during the 1990s, although not race-specific, have also negatively impacted African American women and have torn apart the African American family. It is unlikely that any other group would endure this type of negative public policy. Although Whites (men and women) make up the bulk of drug users and sellers, African Americans and Hispanics make up the bulk of those serving prison sentences for drug abuse.

Ethnic and racial groups are impacted by policies and practices of law enforcement, courts, and corrections. In essence, this chapter argues that various goals of the criminal justice system as reflected in public policy overshadow the disparities that currently exist and are created by these policies. These policies tend to leave people of color even further disconnected from the larger society.[22]

Mandatory minimums were originally designed to produce more fairness within the sentencing guidelines. There has been a racial and ethnic dimension to mandatory minimums, however, that has resulted in not only more nonviolent drug offenders, no matter what group a person belongs to, in prison but also disproportionate levels of sentencing with respect to minority groups in terms of proportion and raw numbers. An example is that the mandatory minimums for crack cocaine vs. powder cocaine exist to this day, and the 20-year anniversary was the year 2006. Understanding this crack cocaine vs. powder cocaine disparity, many officials have pushed to reduce sentencing guidelines for methamphetamines, even though the language used to create sentencing guidelines for both was the same, the term "epidemic" was used with both. The result is that we have efforts to reduce prison time for methamphetamine, while no effort is made to reduce cocaine sentencing. Even though European Americans have been hurt by powder cocaine sentencing under the mandatory minimums law, it has been argued by several scholars that the sentencing for people with crack cocaine offenses tends to be harsher. Drug sentencing guidelines have also impacted the number of female offenders incarcerated. Three strikes laws have also been shown to have a disproportionate impact on racial and ethnic minorities. Given the fact that cumulative advantage and cumulative disadvantage are legacies within the United States, distributive public policy, specifically crime policy, has a more disastrous impact on minorities and furthers racial and ethnic stereotypes. Many released from prisons find that it is difficult for them to reintegrate into society effectively. Community re-entry programs within prisons provide some of the resources that are needed, but according to some inmates, more are needed in this regard.

To quote a comment witnessed by one of the authors while working in a federal law enforcement building and attending a meeting on the need to ensure probable cause exists: "I hear what you're saying, but all I know is that if I see a bunch of Blacks in a car, I'm stopping them."[23] While it is not even remotely asserted that this is the norm of statements by law enforcement personnel, the importance of this quote is that it was actually made in front of the General Counsel for a federal agency while that agency was making a conscious effort to make sure that police stops that might lead to an arrest or drug seizure are justified. Certainly, this statement stuck with this author for a very long time and helped shape the juxtaposition of being serious about addressing the issue of drugs in America while recognizing that not everyone in that fight would "play by the same rules," an interesting lesson for a (at that time) recent 20-something college graduate on the way to join DEA and complete graduate school. Based on this example and what has been covered in this book, it should not be difficult to understand that the plight of African Americans coming from this legacy of slavery and the psychological impact that still exists today with respect to how African Americans are viewed not only by themselves but by society as a whole are still being used as political pawns when used for gaining votes.

Keyterms

Endnotes

1 Quote. Unnamed inmate participating in the Community Reentry to Society Program at the Wrightsville Prison Unit, Wrightsville, AR (March 2009).

2 Harris, Othello, and R. Robin Miller, *Impacts of Incarceration on the African American Family* (New York: Transaction Publishers, 2002).

3 Angeli, David H., "A 'Second Look' at Crack Cocaine Sentencing Policies: One More Try for Federal Equal Protection," *American Criminal Law Review,* (1997), 34.

4 Moore, Joan. "Bearing the Burden: How Incarceration Weakens Inner-City Communities." Part of *THE UNINTENDED CONSEQUENCES OF INCARCERATION: Papers from a conference organized by the Vera Institute of Justice.* January, 1996. Retrieved May 18, 2008 from the publications list of www.cejamericas.org, p. 67.

5 Harding, D. J., "Jean Valjean's Dilemma: The Management of Ex-convict Identity in the Search for Employment," *Deviant Behavior* (November-December 2003), 24(6), 571–595.

6 Case, Patricia F., "The Relationship of Race and Criminal Behavior: Challenging Cultural Explanations for a Structural Problem," *Critical Sociology* (2008), 34(2), 213–238.

7 Smith, Robert C., *Racism in the Post-Civil Rights Era: Now You See It, Now You Don't* (Albany: State University of New York Press,1995), p. 77.

8 Williams, Art S. "The Psychosocial Plight of the African American Male." *Fulfilling Our Dreams by Bringing All Cultures Together: 2007 Monograph Series.* National Association of African American Studies & Affiliates, Scarborough, ME, 2007, p. 296.

9 Sampson, Robert J., and Janet L. Lauritsen. "Racial and Ethnic Disparities in Crime and Criminal Justice in the United States." *Crime and Justice, 21.* Ethnicity, Crime and Immigration: Comparative and Cross-National Perspectives (1997): 311–374.

10 "Too Little Too Late: President Clinton's Prison Legacy." *Justice Policy Institute,* a project of the Center on Juvenile and Criminal Justice, February, 2001. The Justice Policy Institute is a project of the Center on Juvenile and Criminal Justice.

11 Johnston, Sara-Michelle, David Montague, Artemesia Stanberry, and Jaime Byrne, *Methamphetamine and Crack Policies: Different Treatment for Different Drugs?* Working Paper, University of Arkansas at Little Rock (2008).

12 McGlone, Tim, "Supreme Court Rules Judges Can Reduce Crack Cocaine Sentences," *The Virginian-Pilot* (December, 10, 2007).

13 a. In 2005 the Office of National Drug Control Policy estimated its budgets of drug law costs in America to be $14,973,000 for crack-cocaine control and $16,757,000 for methamphetamine (ONDCP, 2005).

   b. The Drug Enforcement Agency estimated the number of federal prison incarcerations for drug crime in 2006 to be 5,623 crack-cocaine offenders and 5,494 methamphetamine (DEA, 2006).

   c. In 2007 the Centers for Disease Control and Prevention estimated the number of drug related deaths in the United States to be 3,258 crack-related and 1,816 methamphetamine related (CDC, 2007).

   d. In 2005 the Office of National Drug Control Policy estimated that America spent $18,000,000 for crack-cocaine health costs and $27,000,000 for methamphetamine.

   e. The Child Welfare League of America estimated that in 2006, there were 4,384 minors (under the age of 18) with parents incarcerated for crack cocaine drug crime, and 1,660 for methamphetamine drug crime (CWLA, 2006).

   f. In 2007 the Office of National Drug Control Policy estimated the number of admission into drug treatment programs in the United States to be 185,236 for crack cocaine and 152,368 for methamphetamine addictions (Facts *Crack; Meth,* 2007).

g. In 2004 the Office of National Drug Control Policy estimated the number of arrests for federal drug crimes to be 3,921 for crack cocaine offenses and 6,090 for methamphetamine (Facts, *Crack; Meth,* 2007).

h. The Drug Enforcement Agency estimated the total amount of crack cocaine confiscated nationally to be 2,189 kilograms and 2,149 kilograms of methamphetamine (DEA, 2006).

14 Schneider, Cathy Lisa, "Racism, Drug Policy, and AIDS," *Political Science Quarterly* (Autumn 1998), 113 (3), 427–446.

15 DeLano, Lynne, "Sexual Assault: Not Part of the Penalty," *Connections: A Bi-Annual Publication of The Washington Coalition of Sexual Assault Programs* (Fall/Winter 2005).

16 "Insights into the Inmate Population, *Washington Post* (Wednesday, May 21, 2003), A9.

17 Simmons, Evett L., "Women the Target: Children the Victims," Delta Research & Education Foundation: Journal Introduction, *The Impact of the Criminal Justice System on Women & Their Families, Journal* (2001), 24.

18 Ibid.

19 Mauer, Marc, and Meda Chesney-Lind, *Invisible Punishment: The Collateral Consequences of Mass Imprisonment* (New York: W.W. Norton and Company, 2002), p. 51.

20 Ibid. pp. 23–24.

21 Ibid.

22 Mann, Coramae Richey, et al. Images of *Color, Images of Crime.* 3rd edition. Cary, NC, Roxbury Press, 2007, p. 243.

23 Statement witnessed by David R. Montague (an employee of a company on contract there) of a U.S. Drug Enforcement Administration employee during a meeting on the importance of probable cause. Meeting was held in the DEA Office of Chief Counsel, Asset Forfeiture Section in Arlington, Virginia (1991).

ACTIVITY 1
Impact by the numbers...

A Chapter 6 Exercise

Instructions:

In the space above, explain what the book talks about in the start of the chapter regarding the 1993 statistics associated with the impact of the 100-1 sentencing disparity.

1993

[Please tear out your completed response so you can turn it in to the instructor]

ACTIVITY 2

In the boxes, describe the chapter terms "otherness"
and "internal inferiorization."

A Chapter 6 Exercise

Otherness	Internal Inferiorization

[Please tear out your completed response so you can turn it in to the instructor]

ACTIVITY 3

Applying a book concept to a real-life issue...

Crack as "Epidemic"   Methamphetamine as "Epidemic"

Instructions:

Using Figure 6.1, please provide some comments in the boxes regarding how crack cocaine and methamphetamine had either similar or different realities associated with them. Keep in mind how the word "epidemic" has been used to describe the impact of both on society. Should legislative response have been similar?

A Chapter 6 Exercise

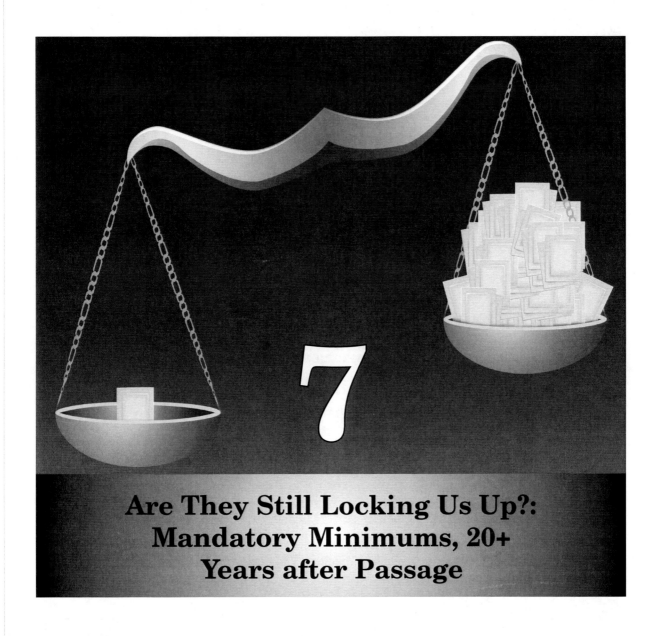

Are They Still Locking Us Up?: Mandatory Minimums, 20+ Years after Passage

Chapter 7 Synopsis: This chapter explores future implications of maintaining the 100-1 disparity. It also discusses what the Congressional Black Caucus must do if it is to have a significant impact on laws that provide such negative policy results for people of color.

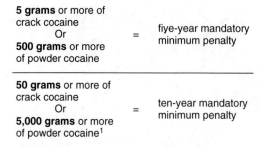

Figure 7.1. Federal Sentencing Guideline Disparity: Federal Law as It Stands Today (no change since 1986 in 100:1 disparity)

The year 2006 marked the 20th anniversary of the passage of these laws. The impact of the laws continues to be devastating for the African American community. According to data included in the National Urban League's annual publication, *The State of Black America,* "black men are more than 6 times more likely than white men to be incarcerated. At the end of 2001, 16.5 percent of the black male population had been to prison, compared to 7.7 percent of Hispanic and 2.7 percent of white men, according to the Bureau of Justice Statistics."[2] The same report contributes the continued rise in incarceration rates since the 1990s to harsher punishments for repeat offenders and harsh drug laws for those in possession of crack cocaine.[3]

On January 3, 2007, Democrats regained control of Congress for the first time in over a decade. Although it was a Democratic Congress that responded to mass media hysteria that crafted mandatory minimum laws for crack and powder cocaine, the jury would still be out as to whether the newly minted Democratic Congress would work to undo what was done 20 years ago. The politics of crime was still evident. Prior to the 2006 elections that gave Democrats control of Congress, the old tactics of painting Democrats as being soft on crime came up.

Roy Blunt Jr., former Republican majority whip of the United States House of Representatives, issued a press release on Thursday, October 19, 2006, about what he envisions the agenda of a Democratic-controlled House would be. Of course, he went with the tactic that some of the most liberal Democrats would chair committees and thus would implement a pro-tax, pro-big government agenda. Roy Blunt stated in his press release the following:

"This list of the bills most likely to be championed by committee chairmen in a Pelosi-led House of Representatives would be great fodder for the late night talk show hosts if it weren't true," House Majority Whip Roy Blunt said. "Instead, it's just plain scary. While Republicans fight the War on Terror, grow our robust economy, and crack down on illegal immigration, House Democrats plot to establish a Department of Peace, raise your taxes, and minimize penalties for crack dealers. The difference couldn't be starker."[4]

As has been shown in this research, Blunt conveniently ignored the sad reality that a Democratic-led Congress during the 1980s passed among the harshest drug sentencing laws, including mandatory minimums for crack and powder cocaine that treats a derivative of one drug much, much more harshly than the powder form of the drug. What he also ignored is that it was a Republican-led Congress faced with an epidemic of methamphetamines in rural, predominantly White areas of the country that formed The Congressional Caucus to Fight and Control Methamphetamine also known as the "Meth Caucus" and that the same Republican majority addressed the issue of methamphetamine use with compassion not a steady drive to the House floor demanding more prisons. If one looks at the website of the "Meth Caucus," one would see that the members do not emphasize throwing everyone in jail, rather, they promote an understanding of the drug and comprehensive efforts to address the abuse of meth. We often heard about crack babies in the 1980s that helped to justify the harsh treatment of crack users. We now have "meth babies," and they are overwhelming the foster care system. The meth epidemic includes a long-term environmental impact of meth labs: Entire neighborhoods are placed in danger when meth is cooked in homes, meth users engage in id theft, and so on. The media have covered these problems, some critics say to the point of the same type of sensationalism seen in the 1980s, but congressional response is different. Roy Blunt and Republicans when they were in the majority chose not to treat meth users as Democrats have treated crack users. There is a sense of compassion. There is a perception that it is the drug that's making good people go bad. In a *Congressional Quarterly* article on the different legislative approaches to the treatment of the meth vs. crack epidemic, the reporter discussed the concern that many have, that methamphetamine users are treated more sympathetically than crack users. Below are two excerpts from the article:

> When Rep. Elijah E. Cummings visits rural communities in the Midwest that have been ravaged by methamphetamine use, he hears stories of despair and damage not unlike those he heard during the crack epidemic of the 1980s. His hometown of Baltimore includes some of the neighborhoods that were devastated the worst by crack, the last drug epidemic to draw an intense response from the federal government and local law enforcement.

> The similarities exist despite fundamental differences between the populations affected by the two drugs. Meth is used mostly by white people in rural areas, while the epicenters of the crack epidemic were the African-American communities of the inner cities.

> "If you were to close your eyes and listen to how they talk about the effect on communities, how it breaks up families and drives down property values, you would swear they were in any urban community" during crack's heyday, Cummings says.

> What's different this time are the solutions that his congressional colleagues are promoting. The first comprehensive federal anti-meth law, enacted this year, focuses on cutting off the supply of the chemical ingredients used to make the drug—not on toughening punishments for dealers or users.

"There seems to be more of an emphasis on shutting down these meth labs and trying to figure out ways to treat these addicts and then get them back into flow of society," says Cummings, a Maryland Democrat. "We don't get for crack or heroin that kind of support for prevention, treatment and rehabilitation."[5]

Congressman Cummings is a member of the CBC and former chair of the body. Consider the following excerpt from the same article from other members, including Republican members of Congress:

Users as Victims

The lawmakers most vocally concerned about meth reject the notion that they're sympathetic to meth users because they tend to come from a higher-income, less urban and more white demographic than users of other narcotics.

In fact, Republican Mark Souder, who sponsored the House version of the anti-meth legislation enacted this year, says he and his northeastern Indiana constituents have less compassion for meth users than for other addicts. "When you come from areas where you see opportunities exist and you get whacked out on drugs, the sympathy is less than for in urban areas where they have no jobs or may not have fathers," he says.

But when many members talk about meth users, their sympathy often shines through.

"I view many of them as victims," says GOP Rep. Ken Calvert of Southern California.

Kennedy invoked "the tragic story of a young girl named Megan from a beautiful town" in his state when he appeared before a House Judiciary panel last fall to promote his own meth-fighting legislation. She got hooked on meth in seventh grade and turned to prostitution to pay for her habit, he said, and "In the face of so much suffering, we have an obligation to act."

In an interview later, Baucus said he was "quite certain" he would have reacted the same way to similar testimony by crack addicts. But, minutes later, he conceded that he feels more sympathy for meth users because "there are more kids involved, it's harder to solve, addictiveness is higher than crack or heroin."

The greater sympathy expressed by members of Congress, such as Baucus, is not much different than how African-American members responded to crack: Lawmakers are most concerned with problems that affect their constituents most directly. The problem is how little overlap there is between those two groups of lawmakers. Of the 138 members of the Congressional Meth Caucus, 127 are white.[6]

The hearing referenced took place when Blunt and Republicans were in the majority-and expressing what appeared to be a soft on drugs mentality as it related methamphetamine but in his press release, issued before the mid-term congressional elections in 2006, he attempted to lead the public to believe that Democrats would let crack users out of jail. Yet, Democrats do not confront him on this. Democrats' unwillingness to confront such demagoguery on this issue will continue to result in an insincere effort to seriously respond to the treatment of powder and crack cocaine. In other words, the likelihood of a "Pelosi House" putting a cocaine-equitable sentencing bill on the floor to be voted on is slim out of fear that one Democrat may lose his or her seat because Republicans will demagogue this issue. This leaves the impression that saving one Democratic seat and maintaining control of the House is more important than saving the lives of the young Black men and women disproportionately incarcerated and their communities disproportionately impacted.

Blunt's speech and Pelosi's apparent unwillingness to make this a priority for the 110th Congress ignores the fact that Republican senators have stated that mandatory minimums for crack are unjustifiable. Several years ago, it was Orrin Hatch (R-Utah) and Spencer Abraham (R-MI) who tried to address the issue in the Senate. A press release issued on July 25, 2006, by Senator Jeff Session's (R-AL) office stated the following:

U.S. Sens. Jeff Sessions (R-AL), Mark Pryor (D-AR), John Cornyn (R-TX) and Ken Salazar (D-CO)—all former state Attorneys General—today introduced legislation that would reduce the crack-powder cocaine sentencing disparity from 100-to-1 to 20-to-1. The bill, the Drug Sentencing Reform Act of 2006, would reduce the disparity for triggering the mandatory minimum sentences for crack and powder cocaine from 100-to-1 to 20-to-1 by reducing the penalty for crack cocaine and increasing the penalty for powder cocaine. The underlying goal of the bill is fairness—treating similar drugs more equally when it comes to sentencing.

Sessions said: "This bill would bring measured and balanced improvements in the current sentencing system to ensure a more just outcome—tougher sentences on the worst and most violent drug offenders and less severe sentences on lower-level, non-violent offenders. The 100-to-1 disparity in sentencing between crack cocaine and powder cocaine is not justifiable. Our experience with the guidelines has convinced me that these changes will make the criminal justice system more effective and fair. It's time to act."[7]

Congressman Blunt's attempt to paint Democrats as being soft on crime continues to ignore that this fear of being tainted as soft on crime is what led to the crack-powder disparity in the first place. Democrats "outcrimed" Republicans. These harsh laws led to an explosion of a prison system that included a majority of African American and Hispanic drug offenders, an explosion of the prison industrial complex, an increase in HIV/AIDS among the prison population, overcrowding conditions leading to prison rape, a reduction in prison education programs, and so on. Returning to the aforementioned Senator Sessions' press release:

Cornyn (R-TX) said: "Though we have made great strides in the war on drugs in recent years, Congress must remain vigilant in addressing this problem where and when it is required. Today, more high school students use powder than crack. In 2005, the rate of powder cocaine use among 12th Graders was almost three times as high as the rate of crack cocaine use. It is important that our drug laws reflect those troubling statistics which is what this legislation seeks to do."[8]

This sounds like feel-good liberal language, but it's coming from Majority Whip Blunt's law-and-order Republicans, not Pelosi's Democrats. We can see if Mr. Blunt's predictions have come true on the issue of mandatory minimums for crack by exploring Nancy Pelosi's first 100 days as Speaker of the House of Representatives.

110th Congress (January 2007–January 2009)

As a result of the 2006 mid-term elections, Democrats regained the majority in the House of Representatives. They selected Nancy Pelosi as their Speaker of the House, the first female to hold such a position. CBC member James Clyburn was selected as Majority Whip, only the second African American to hold such a position. For those interested in mandatory minimum laws, the possibility that after 20 years the laws would be overturned, at least that the disparity between the treatment for crack and powder would be eliminated, never seemed stronger. There was a belief that Conyers and Rangel and the CBC would convince Speaker Pelosi of the perceived racism contained within this law. Clyburn in his seat in the Democratic leadership would, some may have believed, inform her about how this law has impacted the African American community. Surely someone would say that we have reached the 20th anniversary of these laws and even conservative credentialed Republicans have recognized the unfair nature of this law.

During Pelosi's 100 days, Rangel introduced the bill he has introduced since the early 1990s to eliminate the 100:1 disparity between crack and powder. His bill, HR 460, the Crack Cocaine Equitable Sentencing Act, contains a total of 10 co-sponsors, just five of which were CBC members.[9] One can begin to get the idea that much like Conyers' HR 40, it is merely symbolic legislation to give him and CBC members a means to say, well, we have introduced legislation, but you know, we do not control Congress. The difference with the introduction of such legislation during the 110th Congress is that Democrats did control Congress and many CBC members were in powerful and in leadership positions. If the first session of the 110th Congress is any indication of what Congress would do to address mandatory minimums, chances that the law would be overturned would be slim. However, this did not mean that drug policies would not be addressed. The bipartisan Meth Caucus was successful in getting a bill on the House floor. During Pelosi's first 100 days as Speaker, a bill was on the floor that further addressed the impact methamphetamines are having on solid, upstanding communities. HR 365, the Methamphetamine Remediation Research Act of 2007, mainly addressed ways to clean up areas affected by meth, but it continued to demonstrate that meth, not crack, was on the mind of Congress and one has to ask why. African American members of Congress weren't oblivious to this bill as Congresswoman Shelia Jackson Lee spoke on this bill. In her extension of remarks, she stated, in part:

. . . . Methamphetamine labs not only damage individuals, they affect our children and our environment. As the founder and co-chair of the Congressional Children's Caucus, I am horrified by the effects methamphetamine labs have on children. Children living at methamphetamine labs are at increased risk for severe neglect and abuse, both physical and sexual abuse. A child raised in or near a methamphetamine lab environment experiences stress and trauma that significantly affect his or her overall safety and health, including behavioral, emotional, and cognitive functioning. Hazardous living conditions and filth are common in methamphetamine lab homes where explosives and loaded guns are often present and in many instances, within easy reach. The safety and development of our children are negatively influenced by living in methamphetamine lab homes. Mr. Speaker, these dire problems require immediate action and H.R. 365 does this appropriately. I urge my colleagues to join me in the fight against the methamphetamine epidemic by supporting H.R. 365, the Methamphetamine Remediation Research Act of 2007.[10]

Congresswoman Sheila Jackson Lee, like others who spoke on the bill, included in her comments concern about the rising use of meth and the devastating impact of meth labs. She also mentioned that death rates from meth have surpassed that of crack in states such as Oklahoma. Those optimistic that the Congress would focus on crack instead saw a bill addressing the meth epidemic from a compassionate point of view debated on the floor of the House of Representatives. Again, it was not as if some members of the CBC were oblivious to the issue of crack. Just a couple of weeks after the aforementioned meth bill was passed, Congressman Danny Davis introduced and spoke on the floor about a bill recognizing the significance of Black History Month (H. Res 198). After he addressed the struggles and accomplishments of African Americans, he concluded by saying the following:

While 5 percent of the world's population lives in the United States, we have 25 percent of the world's prison population in United States jails and prisons. Nationally, the Bureau of Justice statistics reports that the United States incarcerates 2 million people. Whites are about 36 percent, compared to 46 percent for blacks in prison.

As some of us know, the majority of people in prison are attributed to drug convictions. The law is not equally applied when it comes to drug offenses involving crack and powder cocaine. Five grams of crack cocaine brings a mandatory sentence of 5 years, compared to 5 grams of powder cocaine, which has no sentencing requirements, and the possessor of powder may get probation. Of course, a disproportionate number of the individuals who use crack cocaine are African Americans.

These are just a few barriers that many African Americans confront every day. And so when we honor Black History Month, we are recognizing the struggles and achievements of African Americans.[11]

The first session concluded without a bill specifically dealing with crack cocaine making it to the House floor, however, events outside of Congress (a Supreme Court ruling and USSC guidelines) would push the issue with Congress as it entered the second session of the 110th Congress.

Second Session of the 110th Congress

As the first session of the 110th Congress came to an end, two very important decisions made by the USSC and the United States Supreme Court respectively would put pressure on Congress to act on changing the 100-1 disparity between crack and powder cocaine. In May 2007, the USSC sent its fourth report to Congress on federal sentencing guidelines for crack cocaine. Much of the report replicated past reports sent to Congress on this subject. As was the case in 1995, the USSC issued an amendment to Congress to reduce the penalty between crack and powder cocaine. To quote from a press release issued by the USSC on April 27, 2007:

> The Commission's amendment modifies the guideline drug quantity thresholds to provide guideline sentencing ranges that include the statutory mandatory minimum penalties for crack cocaine offenses. Accordingly, under the amendment, a first-time trafficking offense involving 5 grams of crack cocaine will receive a guideline sentencing range of 51 to 63 months, and a first-time trafficking offense involving 50 grams or more of crack cocaine will receive a guideline sentencing range of 97 to 121 months, before accounting for other relevant factors under the guidelines. Under the statutory mandatory minimum penalties, however, a five- and ten-year sentence will still be required, respectively. As a result, the Commission's amendment provides some relief to crack cocaine offenders impacted by the disparity created by federal cocaine sentencing policy.

> The Commission emphasized and expressed its strong view that the amendment is only a partial solution to some of the problems associated with the 100-to-1 drug quantity ratio. Any comprehensive solution to the 100-to-1 drug quantity ratio would require appropriate legislative action by Congress.[12]

As was the case in 1995, Congress had the option of voting against this amendment or allowing it to take effect on November 1, 2007, by doing nothing. To its credit, Congress allowed the amendment to take effect. The USSC took the amendment a step further when it voted on December 11, 2007, that the amendment would be retroactive. In a press release the USSC wrote the following:

> The United States Sentencing Commission unanimously voted today to give retroactive effect to a recent amendment to the Federal Sentencing Guidelines that reduces penalties for crack cocaine offenses. Retroactivity of the crack cocaine amendment will become effective on March 3, 2008. Not every

crack cocaine offender will be eligible for a lower sentence under the decision. A Federal sentencing judge will make the final determination of whether an offender is eligible for a lower sentence and how much that sentence should be lowered. That determination will be made only after consideration of many factors, including the Commission's direction to consider whether lowering the offender's sentence would pose a danger to public safety. In addition, the overall impact is anticipated to occur incrementally over approximately 30 years, due to the limited nature of the guideline amendment and the fact that many crack cocaine offenders will still be required under Federal law to serve mandatory five-or ten-year sentences because of the amount of crack involved in their offense.[13]

According to FAMM, this amendment would affect nearly 20,000 currently incarcerated individuals.

On December 10, 2007, the United States Supreme Court ruled (7–2) on a case that returned some discretion to judges in the sentencing of crack cocaine offenders. *Kimbrough v. United States* involved the sentencing of a crack offender below the recommended guidelines. Derrick Kimbrough, an African American, Gulf War veteran with no prior felony convictions, pleaded guilty to four offenses, including possession with an intent to distribute more than 50 grams of crack. Under the federal sentencing guidelines, he could have been sentenced to serve 19-22.5 years (228–270 months) in prison. The judge in his the case, Raymond Jackson, sentenced him to 15, calling the case "another example of how crack-cocaine guidelines are driving the offense level to a point higher than is necessary to do justice."[14] The judge also noted that if Kimbrough had only possessed powder cocaine, his guidelines would have been far lower: 97–106 months.[15] While the court ruled overwhelmingly in favor of Judge Jackson's power to use judicial discretion, Judge Clarence Thomas, in his dissenting opinion, argued that Congress intended for the sentencing guidelines to be mandatory, thus forcing judges to adhere to the guidelines.[16] This is an important comment from Justice Thomas in that it puts the ball in the court of the United States Congress to revisit crack sentencing under the federal sentencing guidelines. It is important to also note that in spite of the USSC's decision and the Supreme Court's rulings that the five-year mandatory sentence remains in place, it is those sentences above the five-year sentence that will be eligible for reduction. This means that unless Congress does something to address the mandatory minimums for crack, nonviolent offenders sentenced to "just" five years will have to serve out a full five years.

On December 11, 2007, Congressman Rangel wrote an op-ed piece that can be found on his website entitled "Supreme Court, Sentencing Commission Send Strong Message on Crack Cocaine Sentencing." In this op-ed, he writes the following:

The Commission and the Court have done all they can. Now, it's our turn. The impetus falls on Congress to end the sentencing inequity that slaps the same 5-year sentence for possessing 500 grams of powder as it does for 5 grams of crack. That's a 100-to-1 disparity—and an average difference of 40 months in jail time—for two drugs experts say have no significant differences. Well, here's one significant difference: Over 80 percent of sentenced crack offenders are Black. Targeted by law enforcement, Blacks account for 38 percent of drug arrests and 59 percent of convictions, although they are only 13 percent of drug users.

No one condones the suffering inflicted on society by drug abuse and crime, nor should we accept the needless devastation caused by disproportionately harsh drug laws. The numbers paint a grim picture: 500,000 of this country's 2.2 million prisoners are locked up for drug crimes, the majority on petty charges with no history of violence or high-level drug dealing.

Fair drug sentencing would restore confidence in the criminal justice system and do away with the disparity that has left children fatherless and families broken. We cannot shortchange this, or future, generations and threaten our competitive standing in the world by ignoring failing schools, sky-high dropout rates, an unskilled workforce, poverty, and hopelessness. We should not perpetuate injustice. Better yet, we simply cannot afford to.[17]

The second session of the 110th Congress did respond by holding two hearings (one in the House and one in the Senate), both during Black History Month (Congressman Bobby Scott previously held a forum on the subject). Also during the month of February the PEW Charitable Trusts issued a widely covered and quoted report stating that 1 in 100 Americans are incarcerated, 1 in 9 African Americans are incarcerated.[18] Also, on February 12, 2008, the United States Senate Committee on the Judiciary's Subcommittee on Crime and Drugs held a hearing entitled "Federal Cocaine Sentencing Laws: Reforming the 100-1 Crack/Powder Disparity" featuring members of Congress, federal attorneys, and members of the USSC among others. The committee is chaired by Senator Joe Biden. In his opening statement, he said:

Senators Byrd, Dole and I led the effort to enact the Anti-Drug Abuse Act of 1986 which established the current 100-to-1 disparity. Our intentions were good, but much of our information was bad. Each of the myths upon which we based the sentencing disparity has since been dispelled or altered. We now know:

- Crack and powder cocaine are pharmacologically identical. They are simply two forms of the same drug.
- Crack and powder cocaine cause identical physiological and psychological effects once they reach the brain.
- Both forms of cocaine are potentially addictive.
- The two drugs' effects on a fetus are identical. The "generation of crack babies" many predicted has not come to pass. In fact, some research shows that the prenatal effects of alcohol exposure are "significantly more devastating to the developing fetus than cocaine."
- Crack simply does not incite the type of violence that we feared. Gangs that deal in other types of drugs are every bit as violent as the crack gangs.

After 21 years of study and review, these facts have convinced me that the 100-to-1 disparity cannot be supported and that the penalties for crack and powder cocaine trafficking merit similar treatment under the law.

The past 21 years has also revealed that the dramatically harsher crack penalties have disproportionately impacted the African American community: 82% of those convicted of crack offenses in 2006 were African American.

With the starting premises now debunked, last June I introduced the Drug Sentencing Reform & Cocaine Kingpin Trafficking Act, which eliminates the disparity between crack and powder offenses. It does so without raising penalties for powder because there is not a shred of evidence that shows powder penalties are inadequate.

My bill also eliminates the five-year mandatory minimum sentence for simple possession of crack, the only mandatory minimum for possession of a controlled substance.[19]

Two weeks later, the House of Representatives Judiciary's Subcommittee on Crime, Terrorism, and Homeland Security chaired by Congressman Bobby Scott held a hearing entitled "Cracked Justice: Addressing the Unfairness in Cocaine Sentencing." This hearing also featured witnesses that included members of Congress, such as Congressman Rangel, who introduced bills relating to crack cocaine, victims of the sentencing laws, attorneys, and other interested parties. This was not a hearing on a specific piece of legislation. Until that hearing occurs, it is unlikely that the 110th Congress will vote on a bill addressing the disparity. There were a few bills that members of the CBC could pressure the committee and the House leadership to put on the floor: HR 460, introduced by Charles Rangel; HR 4545, introduced by Congresswoman Sheila Jackson Lee; and HR 5035 introduced by Congressman Bobby Scott. The Senate has a bill related to HR 4545 that was to be considered in a hearing on February 12, 2008.

The Senate version was sponsored by Republican Senator Jeff Sessions. With a bipartisan bill, the CBC chairing the Judiciary full committee and subcommittees, a Democratic majority, and favorable language toward reducing the disparity by major presidential candidates, the U.S. Supreme Court, and the USSC, the 110th Congress stood the best chance to finally overturn mandatory minimums for crack. But if history is any judge, the CBC would not pressure the leadership to take a stand.

On April 1, 2008, Congressman John Conyers managed a bill on the floor that would make March "National Criminal Justice Month" (H Res 945). Below is text of his own words. It is important to include his comments intact because it provides the reader with further insight on how members of the CBC felt about the massive incarceration of Black men and women as a result of mandatory minimum laws for crack. He stated:

. . . Mr. Speaker, I yield myself such time as I may consume.

Mr. Speaker, Members of the House, the measure before us calls attention to a critically important issue, the state of our Nation's criminal justice system.

We do this by designating March as National Criminal Justice Month, because it will serve to raise awareness of the causes and consequences of crime, as well as our crime prevention efforts. It is a subject and an area that, for too long, we have not paid close attention to, and it is our feeling that this designation will have a great impact upon our work. Millions of Americans have been victimized by crimes, and many millions more pass through our criminal justice system. We have more than 2 million Americans behind bars, I am sad to say. This means that almost one out of every 100 Americans is incarcerated. Among African American men between the ages of 20 and 34, one in nine are behind bars. What a tragedy. What a waste of human life and potential. The New York Times observed, "We have become a prison nation."' [From the New York Times, Mar. 10, 2008] *Prison Nation.*

After three decades of explosive growth, the nation's prison population has reached some grim milestones: More than 1 in 100 American adults are behind bars. One in nine black men, ages 20 to 34, are serving time, as are 1 in 36 adult Hispanic men. Nationwide, the prison population hovers at almost 1.6 million, which surpasses all other countries for which there are reliable figures. The 50 states last year spent about $44 billion in tax dollars on corrections, up from nearly $11 billion in 1987. Vermont, Connecticut, Delaware, Michigan and Oregon devote as much money or more to corrections as they do to higher education. These statistics, contained in a new report from the Pew Center on the States, point to a terrible waste of money and lives. They underscore the urgent challenge facing the federal government and cash-strapped states to reduce their overreliance on incarceration without sacrificing public safety . . . .

. . . . Recently, the Supreme Court and the United States Sentencing Commission announced sensible changes in the application of harsh mandatory minimum drug sentences. These are signs that the country may finally be waking up to the fiscal and moral costs of bulging prisons. Each year, we on all of our criminal justice systems spend more than $200 billion. The Pew Center Report states that Connecticut, Delaware, my own State of Michigan, Oregon, and Vermont spend as much or more money on corrections as they do on higher education. I think this is a disgraceful circumstance, and the policies of simply incarcerating increasing numbers of Americans without real opportunities for rehabilitation fail those who go through the criminal justice system, but, more than that, it hurts and diminishes every American.

Mr. Speaker, I reserve the balance of my time.[20]

Why this Bill is Still Important

While there has been more action than normal in terms of committee hearings, it has been sources outside of Congress that have concretely addressed the problems of sentence disparities. The 110th Congress did see more action than normal as measured by committee hearings on drug policies, however, key occurrences outside of congress by the U.S. Supreme Court and the USSC have concretely addressed the problems of sentencing disparities. During the 110th Congress, a historic presidential election was in process. Both Democratic and Republican candidates have expressed during debates that mandatory minimums are harsh and should be addressed. It is an acknowledgment that perhaps Congress did go overboard, or at the very least, after 20 years, it is time for the policy to be reassessed. A chief of staff of an African American member of Congress once told coauthor Artemesia Stanberry in 2000 that if George Bush pushed for a change in mandatory minimum laws for crack, his boss would vote for him in a heartbeat.

According to the Sentencing Project, the major presidential candidates have said that this needs to be addressed,[21] yet the CBC is divided. The reality behind those words spoken by the chief of staff is that the Black community and many people in Black represented districts that have been extremely impacted by this, do not have the power to persuade the Democratic party that this issue is bigger than mere politics. In this case, as many critics of the CBC would argue, we do not know who are the biggest losers in this game of partisan politics, nonviolent drug offenders serving five-year minimums or members of the Congressional Black Caucus who continue to prove that the party and not its core mission statement matters. Party politics is complicated, as is addressing crime related issues. Our intent is not to draw a negative critique of the CBC, rather, this work provides some insight into the complex nature of representation, the politics of race and crime, and partisan politics.

Keyterms

Endnotes

1 "Special Report to Congress: Cocaine and Federal Sentencing Policy (as directed by section 280008 of Public Law 103-322)," The United States Sentencing Commission, Washington, DC, February 1995, p. v.

2 The National Urban League, *The State of Black America: Portrait of the Black Male* (Silver Spring, MD: The Beckham Publications Group, 2007), p. 14.

3 Ibid., p. 214.

4 "Pelosi's House." This press release can be found on the House Republican Whip's (Roy Blunt) website. It was accessed on May 24, 2008, from http://republicanwhip.house.gov/News/DocumentQuery.aspx?Year=2006

5 Stern, Seth, "Meth vs. Crack: Different Legislative Approaches," *Congressional Quarterly* (June 5, 2006). Retrieved on May 25, 2008, from the November Coalition at www.november.org/stayinfo/breaking06/Meth-Crack.html

6 Ibid.

7 "Sens. Sessions, Pryor, Cornyn and Salazar Introduce Drug Sentencing Reform Act," Tuesday, July 25, 2006. Retrieved from Senator Sessions' website on May 25, 2008, http://sessions.senate.gov/public/index.cfm?FuseAction=PressShop.NewsReleases&ContentRecord_id=d57f9580-7e9c-9af9-7727-d70caace37f1&Region_id=&Issue_id=

8 Ibid.

9 The authors revisited this legislation during the second session of the 110th Congress (May 24, 2008) and found that there were just 24 co-sponsors, including 12 CBC members. Information retrieved from http://thomas.loc.gov/cgi-bin/bdquery/z?d110:HR00460:@@@P. Neither this bill nor similar bills had reached the House floor during the 110th Congress as of May 24, 2008.

10 "Support of HR 365, Methamphetamine Remediation Research Act of 2007" (Extensions of Remarks, February 09, 2007), retrieved on May 24, 2008, from http://thomas.loc.gov/cgi-bin/query/D?r110:1:./temp/~r110n9B1xC::

11 Congressional Record, March 12, 2007, H 2416.

12 "United States Sentencing Commission Votes to Amend Guidelines for Terrorism, Sex Offenses, Intellectual Property Offenses, and Crack Cocaine Offenses." April 27, 2007, press release can be accessed by the following link: www.ussc.gov/press.htm.

13 "Commission Votes Unanimously to Apply Amendment Retroactively for Crack Offenses: Effective Date Set for March 3, 2008." December 1, 2007, accessed by the following link: www.ussc.gov/press

14 "Justices: Judges Can Slash Crack Sentences." Article is located at www.cnn.com/2007/US/law/12/10/scotus.crack.cocaine

15 www.supremecourtus.gov/opinions/07pdf/06-6330.pdf, p. 1.

16 Ibid., p. 35.

17 www.house.gov/apps/list/hearing/ny15_rangel/cracksentencing121107.html

18 The report, issued on February 28, 2008, is entitled "One in 100: Behind Bars in America, 2008."

19 http://judiciary.senate.gov/member_statement.cfm?id=3089&wit_id=97

20 The quotation comes from an electronic version of the Congressional Record, which can be accessed by the following link: http://thomas.loc.gov/cgi-bin/query/D?r110:1:./temp/~r110DtqmVT:

21 A full report by the Sentencing Project can be found on its website. The report, published March 2008, is entitled "2008 Presidential Candidates' Platform on Criminal Justice." It can be retrieved at www.sentencingproject.org/PublicationDetails.aspx?PublicationID=611

ACTIVITY 1
More than 20 years of impact...

A Chapter 7 Exercise

Instructions:

2006 marked the 20th anniversary of the 100:1 sentencing disparity. In the space above, explain what the the chapter refers to (in detail) when it cites the 2001 statistics of its report The State of Black America. What does it say is important about incarceration rates since the early 1990s?

2009 - Now

[Please tear out your completed response so you can turn it in to the instructor]

ACTIVITY 2

In the box below, describe what the chapter calls "users as victims."
Please be sure to incorporate the actions of legislators.

A Chapter 7 Exercise

ACTIVITY 3

Applying a book concept to a real-life issue...

First Session

Second Session

Instructions:

Within the two boxes (First Session and Second Session), please discuss the similarities and differences between the first session and second session of the 110th Congress as covered in the chapter.

A Chapter 7 Exercise

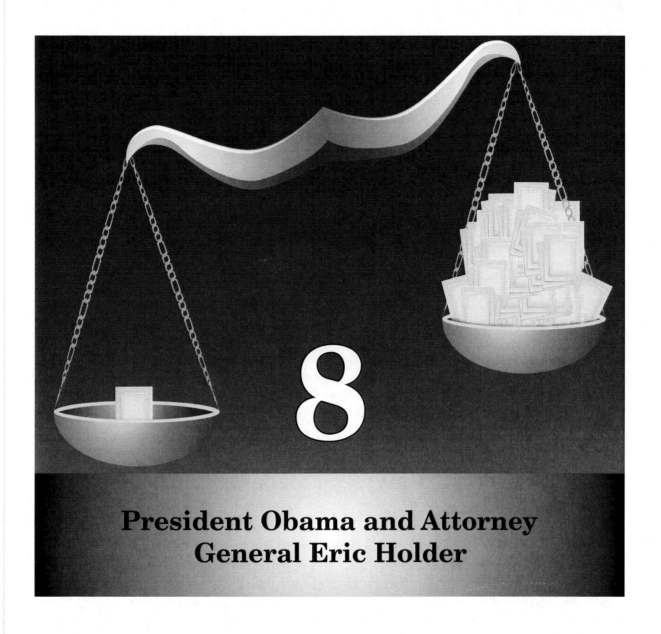

President Obama and Attorney General Eric Holder

Chapter 8 Synopsis: Likewise, we must keep working to build a more effective, more efficient, more equitable system of criminal justice. A system of justice that focuses not just on punishing criminals, but also on preventing crime. A system of justice that focuses not just on locking people away, but also on integrating former offenders back into their communities so they can build productive, law-abiding lives. And a system of justice that applies the same penalties for offenses involving cocaine—regardless of its form.[1]

President Obama was sworn in as the 44th president of the United States on January 20, 2009. He was the first member of the Congressional Black Caucus to become president of the United States and was the only sitting African American Senator since Carol Moseley Braun (D-IL) left the U.S. Senate in 1999 after serving just one term. The dearth of African Americans in statewide positions forces African Americans to run deracialized campaigns, meaning they have to appeal to White voters while garnering African American support. Hamilton believed that "in order for the Democratic Party to be successful and thwart attempts by Republicans to use race as a divisive issue, Democrats needed an agenda to deemphasize race."[2] As we have mentioned in earlier chapters, mandatory minimums for crack cocaine was driven by campaign politics. As such, the balance that an African American presidential candidate who needs to introduce himself to the African American community while maintaining support of the White community, that, according to studies, tend to be more likely to support increasing prison terms for those selling drugs[3] would have to be delicate on the issue. As president, one of his key appointments was Eric Holder to the Office of Attorney General. Both individuals made history in becoming the first African American president and the first African American Attorney General of the United States, respectively. We've demonstrated how mandatory minimum laws for crack cocaine have disproportionately impacted the African American community. Both Obama and Holder had hinted before and after they came to hold their current positions as president and attorney general, respectively, how they stood on these laws and on drug culture in the inner city community in general. In his book, *The Audacity of Hope: Thoughts on Reclaiming the American Dream*, Obama expressed an understanding of what drives the drug culture and his belief that if jobs returned to the inner cities and if businesses hired young people and ex-felons, that, in his words, "they will aspire to something better."[4] As a former community organizer, his experience with working with communities devastated by drugs and high incarceration rates has shaped his worldview. Further, he stated while a U.S. Senator and during the campaign that he had a desire to see reforms in the crack-powder disparity.

Attorney General Holder has an extensive career in the justice system and his appointments include many firsts, including being nominated by President Bill Clinton to become the Deputy Attorney General.[5] He was appointed by President Reagan to be on the D.C. Superior Court, he was appointed by Clinton to serve as U.S. Attorney, and in 1997, after a few years in the private sector, he was appointed to serve as Deputy Attorney General. As a former prosecutor, Holder was considered to be tough on crime, but his experience with being racially profiled provided him with a sense of fairness about how the law should be applied. As an undergraduate student at Columbia University, Holder and his classmates were stopped by the police while driving. This experience "impressed on Holder the dangers of using the law as a blunt instrument, a lesson he applied years later in overseeing a racial-profiling settlement with the New Jersey state police."[6] Holder was known as being tough on violent criminals, but just as interested in preventing crime, making him multidimensional when it came to addressing crime issues.[7]

This is what seemed to distinguish Obama's approach to reducing and/or eliminating the disparity from previous administrations. Indeed, at a Senate Judiciary Hearing on sentencing reform, just a few months into the Obama Administration, Obama's Assistant Attorney General, Lanny Breuer, stated the following:

> Ensuring fairness in the criminal justice system is also critically important. Public trust and confidence are essential elements of an effective criminal justice system—our laws and their enforcement must not only be fair, but they must also be perceived as fair. The perception of unfairness undermines governmental authority in the criminal justice process. It leads victims and witnesses of crime to think twice before cooperating with law enforcement, tempts jurors to ignore the law and facts when judging a criminal case, and draws the public into questioning the motives of governmental officials.[8]

Unlike previous administrations, President Obama sought to make a statement on mandatory minimums for crack/power cocaine very early in his presidency.[9] Statements made by the U.S. Department of Justice reinforced his desire to see sentencing reforms.

Candidate Obama

Obama wrote the introduction to the National Urban League's annual report, entitled "The State of Black America, 2007," where he discussed the two stories of Black America, one of extraordinary success that includes African Americans as heads of corporations, leading Ivy League schools, an African American coach leading his team to win the Superbowl, African Americans serving as Secretary of State, and a high college gradua-tion rate among African American women; the other being high poverty rates, high drop-out rates among African American males, joblessness, and a high rate of HIV/AIDs in the African American community and so on.[10] After mentioning these two Black Americas, he wrote: "This sad story is a stark reminder that the long march toward true and meaningful equality in America isn't over. We have a long way to go."[11] This is an important setup to how Obama would characterize the issue of mandatory minimums for crack cocaine as a civil rights issue that needs to be addressed for the benefit of communities impacted by massive incarceration and society on the basic issue of fairness and equality.

During his last year in the U.S. Senate, Senator Obama was one of seven co-sponsors of S 1711, the Drug Sentencing Reform and Kingpin Trafficking Act of 2007. This legislation was introduced by Senator Joe Biden (now Obama's vice president) on June 27, 2007. The legislation, entitled Drug Sentencing Reform and Cocaine Kingpin Trafficking Act of 2007, "amends the Controlled Substances Act and the Controlled Substances Import and Export Act to increase the amount of a controlled substance or mixture containing a **cocaine** base (i.e., **crack cocaine**) required for the imposition of mandatory minimum prison terms for **crack cocaine** trafficking to eliminate the sentencing disparity between **crack** and powder **cocaine**. (It also) Eliminates the five-year mandatory minimum prison term for first-time possession of **crack cocaine**.[12]

Obama co-sponsored this legislation on March 11, 2008. His major opponent in the 2008 Democratic presidential primaries, Senator Hillary Clinton, signed on to this legislation on December 13, 2007.[13] Whether it was campaign politics that resulted in his signing the legislation or a sincere desire to address the issue, this is an indication that mandatory minimums would be addressed. Indeed, during the 2008 presidential campaign, the Congressional Black Caucus sponsored presidential debates and they issued a questionnaire to the top two candidates in the primary election as well as the candidates on the general election ticket (Senator Obama and Senator McCain) about several issues, including sentencing disparities. On both questionnaires, Obama expressed an interest in eliminating the disparities in sentencing. Based on an analysis conducted by the NAACP and legal scholar Vernelia Randall, "Sentencing Disparities: Eliminate Crack/Cocaine Disparity," "as president, Obama will work in a bipartisan way to eliminate these disparities. He will also repeal mandatory the minimum sentence for first-time offenders convicted of simple possession of crack, as crack is the only drug that a non-violent first-time offender can receive a mandatory minimum sentence for possession."[14]

Candidate Obama made all indications that crack cocaine was something that he wanted to address should he be elected president. This was clearly an issue that the CBC supported.

Eric Holder, Attorney General

Eric Holder's confirmation hearing took place on January 15, 2009, the actual birthday of Dr. Martin Luther King, Jr. Senator Leahy, in his opening statement, talked about the significance of the November elections, the inspiration of President Obama, who was to be sworn in a few days later, and the significance of Holder's nomination. In part, he said:

> We Americans have cause and occasion to reflect during the next
> several days about our great country. The inauguration of our new
> President is Tuesday; Monday is the holiday the country has set
> aside to celebrate and rededicate ourselves to the cause of freedom
> and equality. Today is the anniversary of the birthday of the extraordinary
> man for whom that holiday is named. With this hearing,
> we take another step up the path toward the time Dr. King
> foresaw: when people are judged by the content of their character.
> Eric Holder has the character to serve as the Attorney General of
> the United States of America. He passes any fair confirmation
> standard. His record of public service has earned him strong support
> from law enforcement organizations, civil rights groups, victims'
> rights advocates, former members of the administration of
> President Reagan, the President who first nominated him as a
> judge, and from those of President Bush, and many others.[15]

It was Senator Ben Cardin (D-MD) who asked Holder specifically about mandatory minimum laws for crack cocaine. Below is the exchange:

Senator CARDIN. Well, again, I thank you for that.
I'll mention one other area that I think shows a disparity, a racial
disparity, in our country. We've had a lot of discussion about
the crack cocaine issue. When you take a look at the statistics, African
Americans now serve virtually as much time in prison for
drug offenses as whites do for violent crimes; 37 percent of the people
arrested for drug violations, 59 percent of the convictions and
74 percent of those sentenced for drug offenses are African American,
even though they represent only 15 percent of the people.
My point is this. We know we have disparities in our laws, we
know we have disparities in the way prosecution is centered, and
it's very clear that's true in regards to crack cocaine. We need a
strategy to make sure that we rid ourselves of those types of practices
in this country. I don't want to be soft on those who are violating
our criminal statutes. I want to make sure that we are
tough.
Drugs are a huge menace to our society and I want to do everything
I can to make sure we have effective laws, but let's make
sure it is fairly applied in this country. I would like to have your
commitment that you will work with us and come up with a strategy
where we can have, I think, a fairer system of justice, and a
tough system as well.

Mr. HOLDER. I think that's right. We have to be tough, we have
to be smart, and we have to be fair. Our criminal justice system
has to be fair. It has to be viewed as being fair. When I was a judge
here in Washington, DC, I saw, in the people who served on juries
here, a knowledge, a recognition that, at least in their minds, parts
of the criminal justice system were not fair, and you saw it in some
of the verdicts that I saw in cases that I presided over.
When I would speak to jurors afterwards and say, you know, why
did you vote this way in a case where it seemed to me the government
had all the evidence, that proved all the elements of the
crime, and they talk about inadequacies in the criminal justice system, disparate penalties, and say that, you know, I really am not
going to be part of that. And so I think those are the kinds of attitudes
that we have to recognize that are out there and come up
with a system, as you say, that is tough, smart, and fair.[16]

It is the sentiment about fairness and trust in the system that Obama and Holder
expressed in the context of needing to reform the laws. With these signals coming
from the President of the United States and the Chief Law Enforcement Officer of the
United States, Congress would receive its signal that now is the time to change the
100-1 disparity that had been in place since 1986. Would they take up this opportunity,
or, like so many previous Congresses, will legislation be introduced only to remain in

committee without a chance of becoming law? In the next chapter, we will discuss significant changes made to the disparity in sentencing between crack and powder cocaine.

Keyterms

President Obama   203

President Clinton   204

Senator Moseley Braun   204

Audacity of Hope: Thoughts on Reclaiming the American Dream   204

Assistant Attorney General Lanny Breuer   205

U.S. Department of Justice   205

Candidate Obama   205

Controlled Substances Import and Export Act   205

Cocaine base (crack cocaine)   205

Sentencing disparity between powder cocaine and crack cocaine   204

First-time possession of crack cocaine   205

Senator Clinton   205

Vernelia Randall   206

Dr. Martin Luther King, Jr.   206

Senator Leahy   206

Senator Cardin   207

Eric Holder   204

Attorney General as Federal Chief Law Enforcement Officer   205

Confirmation Hearing   206

Endnotes

1 "Attorney General Eric Holder at the Clarence M. Mitchell, Jr. Memorial Lecture Luncheon at the NAACP's Centennial Convention," 2000. New York, www.justice.gov/ag/speeches/2009/ag-speech-090713.html, accessed on May 2, 2011.

2 Stanberry, A., Ford, P. K., and Adams, M. 2010. The Georgia Presidential primaries: A case study of the role of race and class in the selection of a presidential nominee, in *African Americans in Georgia: A reflection of Politics and Policy in the New South*, ed. by P. K. Ford, 56. Macon Georgia: Mercer University Press.

3 Peffley, M., and Hurwitz, J., 2010. *Justice in America: The Separate Realities of Blacks and Whites*. New York: Cambridge University Press.

4 Obama, B, *The audacity of hope: thoughts on reclaiming the American dream*, 258. New York: Crown Publishers, 2006.

5 "Meet the Attorney General," www.justice.gov/ag/meet-ag.html (accessed May 2, 2011).

6 Weisskopf, M. 2009. "Eric Holder: The Prosecutor," *Time Magazine,* accessed May 2, 2011,www.time.com/time/magazine/article/0,9171,1877386-2,00.html (accessed May 2, 2011).

7 Ibid.

8 "Restoring Fairness to Federal Sentencing: Addressing the Crack-Powder Disparity," Senate Judiciary Committee, Subcommittee on Crime and Drugs, Senate Hearing 111-559. 2009 http://frwebgate.access.gpo.gov/cgi-bin/getdoc.cgi?dbname=111_senate_hearings&docid=f:57626.pdf (accessed on May 2, 2011).

9 Nadelmann, E. 2011. "Obama Takes a Crack at Drug Reform, *The Nation*, www.alternet.org/drugs/148078/obama_takes_a_crack_at_drug_reform?page=1 (accessed April 27, 2011).

10 Jones, S. J., ed. 2007. *Forward: The State of Black America*, 9–10. New York: The Beckham Publications Group, Inc.

11 Ibid.

12 "S. 1711, The Drug Sentencing Reform and Cocaine Kingpin Trafficking Act of 2007" (Bill Text, 110th Congress (2007-2008), S. 1711 IS), http://thomas.loc.gov/cgi-bin/query/D?c110:1:./temp/~c110X4msjY:: (accessed April 27, 2011)

13 Ibid.

14 "Obama's Platform on Eliminating Racial Inequality," prepared by Professor Vernellia Randall, http://academic.udayton.edu/race/2008ElectionandRacism/Obama/Obama00.htm#References and Minimal Differences Between Clinton, Obama: Review the NAACP's Questionnaire and a Legal Scholar's Study of Candidates' Campaign Stances. 2008. www.blackagendareport.com/index.php?option=com_content&task=view&id=518&Itemid=1 (accessed May 3, 2011).

15 Confirmation Hearing of Eric H. Holder, Jr. Nominee to be Attorney General of the United States. 2009 (Washington, DC: United States Senate Judiciary Committee), http://frwebgate.access.gpo.gov/cgi-bin/getdoc.cgi?dbname=111_senate_hearings&docid=f:56197.pdf (accessed May 3, 2011).

16 Ibid., 131.

ACTIVITY 1
From CBC Member to President...

A Chapter 8 Exercise

Instructions:

In January 2009, Barack Obama became the first member of the CBC to be elected president of the United States. In the space above, explain the significance of this event for the CBC as an organization.

2009 - Now

[Please tear out your completed response so you can turn it in to the instructor]

ACTIVITY 2

In the box below, describe the potential importance of having Eric Holder as Attorney General not only for the Obama Administration, but also for those advocating change in drug sentencing.

A Chapter 8 Exercise

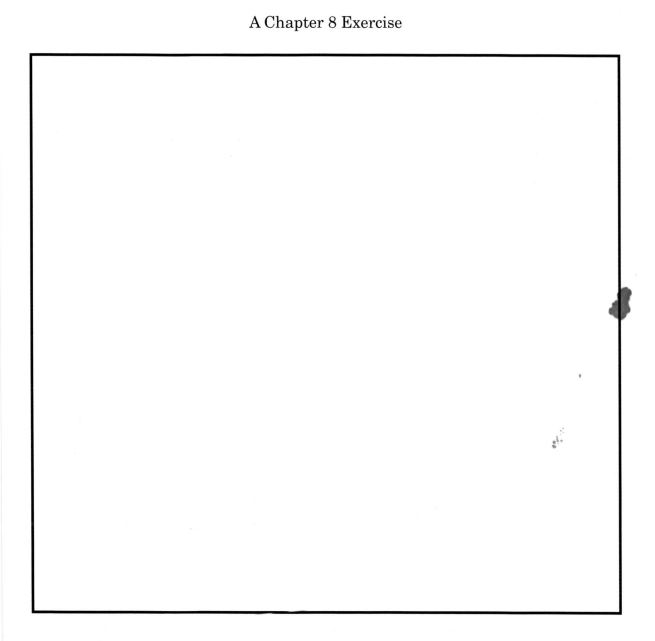

[Please tear out your completed response so you can turn it in to the instructor]

ACTIVITY 3

Applying a book concept to a real-life issue...

Candidate Obama   Attorney General Holder

Instructions:

> Within the two boxes (Candidate Obama and Attorney General Hold-
> er), please discuss the individual details of what makes each of them
> unique as covered in the book.

A Chapter 8 Exercise

Is There Light at the End of the Tunnel?: A 2010 Odyssey from 100:1 to 18:1

Chapter 9 Synopsis: Many have argued that this 100-to-1 disparity is arbitrary, unnecessary, and unjust, and I agree. And I might say at the outset in full disclosure, I am the guy that drafted this legislation years ago with a guy named Daniel Patrick Moynihan, who was the Senator from New York at the time. And crack was new. It was a new "epidemic" that we were facing. And we had at that time extensive medical testimony talking about the particularly addictive nature of crack versus powder cocaine. And the school of thought was that we had to do everything we could to dissuade the use of crack cocaine. And so I am part of the problem that I have been trying to solve since then, because I think the disparity is way out of line. The current disparity in cocaine sentencing I do not think can be justified on the facts we know today and the facts we operated on at the time we set this up.

–Senator Joe Biden, February 12, 2008[1]

111th Congress (January 2009–January 2011)

The 111th Congress was historic in nature in that it was the first Congress in session during the first year of the presidency of the first African American to hold this position. We've mentioned in previous chapters the views of President Obama and Attorney General Eric Holder on mandatory minimums for crack cocaine. With Democrats controlling the House, Senate, and White House, and with significant Republican support for reforming these laws, would the 111th Congress finally bring about change? On June 24, 2009 the Congressional Black Caucus (CBC) held a symposium entitled "The Failed Politics of Sentencing Reform: Seriously Rethinking Sentencing Reform." The forum included Supreme Court Justice Stephen Breyer, Attorney General Eric Holder, Families Against Mandatory Minimums (FAMM) founder Julie Stewart, Eric Sterling, who helped to craft drug sentencing laws during the 1980s, and CBC members, all expressing urgency to end the 100-1 disparity now. This is important to note because mandatory minimum laws for crack and powder cocaine were passed in 1986. Nearly 25 years later, African American members of Congress are joined by the first African American Attorney General in urging their colleagues in Congress to end the disparity in the treatment of crack and power cocaine. The forum also included then current African American chair of the House Judiciary Committee, Congressman John Conyers, and the African American Chair of subcommittee on crime, Congressman Bobby Scott. They were speaking before a sympathetic audience. The struggle for the CBC to change these laws at a time when there is an African American president and attorney general in support of the laws being reformed is the story of the relationship African American legislators have had with their own party in an attempt to maintain power while attempting to also respond to the needs of their core constituency. Soon after the forum, the House Judiciary Subcommittee on Crime, Terrorism, and Homeland Security, chaired by Rep. Bobby Scott, held hearings on and voted out HR 3245, the Fairness in Cocaine Sentencing Act of 2009, which eliminates the 100-1 crack-powder cocaine disparity. On July 29, 2009, the full Judiciary Committee, for the first time since the 100-1 disparity was enacted, voted (16–9) to pass the measure out of committee so that the full House of Representatives could vote on it. This is historic in nature. It came at a time when there was an African American president and attorney general expressing a desire to see the law changed, African Americans chairing the subcommittee and full committee, an African American Majority Whip, and a Democratic controlled Congress. The first session of the 111ᵗʰ Congress had presented the best chance to correct a bill that has led to a high level of incarceration of African Americans. In a press release dated July 29, Congressman Conyers said the following about the significance HR 3245:

> "We have taken a big step today toward ending the disparity that exists between crack and powder cocaine sentencing," said Conyers. "African Americans serve almost as much time in federal prison for a drug offense (58.7 months) as whites do for a violent offense (61.7 months), largely due to sentencing laws such as the 100-to-1 crack-powder cocaine disparity. Since 1980, the number of offenders in federal prisons for drug offenses has skyrocketed from less than 5,000 to almost 100,000 in 2009. Currently, drug offenders represent 52% of all federal prison inmates."

On the Senate side, on October 15, 2009 Senator Richard Durbin (D-IL) introduced S. 1789, the Fair Sentencing Act of 2010. As noted by Families Against Mandatory Minimums:

> *The Fair Sentencing Act would: Replace the 100-to-1 ratio with an 18-to-1 ratio (28 grams would trigger a 5-year mandatory minimum and 280 grams would trigger a ten-year mandatory minimum)Eliminate the five-year mandatory minimum for simple possession of crack cocaine;Call for increased penalties for drug offenses involving vulnerable victims, violence and other aggravating factors; andRequire a report on the effectiveness of federally funded drug courts.*[2]

S. 1789 passed the entire Senate by Unanimous Consent and was referred to the House Committee on the Judiciary, and the House Committee on Energy and Commerce. The problem with the Senate bill is that it did not eliminate the disparity, rather it creates a 18-1 disparity, meaning there remains a different treatment for the same drug. As noted by FAMM, the House bill "would remove references to 'cocaine base' from the U.S. Code, effectively treating all cocaine, including crack, the same for sentencing purposes."[3] This is the ideal situation. However, both the House and Senate bills lack retroactivity, meaning that the people sentenced to 5, 10, 15, 20 years on what many have declared an unjust law and treatment of crack far worse than powder will not benefit from the corrections. For example, someone sentenced prior to the passage of this legislation for possessing 5 grams of crack would have to still serve four more years of his sentence. This bill passed, but without a recorded vote, and was sent to President Obama. Here is how it is listed on Thomas, the Library of Congress' website for federal legislation:

S.1789 Latest Title: Fair Sentencing Act of 2010 **Sponsor: Sen Durbin, Richard** [IL] (introduced 10/15/2009) Cosponsors (23) **Related Bills:** H.R.265 **Latest Major Action:** Became Public Law No: 111-220 [GPO: Text, PDF]

MAJOR ACTIONS:

10/15/2009	Introduced in Senate
3/15/2010	Committee on the Judiciary. Reported by Senator Leahy with an amendment in the nature of a substitute. Without written report.
3/17/2010	Passed/agreed to in Senate: Passed Senate with an amendment by Unanimous Consent.
7/28/2010	Passed/agreed to in House: On motion to suspend the rules and pass the bill Agreed to by voice vote.
7/28/2010	Cleared for White House.
7/29/2010	Presented to President.
8/3/2010	Signed by President.
8/3/2010	Became Public Law No: 111-220 [Text, PDF]

Here's what Attorney General Holder said about the passage of the bill:

Department of Justice
Office of Public Affairs

FOR IMMEDIATE RELEASE

Wednesday, July 28, 2010

Statement of the Attorney General on Passage of the Fair Sentencing Act

I congratulate the House of Representatives on today's passage of the Fair Sentencing Act. The bill greatly reduces the unwarranted disparity in sentences for crack and powder cocaine offenses, and will go a long way toward ensuring that our sentencing laws are tough, consistent, and fair.

By sending the bill to the President, the House has taken an important step toward more just sentencing policies while enhancing the ability of law enforcement officials to protect our communities from violent and dangerous drug traffickers.

This day was long in coming, and I want to express my appreciation to the members of the House and Senate who worked tirelessly to bring about this result. Particular thanks are due to Majority Whip Clyburn, House Judiciary Committee Chairman Conyers and Crime Subcommittee Chairman Scott, and to the bipartisan leadership of the Senate Judiciary Committee, including Chairman Leahy, Ranking Member Sessions and Senators Durbin and Graham.

I join them in celebrating this achievement, and look forward to working with them to implement the new law."

10-867

Attorney General[4]

S. 1789 was passed without fanfare. Unlike the Anti-Drug Abuse Act of 1986 when members of Congress were attempting to "outcrime" one another and gleefully went on record for supporting tough crime bills, members did not seem to want to take a vote on this bill to show that they are just as concerned by fairness and equity as they were in locking people up and throwing away the key. The president on August 3, 2010, signed the bill into law. According to a White House press release: "President Barack Obama signs the Fair Sentencing Act in the Oval Office, Aug. 3, 2010. Joining the President are, from left, Gil Kerlikowske, Director of the Office of National Drug Control Policy, Attorney General Eric Holder, Sen. Patrick Leahy, D-Vt., Rep. Bobby Scott, D-Va., Senate Majority Whip Richard Durbin, of Ill., Sen. Jeff Sessions, R-Ala., Sen. Orrin Hatch, R-Utah, and Rep. Sheila Jackson Lee, D-Texas, and Sen. Lindsey Graham, R-SC. (Official White House Photo by Pete Souza).[5]

After public protestations in 1980s and President Reagan's speeches about fighting drugs being the patriotic thing to do, the first Black president, although bipartisan support is evident, felt as if the political climate wasn't such that he could publicly celebrate the achievement that an unjust law was moving closer to being just.

The 111th Congress was not only significant in passing legislation that removes mandatory minimums for simple possession and for reducing the disparity in the treatment of the two drugs, but it has also shown some leadership in the politicians in Congress are thinking about the drug war. Indeed, Senator Jim Webb (D-VA) introduced the National Criminal Justice Commission of 2009 that endeavors to undertake an 18-month, top-to-bottom review of the entire criminal justice system and offer concrete recommendations for reform.According to Senator Webb's website:

> Why We Urgently Need this Legislation: With 5% of the world's population, our country now houses 25% of the world's reported prisoners.Incarcerated drug offenders have soared 1200% since 1980.Four times as many mentally ill people are in prisons than in mental health hospitals.Approximately 1 million gang members reside in the U.S., many of them foreign-based; and Mexican cartels operate in 230+ communities across the country.Post-incarceration re-entry programs are haphazard and often nonexistent, undermining public safety and making it extremely difficult for ex-offenders to become full, contributing members of society.America's criminal justice system has deteriorated to the point that it is a national disgrace. Its irregularities and inequities cut against the notion that we are a society founded on fundamental fairness. Our failure to address this problem has caused the nation's prisons to burst their seams with massive overcrowding, even as our neighborhoods have become more dangerous. We are wasting billions of dollars and diminishing millions of lives."[6]

The 111th Congress ended without passing this act.

Where Are We Now?

While S. 1789 is law and has made significant changes to the 1986 Anti-Drug Act, there is still a significant disparity in the treatment of crack and powder cocaine. There is a general acknowledgment, as we have shown, that there are no pharmaceutical differences between crack and powder cocaine, so having the 500-gram threshold for powder and the 28-gram threshold for crack continues to be problematic. Further, S. 1789 is not retroactive, meaning those sentenced a day before the bill became law would not benefit from it. There is an effort by Families Against Mandatory Minimums, the Criminal Justice Policy Foundation, the American Civil Liberties Union, the Sentencing Project, and other groups to request that the U.S. Sentencing Commission to make a recommendation to Congress to make the provisions in S. 1789 retroactive. Given the role of Families Against Mandatory Minimums, an interest group that was organized for the purpose of reforming mandatory minimum laws in reforming the crack-powder cocaine disparity, we would like to conclude this chapter with a call for action from the group.

On April 30, 2011 the United States Sentencing Commission announced that they would be taking public comments about "how to make the permanent crack guideline reduction apply so that people serving sentences for crack cocaine might benefit with the shorter sentence."[7] The USSC requested public comments on how the sentencing guidelines from crack cocaine could be retroactive. Activists around the country, including member of FAMM sent comments to the USSC. On June 30, 2011, the USSC held a vote. This historic vote made the U.S. Sentencing Guidelines included in S. 1789 retroactive, unless Congress says otherwise. Below is a press release from USSC following the vote:

U.S. Sentencing Commission One Columbus Circle NE Washington, DC 20002-8002

NEWS RELEASE
For Immediate Release June 30, 2011
Contact: Jeanne Doherty Acting Public Affairs Officer (202) 502-4502
U.S. SENTENCING COMMISSION VOTES UNANIMOUSLY TO APPLY FAIR SENTENCING ACT OF 2010 AMENDMENT TO THE FEDERAL SENTENCING GUIDELINES RETROACTIVELY
Effective Date of Retroactivity Set for November 1, 2011

WASHINGTON, D.C. (June 30, 2011) — The United States Sentencing Commission voted unanimously today to give retroactive effect to its proposed permanent amendment to the federal sentencing guidelines that implements the Fair Sentencing Act of 2010. Retroactivity of the amendment will become effective on November 1, 2011 — the same day that the proposed permanent amendment would take effect — unless Congress acts to disapprove the amendment.

"In passing the Fair Sentencing Act, Congress recognized the fundamental unfairness of federal cocaine sentencing policy and ameliorated it through bipartisan legislation," noted Commission chair, Judge Patti B. Saris. "Today's action by the Commission ensures that the longstanding injustice recognized by Congress is remedied, and that federal crack cocaine offenders who meet certain criteria established by the Commission and considered by the courts may have their sentences reduced to a level consistent with the Fair Sentencing Act of 2010."

Not every federal crack cocaine offender in federal prison will be eligible for a lower sentence as a result of this decision. The Commission estimates, based on Fiscal Year 2010 sentencing data, that approximately 12,000 offenders may be eligible to seek a sentence reduction. The average sentence reduction for eligible offenders will be approximately 37 months, and the overall impact on the eligible offender population will occur incrementally over decades. The average sentence for these offenders, even after reduction, will remain about 10 years. The Bureau of Prisons estimates that retroactivity of the Fair Sentencing Act of 2010 amendment could result in a savings of over $200 million within the first five years after retroactivity takes effect.

The Commission's vote to give retroactive application to the proposed amendments to the federal sentencing guidelines does not give retroactive effect to the Fair Sentencing Act of 2010. Only Congress can make a statute retroactive. Many crack offenders will still be required under federal law to serve mandatory five- or 10-year sentences because of the amount of crack cocaine involved in their offenses. A federal sentencing judge will make the final determination of whether an offender is eligible for a lower sentence and by how much that sentence should be lowered in accordance with instruction given by the Commission. The ultimate determination will be made only after consideration of many factors, including the Commission's instruction to consider whether reducing an offender's sentence would pose a risk to public safety. "The Commission is aware of concern that today's actions may negatively impact public safety. However, every potential offender must have his or her case considered by a federal district court judge in accordance with the Commission's policy statement, and with careful thought given to the offender's potential risk to public safety. The average sentence for a federal crack cocaine offender will remain significant at about 127 months," explained Judge Saris.

The Commission made its decision on retroactivity after significant deliberation and many years of research on federal cocaine sentencing policy. The Commission has issued four research reports to Congress on federal cocaine sentencing policy, testified numerous times before Congress, and held several public hearings on the topic of federal cocaine sentencing policy. The Commission solicited public comment on the issue of retroactivity and received over 43,500 written responses, the overwhelming majority of which were in favor of retroactivity. On June 1, 2011, the Commission held a full day hearing at which it heard from 20 experts and advocates within the criminal justice community. The Commission also carefully considered the views it received from Congress, the federal judiciary, and the Department of Justice.

The Commission considered a number of factors during its deliberations, including the purpose of the Commission's amendment implementing the Fair Sentencing Act of 2010, which lowers the penalties for crack cocaine offenses consistent with the Act, the limit on any reduction allowed by the amendment, whether it would be difficult for the courts to apply the reduction, and whether making the amendment retroactive would raise public safety concerns or cause unwarranted sentencing disparity in the federal system. Ultimately, the Commission determined that the statutory purposes of sentencing are best served by retroactive application of the amendment.

In December 2007, the Commission voted to give retroactive effect to its 2007 crack cocaine amendment effective March 3, 2008, and the process was smoothly coordinated among the courts, probation officers, U.S. Attorney offices, and the federal public defenders community. Since that time, the federal district courts have proc-essed 25,515 motions, granting 16,433 motions for a reduced sentence and denying 9,082. The Commission has conducted a study of the recidivism rate of those offend-ers who received a reduced sentence as a result of the 2007 amendment as com-pared to a similarly situated group of federal crack cocaine offenders who served their normal term of imprisonment and determined that there is no statistically significant difference in recidivism rates between the two groups of offenders.[8]

We felt it appropriate to include the entire press release from the USSC. Inter-est groups and advocates were successful in encouraging people to respond to the USSC's call for action. There may be others reading this book who have been affected and/or have compassion about an issue, as is the case with Julie Stewart, president and founder of FAMM, Eric Sterling, Nkechi Taifa, and others who have dedicated their lives to making a difference. As scholars, we want to provide the tools you need to become engaged as activists, we want to make a difference in our society and in our world.

It is important to keep in mind that the Fair Sentencing Act is not retroactive. Con-gress, in crafting the Fair Sentencing Act, could have included a provision to make the legislation retroactive, meaning that those sentenced to 5 years in prison for possess-ing 6 grams of crack cocaine, for example, under the old 100:1 mandatory minimum law, would have been eligible for a sentence reduction. Because Congress did not make the statute retroactive, then they will have to serve out the mandatory minimum sentence given. Instead, Congress included a provision in the Fair Sentencing Act that "gave the Commission emergency amendment authority to temporarily change the guidelines to implement the statutory changes and to add certain enhancements and reductions to the guidelines.[9] This would particularly come into play for those who have served a decade or more in prison and are seeking a reduction in their sentences based on the guidelines (i.e., range from 100 to 120 months for a given offense). The USSC did craft an amendment to the guidelines based on the Fair Sentencing Act and made the guidelines retroactive. Of the 12,634 cases received by federal judges responsible for reviewing the requests, approximately 7,539 (59.7%) sentence reduc-tions were granted.[10] This is certainly a step in the right direction, but Congress must do more to address mandatory minimum laws for powder and crack cocaine that were part of the 1986 Anti-Drug bill. Members of Congress now understand that the sen-tences that resulted in the creation of the bill were draconian in nature and that those sentences, coupled with the 1988 Anti-Drug bill, resulted in far too may people serving very long sentences for first time offenses—individuals such as Clarence Aaron out of Mobile, Alabama, who received three life sentences. We will return to Aaron's case in an upcoming chapter. It should not be politically difficult to add retroactivity to the bill language. Congressman Bobby Scott (D-VA) has introduced a bill that would make the provisions of the Fair Sentencing Act retroactive. H.R. 2369, the Fair Sentencing Clarification Act of 2013, was introduced in June 2013 and has seven co-sponsors as of May 2014.[11] It is one of the bills introduced in the 113th Congress to address drug sentencing laws and mass incarceration. Will any of the bills become law before the conclusion of the 113th Congress?

113th Congress

In addition to the Fair Sentencing Act, Congressman Bobby Scott also introduced H.R. 2372, the Fairness in Cocaine Sentencing Act of 2013, which "Amends the Controlled Substances Act and the Controlled Substances Import and Export Act to eliminate increased and mandatory minimum penalties for drug offenses involving mixtures or substances which contain cocaine base (i.e., crack cocaine)."[12] There are four co-sponsors of this legislation: Steve Cohen (D-TN), John Conyers (D-MI), Alcee Hastings (D-FL), and Mel Watt (D-NC). (Mel Watt is no longer in the U.S. Congress as he was nominated by President Obama to serve as the Director of the Federal Housing Finance Agency. His nomination was approved by the U.S. Senate). The bill that has received the most attention, however, is the Smarter Sentencing Act of 2013 (H.R. 3382), which has the strongest chance of passing before the conclusion of the 113th Congress. The Smarter Sentencing Act is a bipartisan bill introduced by Congressman Raul Labrador (R-ID) and Congressman Bobby Scott (D-VA) on October 30, 2013. The Senate version of this bill, S. 1410, the Smarter Sentencing Act, was introduced on July 31, 2013 by Senator Richard Durbin (D-IL). The original co-sponsors of the Senate bill are Senator Patrick Leahy (D-VT) and Senator Mike Lee (R-UT). The following is from a press release issued by Congressman Labrador regarding the House version of the bill:

> "WASHINGTON, D.C.—Rep. Raúl Labrador (R-ID) and Rep. Robert C. "Bobby" Scott (D-VA), members of the House Judiciary Committee, introduced a landmark bipartisan bill today to bring common sense and flexibility to federal criminal sentencing laws. Their bill—the Smarter Sentencing Act—would allow courts to make individualized assessments in nonviolent drug cases, ensuring that limited resources are focused on the most serious offenders, while maintaining public safety.
>
> "We must be strict, but also smart, when it comes to federal criminal sentencing," said Rep. Labrador. "The 'one-size-fits-all' approach Congress put on the books has tied the hands of judges without improving public safety. Nearly half of the inmates filling our federal prisons are incarcerated for drug offenses. Many of them do not need overly harsh penalties. And yet judges are forced to impose these penalties, even if they don't want to."[13]

It is important to note that this bill will not eliminate mandatory minimum penalties, but the final version of the bill passed by Congress may make the Fair Sentencing Act retroactive. Instead, it seeks to allow more discretion for judges in giving a sentence that fits the crime and circumstances as opposed to sentencing an individual based on what the sentencing guidelines and the mandatory minimum penalties are. So a first time offender such as Clarence Aaron likely would not have received three life sentences were this legislation actual law when he was convicted. The bill also promotes sentencing consistent with the Fair Sentencing Act, and it expands the Federal Safety

Valve legislation, we've referenced in previous chapters. Also from Congressman Labrador's press release:

"The bill Rep. Scott and I are introducing today will empower judges to determine, on an individual level, when the harshest sentences should apply. This approach will improve justice, reduce the burden on taxpayers, and actually improve safety by enabling the justice system to focus on the most violent offenders. I am proud of the large number of groups—representing the whole ideological spectrum—who are supporting our bill, and I will work with my colleagues in a bipartisan way to get it passed.

During the past 30 years, the number of inmates in federal custody has grown by 500 percent, with nearly half of them serving sentences for drug offenses. Spending on federal incarceration has grown by more than 1100 percent. Today, it costs about $29,000 per year to house just one federal inmate. The Smarter Sentencing Act could save up to $1 billion in incarceration costs."[14]

The economic incentives to reform the criminal justice system are strong, as evident in Congressman Labrador's statement. Many states have faced tremendous challenges in funding its prison system and in dealing with the consequences of prison overcrowding. However, there is also a human cost involved. As the *New York Times* cite in an editorial, "The severity is evident in the devastation wrought on America's poorest and least educated, destroying neighborhoods and families. From 1980 to 2000, the number of children with fathers in prison rose from 350,000 to 2.1 million. As race and poverty overlap so significantly, the weight of our criminal justice experiment continues to fall overwhelmingly on communities of color and particularly on young black men."[15]

As mentioned, the bill Labrador and Scott introduced is a bipartisan bill, not only because the two individuals that crafted the bill are members of the Republican and Democratic Party, but also because they were joined by seven other original co-sponsors from both parties. Those individuals are as follows: John Conyers (D-MI), Henry "Hank" Johnson (D-GA), Cedric Richmond (D-LA), Spencer Bachus (R-AL), Steve Cohen (D-TN), Hakeem Jeffries (D-NY), and Rodney Davis (R-IL). Each of these members, save for Rodney Davis, are on the House Judiciary Committee. In addition, Scott, Conyers, Johnson, Richmond, and Jeffries are members of the Congressional Black Caucus. As of May 28, 2014, there are a total of 32 co-sponsors of this bill.

While hearings have not taken place on the House side regarding the Smarter Sentencing Act of 2013, the United States Senate Committee on the Judiciary held a hearing entitled "Reevaluation the Effectiveness of Mandatory Minimum Sentencing." The hearing was held on September 18, 2013. While the hearing did not specifically focus on the Smarter Sentencing Act, it was Chaired by Senator Patrick Leahy, who is an original co-sponsor S. 1410, the senate version of the Smarter Sentencing Act. Senator Leahy, in his opening statement, discussed the need to reform mandatory minimum sentencing laws and cited an example of how draconian these laws have been. Here is an excerpt from his opening statement:

"Take for example Weldon Angelos, a 23-year-old with no criminal history who received a 55-year mandatory minimum sentence for selling $350 worth of marijuana on three occasions while in possession of a firearm. There is no question that Mr. Angelos committed a crime and deserved to be punished. But 55 years? Mr. Angelos will be in prison until he is nearly 80 years old. His children, only 5 and 6 at the time of his sentencing, will be in their 60s. American taxpayers will have spent more than $1.5 million locking him up."

The federal judge who sentenced Mr. Angelos, a Republican appointee, called this sentence "unjust, cruel, and irrational" and noted the sentence, which involved no violence, was much more than the minimum for hijacking, kidnapping, or rape. We must stop and ask ourselves what good does that sentence do society? Mr. Angelos's sister is here today, as are many family members with similar stories of loved ones sent to prison for decades longer than reason and public safety demand. I want to thank them for being here. http://www.judiciary.senate.gov/imo/media/doc/9-18-13LeahyStatement.pdf[16]

In contrast, Senator Charles Grassley (R-IA), the ranking member of the Senate Judiciary Committee, did not see a problem with mandatory minimum sentences. He sees the problem as activist judges attempting to overturn what Congress required with regard to establishing the U.S. Sentencing Commission to establish guidelines. Further, he makes the argument that mandatory minimums do carry some degree of flexibility: Here is just a part of his opening statement:

"Mandatory minimum sentences are not as inflexible as they are often characterized. According to the Sentencing Commission, almost half of all offenders convicted of an offense carrying a mandatory minimum sentence are not given such a sentence. We hear over and over that mandatory minimum sentences are one size fits all or that they are unfair. We hear that low level and first time offenders always receive harsh sentences. That's just not so. The safety valve provision requires judges not to impose mandatory minimum sentences for first time, low-level, nonviolent drug offenders, who have provided all information to the authorities. Mandatory minimum sentences are not imposed on many other offenders because they provide substantial assistance to the government in prosecuting more serious criminals."[17] http://www.judiciary.senate.gov/imo/media/doc/9-18-13GrassleyStatement.pdf

Although there is a bipartisan effort to reform mandatory minimum sentences, there are still strong voices inside and outside of Congress to oppose the Smarter Sentencing Act.

On March 11, 2014, according to what is on www.thomas.gov, the bill was reported out of committee by Senator Leahy with an amendment in the nature of a substitute.

S. 1410 was then placed on the Senate Calendar, meaning that a vote can be scheduled on the bill. On April 8, 2014, Senator Grassley, responding to reports that the Smarter Sentencing Act would be considered on the Senate Floor during the month of April, went to the floor to reiterate his strong opposition to the bill. His purpose was to engage with his colleagues not on the Judiciary Committee who think this bill is a good bill. His statement can be located at http://www.grassley.senate.gov/news/news-releases/grassley-floor-statement-smarter-sentencing-act.[18] He returned to the Senate Floor to discuss this issue in May 2014, during National Police Week, according to his May 13, 2014 press release. He again reiterates his strong opposition to the Smarter Sentencing Act and to the weakening of mandatory minimum laws. In this Floor statement, he references a letter sent to Majority Leader Harry Reid (D-NV) and Minority Leader Mitch McConnell (R-KY) from "a bipartisan group of former Justice Department" officials in opposition to reducing mandatory minimum laws. He also includes other groups in his statement who oppose the Smarter Sentencing Act and any weakening of mandatory minimum laws, including the Federal Law Enforcement Officers Association and the National Narcotics Officers' Association.[19] As of May 28, 2014, the bill has not received a vote on the Senate Floor. There are 23 co-sponsors on S. 1410, which is more than five of those serving in the U.S. Senate. Included as a co-sponsor is Senator Corey Booker (D-NJ), one of two African Americans currently serving in the senate. Senate Majority Leader Harry Reid (D-NV) can schedule a floor vote on the bill at any time.

The Smarter Sentencing Act has received a significant amount of attention from the media and interest groups. Nearly three decades after the death of Len Bias, this bipartisan approach to criminal justice reform may be a signal that Congress is ready to focus on smarter sentencing laws, rather than responding to the latest epidemic with the tough on crime rhetoric that resulted in this travesty of justice.

Conclusion

The year 2014 is a midterm election year so the question is whether or not the U.S. Senate will schedule a vote on this bill before the election, or, at the very latest, shortly after the election concludes. Also, will this bill be reported out of committee on the House side for consideration on the House Floor? While it is possible that Congress will wait until the 114th Congress, which means that the bills will have to be reintroduced, it is important to remember that the Fair Sentencing Act was passed, albeit via voice vote, during a mid-term election year. Also, with states struggling to address the rising costs of mass incarceration, bipartisan legislation introduced that addresses prison overcrowding without eliminating penalties will not leave members vulnerable to the "soft on crime" mantra. The policy window has opened to allow for Congress and state legislatures to address mass incarceration in a sound, comprehensive fashion. By the time, this second edition is published, the reader will know whether or not the Smarter Sentencing Act became law.

Key Terms

Endnotes

1 "Federal Cocaine Sentencing Laws, Reforming the 100-1 Crack Powder Disparity, United States Senate, Subcommittee on Crimes and Drugs, Committee on the Judiciary, Washington, DC) Tuesday, February 12, 2008.

2 www.famm.org, accessed on April 27, 2011 and Artemesia Stanberry, "Mandatory Minimums for Crack Cocaine: A Change Has Got to Come," May 23, 2010, http://politicsroundtable.blogspot.com/2010/05/mandatory-minimums-for-crack-cocaine.html

3 Ibid.

4 http://www.justice.gov/opa/pr/2010/July/10-ag-867.html

5 www.whitehouse.gov/blog/2010/08/03/president-obama-signs-fair-sentencing-act, accessed on April 27, 2011.

6 http://webb.senate.gov/issuesandlegislation/criminaljusticeandlawenforcement/National-Criminal-Justice-Commission-Act-of-2009.cfm.

7 Crack Cocaine Issue for Public Comment (Washington, DC: Families Against Mandatory Minimums), assessed on May, 2, 2011. http://www.famm.org/NewsandInformation/PressReleases/FAMMUrgesUSSCtoMakeCrackChangesRetroactive.aspx.

8 www.ussc.gov/Legislative_and_Public_Affairs/Newsroom/Press_Releases/20110630_Press_Release.pdf.

9 U.S. Sentencing Commission: Preliminary Retroactivity Data Report, Fair Sentencing Act," April 2014 http://www.ussc.gov/sites/default/files/pdf/research-and-publications/federal-sentencing-statistics/fsa-amendment/20140415-USSC-Crack-Retro-Report-Post-FSA.pdf (assessed May 28, 2014).

10 Ibid, Table 1.

11 Bill text, 113th Congress (2013–2014), H.R. 2369, http://thomas.loc.gov/cgi-bin/query (assessed May 28, 2014).

12 *Congressional Record*, Volume 159, Number 84, Thursday, June 2013, p. H3592, www.Thomas.gov (accessed May 28, 2014).

13 "Labrador and Scott Introduce Bipartisan Bill to Reform Criminal Sentencing Laws, press release, October 30, 2013, http://labrador.house.gov/press-releases/labrador-scott-introduce-bipartisan-bill-to-reform-criminal-sentencing-laws/ (accessed on May 28, 2014).

14 Ibid.

15 "End Mass Incarceration Now," *The New York Times*, http://www.nytimes.com/2014/05/25/opinion/sunday/end-mass-incarceration-now.html?_r=0 (accessed May 26, 2014).

16 "Reevaluation the Effectiveness of Mandatory Minimum Sentencing," September 18, 2013, United States Senate, http://www.judiciary.senate.gov/imo/media/doc/9-18-13LeahyStatement.pdf (accessed June 26, 2014).

17 Ibid, http://www.judiciary.senate.gov/imo/media/doc/9-18-13GrassleyStatement.pdf (accessed June 26, 2014).

18 "Grassley Floor Statement on the Smarter Sentencing Act," press release, April 8, 2014, http://www.grassley.senate.gov/news/news-releases/grassley-floor-statement-smarter-sentencing-act (accessed June 26, 2014).

19 "Grassley Floor Statement on the Smarter Sentencing Act, Part II," press release, May 13, 2014, http://www.grassley.senate.gov/news/news-releases/grassley-floor-statement-smarter-sentencing-act-part-ii (accessed June 26, 2014).

ACTIVITY 1
2010, a Drug Sentencing Odyssey...

A Chapter 9 Exercise

Instructions:

The 111th Congress (January 2009–January 2011) was the first Congress in history to function during the presidency of an African American. In the space above, explain why so many were optimistic that the 111th Congress might have been able to make significant changes to the 100:1 ratio than in the past.

100:1–18:1

[Please tear out your completed response so you can turn it in to the instructor]

ACTIVITY 2

In the box below, describe what Attorney General Eric Holder said about the passage of S.1789 (AKA "Fair Sentencing Act of 2010") sponsored by Senator Richard Durbin.

A Chapter 9 Exercise

ACTIVITY 3

Applying a book concept to a real-life issue...

Questions Posed by the U.S. Sentencing Commission

Instructions:

Within the *Questions Posed by the U.S. Sentencing Commission* box, please explain the details of the questions that the Commission wanted to hear from the public on.

A Chapter 9 Exercise

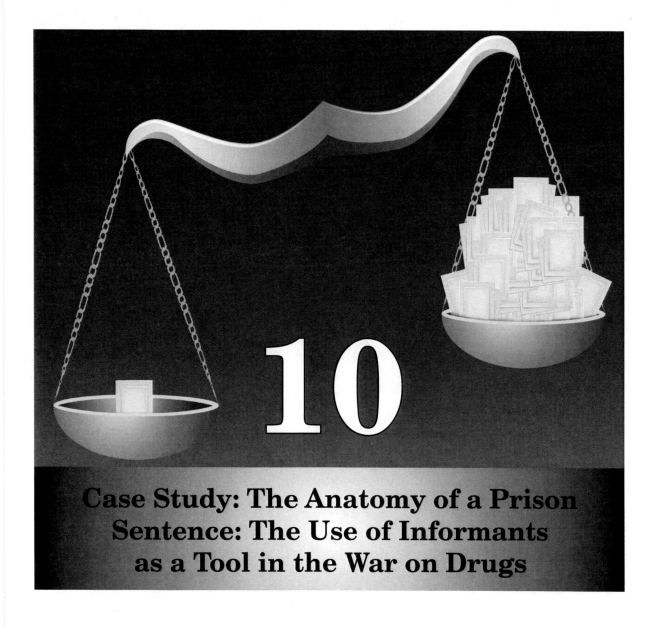

Case Study: The Anatomy of a Prison Sentence: The Use of Informants as a Tool in the War on Drugs

Chapter 10 Case Study: The Anatomy of a Prison Sentence: The Use of Informants as a Tool in the War on Drugs

"You have mothers in prison that—all you're doing now is bringing up children to be bitter against the government. I mean, my son is very bitter. And I know I never saw that in him when I was home. This law has destroyed families."[1]

Dorothy Gaines, mother of 3, sentenced to 19 years and 7 months in prison

Mobile is a moderately sized southern city located in the state of Alabama. The federal district court responsible for trying cases out of Mobile played an active role in the War on Drugs. At the federal level, there is a three tiered court system—the U.S. Supreme Court, the Court of Appeals, and the District Courts. There are 94 district courts, which are trial courts.[2] The southern judicial district of Alabama is where federal drug cases in the Mobile and surrounding areas are prosecuted. During the 1990s, a documentary aired on PBS that spotlighted Mobile as the "snitch capital" of the United States because, as reported in the *Frontline* documentary entitled "Snitch", it had the highest percentages of informants in the country. Within legislation created by Congress in an effort to fight the War on Drugs, Congress had allowed for a downward departure of a conviction IF a defendant would provide "substantial assistance" to the federal government. What this means is that if an individual is caught with 50 grams of crack and is facing a 10-year prison sentence that person can get a lesser sentence if he or she can help the government by providing the names of others involved in the drug trade. However, in 1988, the floodgates opened because Congress allowed for the lowest person in a drug ring to get the time of a Kingpin. As reported by *Frontline*:

NARRATOR: There don't have to be drugs because in federal cases oral testimony is enough. So when a small technical amendment to the mandatory minimums was issued in 1988, it created a huge change in the prosecution of drug offenders. The conspiracy amendment stipulated that the lowest person in a so-called drug conspiracy could be punished with the maximum sentence designed for a kingpin.

ERIC STERLING: If the mandatory minimums were a result of haste and excess by Congress, "conspiracy" as applied to these mandatories was completely by oversight and by accident. It was submitted as part of a simple "technical corrections" amendment. No one even thought at all about what the implications were of applying conspiracy.

NARRATOR: Its implications were enormous and would change thousands of lives.[3]

As one can imagine, many facing very long prison terms were willing to give up names in order to lower a prison sentence. If a defendant is facing 30 years but can get 10 if he or she is able to provide the government with names, then pressure to avoid a lengthy sentence would often prevail. Thus, a genuine mid-level dealer who has information about the people working with him or her would provide the names of street level offenders, and even people innocently associated with a street level offender, and end up getting less time than the people he names, in many cases. Why? Because the street level dealer or even the person who is not involved in the trade but may have been at the home of someone who was involved, has no one to name, or refuse to name names, and, as a result, he or she may get a long sentence because the government has not received assistance. Ethan Brown opens his book entitled *Snitch: Informants, Cooperators, & the Corruption of Justice* with the following quote:

"Twenty years ago defendants were expected by their criminal associates to take their medicine and keep their mouths shut. Now sentences are so strong they all know that when they get caught they're gonna talk, their buddies are gonna talk—*everyone* is gonna talk. There is no more honor among thieves. And that is progress for law enforcement."—Alabama Republican Senator Jeff Sessions[4]

There are real consequences when the sentences are draconian in nature. While Senator Sessions, who was a U.S. Attorney for the southern district of Mobile during the late 1980s and early 1990s, called this progress for law enforcement, it resulted in individuals with a limited or no role in the distribution of drugs to serve extremely long prison sentences. We are not arguing that people involved with drugs should not receive punishment; rather, it is our contention that the punishment should be more in line with the crime. What would have been probation or a 2-year sentence before the 1986 Anti-Drug bill, for example, will now result in a 5, 10, or even a life sentence. If the intent of Congress was to target serious traffickers ("the managers of the retail traffic") and major traffickers ("the manufacturers or heads of organizations who are responsible for creating and delivering very large quantities"), it was the smaller scale street level dealer that was prosecuted under these mandatory minimum penalties.[5] The added addition of the conspiracy amendment swept many in the court system and charged as if they manufactured and managed large level drug deals. According to a 2002 U. S. Sentencing Commission report, "the high concentration of federally sentenced street-level crack cocaine dealers also may indicate that scarce federal law enforcement resources are not being focused on serious and major traffickers, as Congress appears to have desired."[6] Regardless of what Congress desired, Congress set up the initial 100-1 disparity between the treatment of crack versus powder cocaine, which, essentially, rendered those with 5 grams of crack as serious offenders. Again, Congress set up a structure that allowed defendants with 499 grams of powder cocaine to avoid that distinction when it comes to applying a mandatory minimum penalty based on the 100:1 structure. Refer back to Chapter 7 for the sentence structure that existed until the Fair Sentencing Act of 2010. Thus, the Drug Enforcement Agency and federal attorneys were, in targeting low-level dealers, operating within the tools and message that congress was sending—we want crack users in prison, so do your job.

Informants and Lengthy Sentences—Unintended Consequences?

We will provide three brief case studies of people arrested and convicted in Mobile, Alabama, (in the federal court system). These individuals received very long sentences and were granted relief from their sentences via U.S. Presidents and/or the Fair Sentencing Act of 2010. Clarence Aaron, Dorothy Gaines, and Stephanie Nodd served a combined total of approximately 50 years in prison. Aaron and Gaines were highlighted in the aforementioned PBS Frontline documentary. We will discuss their cases in the order that they were released from prison: Gaines (6+ years in prison), Nodd (22+ years in prison), and Aaron (20+ years in prison).

Here is another excerpt from *Frontline*:

Sen. JEFF SESSIONS (R), Alabama: Well, you have to be careful. A good prosecutor must always be careful, and if there's not corroboration on the testimony of a co-conspirator drug dealer, you should not proceed with the case. You should have absolute confidence that the facts given to you are true or you should not proceed.

NARRATOR: Yet after the conspiracy amendment was enacted, the prison population swelled. Within six years, the number of drug cases in federal prisons increased by 300 percent. From 1986 to 1998, it was up by 450 percent. Not only were there more prisoners, but they were serving much longer sentences as a result of conspiracy charges. *[www.pbs.org: More on the laws and statistics]*[7]

Dorothy Gaines was a 39-year-old single mother of three when her house was raided by the Alabama State police in a search for drugs. It was 1993. At the time, she worked as a nursing assistant. There were no drugs or any sign of drugs found in her home. What she discovered was that her former boyfriend, who was also the father of her eldest child, had been arrested on a drug charge. She said she had not spoken to him with any frequency and when they did speak, it was about child support. In 1999, Dorothy Gaines was interviewed for an episode of *This American Life*. The following is an excerpt beginning with a comment from Ira Glass, the producer and host of the show:

"There was bad blood between them. And when he was thrown in prison on drug charges, to get himself a lower sentence he said that she was part of a drug ring.

Dorothy Gaines

I always felt like it was a revenge thing. You know, as I read my paperwork and I talk to my attorney, she told me also that he brought up some things against his own mother. So, you know, I didn't know that."

While the state of Alabama would not pursue charges against Gaines due to lack of evidence, the federal government did. Gaines and her common-law husband were charged with possession of 2 kilos of cocaine with the intent to distribute it.[8] The federal government would bring up several people along with Gaines on a conspiracy charge. She ended up getting the longest sentence of everyone, including the individual who provided the government with names so that his sentence could be reduced. Gaines received a sentence of 19 years and 7 months (235 months). The "kingpin" in her case received less time than she did.[9] Gaines said that when she heard 235 months, she could not really calculate exactly how much time that was at the moment it was read by the judge. She said she heard her children screaming and crying after the sentence was read by the judge. Even a U.S. Marshall cried, according to Gaines, explaining to Gaines that "to see your son hold onto the judge and tell him that my mother's all I got, don't send her away. She said that was the most hurting thing."[10] Her children were 19, 11, and 9 when she went to prison. Her son was 9 years old.

Dorothy Gaines: "Conspiracy" is so broad. Anyone can get caught up in conspiracy-just knowing someone. That's what I constantly tell my kids—just being around someone. But it don't take 20 years to learn your mistake. I know that I got .caught up by being associated.[11]

So this mother of three, who admitted that she did not always associate with the right people, was given a sentence intended for serious traffickers.

"Ira Glass: How did they decide two kilos, since they never actually found any crack cocaine in her home?

Lyn Campbell [Gaines' appeals attorney at the time of the interview]

Well, it was totally based upon, according to the agent that testified, what the kingpin of the conspiracy said. That he had stored a kilo of crack at her house on one occasion. And on another occasion he had brought a kilo through and picked up a kilo of powder from her house that was later converted to crack. So it was totally on what he said.

Ira Glass

If that were not true, why would he say that? What's in it for him just to finger her?

Lyn Campbell

Well, cooperating witnesses get substantial sentencing cuts in the federal system. It's the only real way to get your time reduced. And because he was a leader, and I believe there were some weapons involved with him, he was looking basically at a life sentence. By telling on other people, and by being valuable to the federal government, he ended up with less than 15 years in jail. So he has a big incentive to turn in as many people as he can.

Dorothy Gaines, a working mother living on the outskirts of poverty, had never been on an airplane until she was flown from Mobile, Alabama, to a federal prison in Danbury, Connecticut. The prison did not allow for contact visits, so she was unable to see her children in person until she was transferred to another prison.[12] Her eldest daughter had to leave college to care for her young siblings.[13] The judge in her case had no discretion to consider her circumstances in giving out his sentence, judicial discretion had been weakened as a result of laws passed during the 1980s as we have discussed in previous chapters. However, her judge did show some kindness and sympathy toward her by allowing her time to get her affairs in order and to spend some time with her dying mother.[14] When former U.S. District Judge Alex T. Howard died in 2011, Gaines praised him for helping her to obtain her release. He wrote a letter to President Clinton and had been a critic of the federal sentencing guidelines; he believed that they were unconstitutional. Said Gaines "Judge Howard is my heart,"

Gaines said. "'Judge Howard is the reason I'm free today.'"[15] The compassion of a woman sentenced to 235 years toward a judge who saw her as more than a case number is strong.

Gaines' case, like several in Mobile, Alabama, did garner national news attention given the length of the sentence, and the public appeal of her children and she was able to gain support for a clemency,[16] which was granted by President Clinton in December 2000, as he was leaving office. She served approximately 6 years in prison. In accordance to Article II, Section II, of the U. S. Constitution, the President of the United States "shall have Power to grant Reprieves and Pardons for Offenses against the United States, except in Cases of Impeachment."[17]

Here is how the U.S. Department of Justice lists her sentence commutation:

December 22, 2000

Dorothy Marie Gaines

Offense:	Conspiracy to possess with intent to distribute, and possession with intent to distribute, cocaine base, 21 U.S.C. §§ 841(a)(1) and 846, 18 U.S.C. § 2
District/Date:	Southern Alabama; March 10, 1995
Sentence:	235 months' imprisonment; five years' supervised release
Terms of Grant:	Sentence of imprisonment to expire immediately[18]

Clarence Aaron

Narrator: How the drug laws affect the life of a community can be seen in Mobile, Alabama, which has one of the highest federal drug conviction rates in the country. Take the case of number 33. Clarence Aaron was a 23-year-old student and a promising athlete at Southern University Louisiana. His home was Mobile. He was the only one of Linda Aaron's three children who went to college.[19]

Clarence Aaron was not convicted on a mandatory minimum for crack violation, rather, he, too, was charged and sentenced under the 1988 drug conspiracy law. As written by Dafna Linzer, reporter for ProPublica, "At 24, he was sentenced to three life terms for his role in a cocaine deal, even though it was his first criminal offense and he was not the buyer, seller, or supplier of the drugs. Of all those convicted in the case, Aaron received the stiffest sentence."[20]

Aaron was in his junior year in college. His grandfather, who had been his mentor and helped him with his educational expenses, died.[21] Aaron made a decision that would cost him more than two decades of his life. He introduced someone he knew from Louisiana, where he attended college, to people he knew in Mobile "who were also involved in drugs. He drove them from one city to the other, accompanied by his cousin, and was paid $1,500 for his help."[22]

Dennis Knizley, Defense Attorney: Clarence Aaron was one of the worst cases I've ever had. Clarence tells me that the FBI came to his college classroom and pulled him out of the classroom and arrested him for possession with intent to distribute cocaine.

What makes it the worst case I ever had was there was absolutely no cocaine introduced into evidence. There was no cocaine seen. Nobody—the police had no cocaine. The FBI had no cocaine. There was no scientific evidence, no fingerprints, nothing. The entire case was based upon the testimony of what they call "cooperating individuals."[23]

When the federal government busted the drug ring, everyone knew that they needed to provide the government with assistance in order to avoid a very harsh sentence. The two quotes below from Clarence Aaron and the prosecuting attorney sums up what is problematic with the conspiracy laws:

Clarence Aaron: Miss Ofra, who was I to testify against? I was the last one to be arrested. When I got arrested, all the guys that was involved in our conspiracy was already cooperating. So what do you want me to tell, what they already told? Ain't nothing else I could tell. Only people I could have testified against, the guy that was already cooperating at that particular time already.

J. Don Foster: You know, the tendency to feel sorry for him is in relation to these other people that did cooperate and that did help themselves and got less. And even though they were perhaps guiltier or more culpable, they got less because they helped solve the case. They helped to bring everybody to justice. And the one person or two—I think there were two that went to trial in that case—that didn't, you know, suffered the results or the consequences of the arrogance of thinking that you're—you're going to beat this, that "I'm too good. I'm too good to take a deal."

Clarence Aaron had a clean criminal record and did not have a history of involvement with the drug trade. Nevertheless, he would receive the longest sentence of all involved; including the person the government would consider a serious offender. Aaron would get three life sentences, to be served concurrently. Said Aaron: "I just couldn't believe that when the judge told me that three life sentences running concurrent. When he said that, I was setting in my chair, and I was thinking to myself, I say, "Where in the world do I suppose to start doing three life sentences at? Where am I supposed to start at, in the middle, at the end part of it, where?" I just couldn't believe that this was occurring to me. All I'd seen my whole life, everything that I had strived and stayed out of trouble for all my life, go down the drain, you know?"[24]

A serious offender responds to the situation the government encouraged by providing names to help get a lighter sentence. However, some of the names provided may not actually be involved, at least not enough to merit a 20 year to life drug sentence. As Eric Sterling stated earlier, the person who has minimum involvement can get the time of a kingpin under the provisions added to the 1988 Anti-Drug bill. He also points out what the USSC has reported and that is that less than 11% of those in prison on drug charges are kingpins.[25]

Aaron's case also garnered national attention after the 1999 *Frontline* documentary that included his case. There were calls for his sentence commutation. The Bush (George W.) Administration denied his application for clemency, although it may have been granted had the President been given all of the information available to grant him a relief from his sentence by his U.S. Department of Justice's pardon attorney, Ronald Rodgers. According to an extensive investigation by Dafner Linzer and ProPublica, "In a confidential note to a White House lawyer, Rodgers failed to accurately convey the views of the prosecutor and judge and did not disclose that they had advocated for Aaron's immediate commutation."[26] When Bush left after serving two terms, President Barack H. Obama was elected.

President Obama had not issued many commutations and pardons during the first term of his presidency,[27] but there were calls in the public sphere for him to commute Aaron's sentence, calls from conservative and liberal media and cable news outlets, and from activists such as Dorothy Gaines, who was able to get the attorney who worked on her clemency to help Aaron.[28] On December 19, 2014, during his second term, President Obama commuted Aaron's sentence. Here is how it was listed on the Department of Justice's webpage:

December 19, 2013

Clarence Aaron

Offense: Conspiracy to possess with intent to distribute cocaine and cocaine base, 21 U.S.C. § 846; possession with intent to distribute cocaine, 21 U.S.C. § 841(a)(1); attempt to possess cocaine with intent to distribute (erroneously listed in the judgment as conspiracy to distribute cocaine), 21 U.S.C. § 846

District/Date: Southern Alabama; December 10, 1993 (as amended July 30, 1996)

Sentence: Life imprisonment; 5 years' supervised release

Terms of Grant: Sentence of imprisonment to expire on April 17, 2014, leaving intact and in effect the 5-year term of supervised release with all its conditions and all other components of the sentence.[29]

Aaron went to prison while he was in his 20s, and left prison when he was in his 40s. Given that he was sentenced to life in prison, his freedom was welcomed and embraced by his family and supporters.[30] Aaron is under supervised release for the next 5 years. He has to report to a parole officer and has to take drug tests.[31]

President Obama has taken action to allow for more individuals to apply for and to receive clemency, particularly those who have served at least a decade in prison and who have met various requirements.[32]

Stephanie Nodd

Stephanie Nodd of Mobile, Alabama was 22 years old when she was given a 30-year sentence. While Nodd admitted to selling drugs, she says she was not the major distributor that the prosecutors made her out to be. While not an owner of an airplane to bring drugs into Mobile, Alabama, nor a Kingpin, nor a major supplier, the then 22 year old with young children certainly deserved punishment for getting involved with the sale of drugs, but her punishment, many would argue, was more severe than what was called for in her situation. She spent 22 years in prison before she was released as a result of reforms made in the Fair Sentencing Act of 2010. She was 22 when she entered prison, 44 when she exited (http://blog.al.com/live/2011/11/long-serving_prisoner_from_mob.html).

Nodd's story is somewhat different than that of Gaines and Aaron in that she admits to regularly selling drugs and to encouraging others to sell drugs for her. In addition, she admits to telling the person who ended up testifying against her about how to unload drugs in Mobile, Alabama. For the 4–6 weeks that she knew him, she helped him to pick up money. What she denies is being a drug kingpin that she was portrayed to be when the individual was swept up in a drug ring and began cooperating with the government to get a sentence deduction. But that 1 month that she interacted with him, cost her more than 22 years of her life. Said Nodd: "He blew up the situation bigger than what it was," she said, claiming that her onetime acquaintance lied to get a deal from prosecutors. "I only knew him 4–6 weeks." Nodd said that when prosecutors dangled a plea bargain and a promise of lighter punishment in exchange for her cooperation, she had no information to give. She said that she was unaware of the extent of her possible penalty—up to life in prison—until after the trial.[33] Nodd said that she used the money she made from the 4–6 weeks of interacting with the individual who testified against her to pay bills and to buy groceries and that she was able to move to Boston with her children to begin a new life.

We were living in Boston when I was indicted on drug charges in Alabama. I returned to take responsibility for my mistake. I prayed I would not have to serve any time because of my clean record and limited involvement. I could not have been more wrong. I was put in jail immediately. My lawyer told me that unless I cooperated against some drug dealers in Florida—people I did not know—I would have to take a chance on a trial.

I could not give the prosecutors any information because I did not know anyone in Florida. Meanwhile, John cooperated against everyone, including me. I was eventually charged as a manager in the drug conspiracy and found guilty at trial. Even though I did not have a criminal record, I was sentenced to 30 years in federal prison. The year was 1990. George H.W. Bush was president, and no one knew what email was. I was 23 years old.[34]

Nodd was charged with 18 kilos of cocaine. This got her a 30-year prison sentence. When Nodd entered prison, she had four children and was pregnant with a fifth child.

She gave birth while in prison. Nodd says that while she sold drugs, she never used drugs, nor drank alcohol.[35] It was not until she was in prison that she realized the impact drugs had on people. Nodd said in an interview after she was released that "she thought little about what might happen if she were caught and not at all about the impact of drugs on her customers until years later, when she met crack-addicted inmates in prison. She said her goal is getting young people to see the whole frightening picture."[36]

Stephanie Nodd was released from prison on November, 2011, after serving nearly 22 years in prison. Following the passage of the Fair Sentencing Act of 2010, approximately 317 drug offenders convicted in the southern Alabama federal court in Mobile, Alabama, petitioned for relief under the guidelines the USSC created to conform with the new law. Of those 317, approximately 156 (49%) were granted.[37]

Conclusion

These three cases are just samples of the types of charges that the federal government imposed on citizens in Mobile, Alabama. Providing these profiles are not for the purpose of excusing or rationalizing anything related to the drug trade. Rather, it is to provide the reader with three real examples of individuals receiving very long sentences under the conspiracy laws, and to highlight the types of sentences that the public and Congress were hearing about. The *Frontline* episode aired in 1999. Recall from Chapter 9 Senator Patrick Leahy's mentioning of Weldon Angelos, who was 23 years old when he received a 55-year mandatory minimum penalty, he remains in prison. Do these sentences fit what these individuals actually did or are these types of sentences necessary in the fight against drugs in society? These cases also demonstrate the types of sentences that were and still can be given to drug offenders. Further, over the years comments have been expressed that these drug offenders spend more time in prison than violent offenders. We included this discussion in a previous chapter. Stephanie Nodd said that after telling people in prison how much time she received, she was often asked who did you kill, the presumption being that only convicted murders got those types of sentences. Here is Ira Glass on Dorothy Gaines' sentence: "In the end, her 19-year prison term was higher than the federal mandatory minimum sentence for rape, for kidnapping, for running a slave trade, for criminal sexual abuse of a child, for second degree murder, for conspiracy to commit murder. Her sentence had the same minimum as she would have gotten if she had hijacked a plane or bought and sold children for use in pornography."[38]

Two of the cases we highlighted are women who were arrested and incarcerated. These individuals left young children behind as they began their prison sentences. Nodd gave birth while in prison. Women are the fastest growing population in the prison system. Between 1980 and 2011, the number of women in prison increased by 587%, rising from 15,118 to 111,387.[39] This does not include women in local jails, if included, the number would be more than 200,000.[40] Further, 1 in 33 women in federal prison is pregnant when she enters prison.[41] Families have to deal with a new reality. Dorothy Gaines says her son changed when she was incarcerated, going from an honor student before her imprisonment to failing school after she was incarcerated. She said: "You have mothers in prison that—all you're doing now is bringing up children to be bitter against the government. I mean, my son is very bitter. And I know I never saw that in him when I was home. This law has destroyed families.[42]

Key Terms

Dorothy Gaines 237

Mobile, Alabama 239

Federal District Court 237

Southern Judicial District of Alabama 238

Frontline TV Show 238

War on Drugs 237

Author Ethan Brown 238

Alabama Republican Senator Jeff Sessions 239

2002 United States Sentencing Commission Report 239

Clarence Aaron 239

Dorothy Gaines 237

Stephanie Nodd 239

Ira Glass 240

Lyn Campbell 241

Judge Howard 241

Dennis Knizley 243

Clarence Aaron 239

J. Don Foster 243

Pardon Attorney Ronald Rodgers 244

21 U.S.C. 244

21 U.S.C. § 841(a)(1) 244

21 U.S.C. § 846 244

Endnotes

1 Glass, Ira, "Sentencing," Transcript. *This American Life*: Public Media and Ira Glass. Originally aired on October 22, 1999.

2 http://www.uscourts.gov/FederalCourts/UnderstandingtheFederalCourts/DistrictCourts .aspx (accessed June 26, 2014).

3 Bikel, Ofra, "Snitch." Transcript. *Frontline*, #1797. Air Date: January 12, 1999, http://www .pbs.org/wgbh/pages/frontline/shows/snitch/etc/script.html (accessed June 26, 2014).

4 Brown, Ethan, *Snitch: Informants, Cooperators & the Corruption of Justice*, (New York: PublicAffairs, 2007), p. O.

5 "Special Report to Congress: Cocaine and Federal Sentencing Policy," The United States Sentencing Commission, Washington, DC, May 2002, p. 99.

6 Ibid.

7 "Snitch", *Frontline*.

8 Glass, *This American Life*

9 Ibid

10 Glass, *This American Life*

11 "Snitch," *Frontline*

12 Bernstein, Nell, "Punishment for the Whole Family: California prison officials want to prohibit parents convicted of drug offenses from touching their children—even infants and toddlers—for one year," Salon May 8, 2002. (accessed on May 31, 2014)

13 "Snitch," *Frontline*

14 "Dorothy Gaines Mourns Judge Who Sentenced Her to Prison (Political Skinny), Al.com and Mobile Press Register, February 21, 2011, http://blog.al.com/live/2011/02/dorothy_ gaines_mourns_judge_wh.html (accessed June 26, 2014).

15 Ibid.

16 Saunders, Debra J, "Why Clinton Should Pardon Gaines," SFGate, Tuesday, September 26, 2000. http://www.sfgate.com/opinion/saunders/article/Why-Clinton-Should-Pardon-Dorothy-Gaines-3316047.php (accessed June 26, 2014).

17 United States Constitution.

18 "Commutations, Remissions, and Reprieves Granted by President William Jefferson Clinton," U.S. Department of Justice, http://www.justice.gov/pardon/clinton_comm.htm (accessed May 30, 2014).

19 "Snitch," Frontline

20 Linzer, Dafner, ProPublica, "Clarence Aaron was Denied Commutation, but Bush Team Wasn't Told All the Facts," *Washington Post*, May 13, 2012, http://www.washingtonpost.com/investigations/clarence-aaron-was-denied-commutation-but-bush-team-wasnt-told-all-the-facts/2012/05/13/glQAEZLRNU_story.html (accessed June 26, 2014).

21 Saunders, Debra J, "Freed Prisoner of the War on Drugs, " SFGate, May 2, 2014. http://www.sfgate.com/default/article/Freed-prisoner-of-the-drug-war-5449302.php (accessed June 26, 2014)

22 "Snitch," *Frontline*.

23 "Snitch," *Frontline*

24 Ibid.

25 Ibid. *Frontline*

26 Linzer, Dafner, ProPublica, "Clarence Aaron was Denied Commutation, but Bush Team Wasn't Told All the Facts," *Washington Post*, May 13, 2012. http://www.washingtonpost.com/investigations/clarence-aaron-was-denied-commutation-but-bush-team-wasnt-told-all-the-facts/2012/05/13/glQAEZLRNU_story.html

27 By 2012, President Obama had only granted 22 clemencies out of over 6,000 requests. U.S. DOJ: Office of the Pardon Attorney: Clemency Statistics, http://www.justice.gov/pardon/statistics.htm. http://www.justice.gov/pardon/statistics.htm (accessed June 26, 2014).

28 Saunders, Debra J. "Dorothy Gaines, a Grandmother/ Casualty in the Drug War, SFGate, Monday, April 20th, 2014, http://blog.sfgate.com/djsaunders/2014/04/28/dorothy-gaines-a-grandmothercasualty-in-the-drug-war/ (accessed April 21, 2014)

29 http://www.justice.gov/pardon/obama-comm.html (accessed June 26, 2014).

30 Saunders, "Freed Prisoner of the Drug War."

31 Ibid.

32 "Announcing New Clemency Initiative, Deputy Attorney General James M. Cole Details Broad New Criteria for Applicants," Press Release, April 23, 2014, http://www.justice.gov/opa/pr/2014/April/14-dag-419.html, (accessed April 24, 2014).

33 Kirby, Brendan, "The Money is Addicting, 'former Mobile Dealer Says of Time Selling Crack, December 20, 2011, http://blog.al.com/live/2011/12/that_money_is_addiction_former.html (accessed June 26, 2014).

34 Nodd, Stephanie, "Crack Cocaine: One Woman's Tale," Chicago Tribune, July 28, 2011. http://articles.chicagotribune.com/2011-07-28/site/ct-oped-0728-crack-20110728_1_federal-prison-crack-cocaine-drug-conspiracy (accessed May 30, 2014)

35 Schulzke, Eric, "Parenting From Prison: the Collateral Damage of Harsh Mandatory Minimum Sentencing," Deseret News (National Edition), March 20, 2014. http://www.deseretnews.com/article/865599027/Parenting-from-prison-the-far-reaching-impact-of-mandatory-minimums.html?pg=all (accessed June 26, 2014).

36 Kirby. "The Money is Addicting."

37 "The United States Sentencing Commission Preliminary Retroactivity Data Report-Fair Sentencing Act," United States Sentencing Commission, April 2014.   http://www.ussc .gov/sites/default/files/pdf/research-and-publications/federal-sentencing-statistics/ fsa-amendment/20140415-USSC-Crack-Retro-Report-Post-FSA.pdf   (accessed   June 26, 2014).

38 Glass, This American Life

39 "Incarcerated Women," Fact Sheet. The Sentencing Project, Washington, DC, pg 1. http:// www.sentencingproject.org/doc/publications/cc_Incarcerated_Women_Factsheet_ Dec2012final.pdf (accessed June 26, 2014).

40 Ibid

41 "Parents in State Prisons," Fact Sheet. TheSentencing Project, Washington, DC pg 3. http://www.sentencingproject.org/doc/publications/cc_Parents%20in%20State%20 Prisons%20Fact%20Sheet.pdf (accessed June 26, 2014).

42 Glass, This American Life

ACTIVITY 1

Understanding the Impact of courts . . .

Instructions:

In the space above, please provide understanding on the impact of the Southern Judicial District of Alabama, specifically on the city of Mobile's drug cases.

A Chapter 10 Exercise

[Please tear out your completed response so you can turn it in to the instructor]

ACTIVITY 2

Instructions: In the boxes, the importance of drug cases involving the three individuals listed...

Clarence Aaron

Dorothy Gaines

Stephanie Nodd

A Chapter 10 Exercise

ACTIVITY 3

Applying a book concept to a real-life issue...

21 U.S.C. § 841(a)(1)

21 U.S.C. § 846

Instructions:

Within the two boxes above, please discuss these two federal drug statutes and what you consider important about each one.

A Chapter 10 Exercise

[Please tear out your completed response so you can turn it in to the instructor]

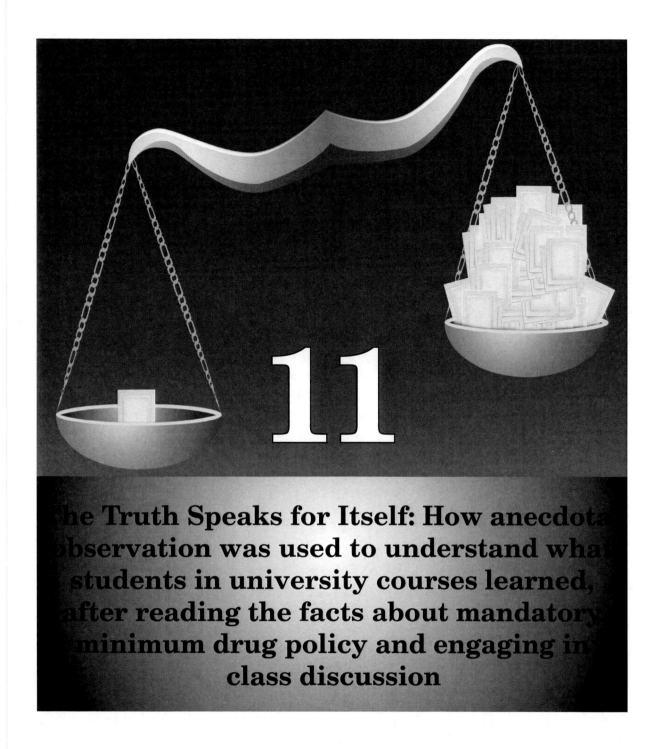

11

The Truth Speaks for Itself: How anecdotal observation was used to understand what students in university courses learned, after reading the facts about mandatory minimum drug policy and engaging in class discussion

Chapter 11 Synopsis: This chapter provides a sampling of understanding students have about the creation of federal sentencing guidelines for crack cocaine and powder cocaine, as well as the efforts and eventual changes by Congress as well as the Attorney General with respect to enforcement of these laws. More importantly, this chapter provides understanding of views about creation of the law and eventual changes to it.

Undergraduate and graduate responses.

Introduction

Given that this text, in the first edition, sought to explain the reality of how the federal sentencing disparity created by Congress regarding powder cocaine and crack cocaine, it also sought to provide clarity on the dilemma the Congressional Black Caucus (CBC) faced. More specifically, as was made clear in the first edition of this book, the CBC sought to address perceptions of a public problem, just like non CBC members of Congress. The problem was that the solution decided upon by Congress was unrealistic in scope and created a sentencing disparity four times more punitive than even the conservative U.S. President Ronald Reagan proposed at the time. A climate of that time therefore incorrectly mandated minimum sentences for these two versions of the same drug which were not only unrealistic but created a negative impact of devastation to the justice system we as a society are dealing with today in 2014. This is a legacy which many professionals within and outside the justice system warned would happen but were ignored. So this chapter's importance is that it provides the first-ever understanding from students who learned (based on anecdotal observation) the story of this disparity and their reaction to how it was created and how it finally changed dramatically starting in 2010.

Providing a History Lesson to only Learn that the Professor was being Taught

When the first edition of Travesty of Justice was published in 2011, it was adopted by professors teaching political science, criminal, justice, sociology, and several other disciplines. The first edition sold well on amazon.com, speaking to a larger community of those interested in the topic. In addition, the first edition sold out at every book signing held for it; largely due to the substantial interest in learning the complexity of the politics and historical realities which created the federal mandatory minimum laws for crack cocaine and powder cocaine.

What was interesting with respect to the first edition, was that the authors anecdotally noticed that students in their specific courses using the first edition, reacted in a manner which the authors considered unusual. Both authors, i.e., Stanberry and Montague, had previously used various books in courses which essentially told a story about some reality, and the responses of students ranged from apathetic to mystified. One of the authors in particular observed that undergraduate students began coming to class each week with increasing anger and disbelief as they delved deeper into the first edition of *Travesty of Justice*. As this type of response seemed to resonate with a large number of students in the class, the authors discussed this reaction and decided to ask the students why they felt the way they did and to be more specific about what message(s) they received from the first edition of the book. More importantly, the authors became curious as to whether or not there was just a general reaction to the book overall, or to actually various sections of the book dealing with not only the creation of the sentencing guidelines but also the eventual change in the guidelines.

The Process: Exploration into Curiosity

The authors agreed that based on the unanticipated anecdotal observations mentioned earlier that some inquiry with students during class period sessions could help shed light on what might become a more formal understanding. Initially, it was observed that class discussion became more intense after students read Chapter 4 which addressed how cocaine as a drug became politicized, then the discussion intensified even more after students completed Chapter 5 which addressed the actual votes within Congress. Finally, it was observed that the shock expressed by students after reading Chapters 4 and 5, turned to a sense of general disgust after reading Chapters 8 and 9 which addressed the appointment of Attorney General Eric Holder and the eventual reduction in the guidelines from 100:1 down to 18:1 in terms of disparity. The terms "anger," "frustration," and "disgust" are terms that students used during several semesters of these discussions, meaning that the authors did not suggest to the students which words best to describe their feelings via class discussions. This is an important distinction in that it was the repeated use of these terms in particular, more than other terms used, which indicated to the authors that a more substantive understanding of student views was needed.

The Opportunity to Learn and give Back Simultaneously

As professors, we (the authors) understand the realities associated with empiricism; that is, that there are processes involved when adding to the "body of knowledge" on any particular subject. That said, approaching "how" to obtain any new understanding, takes careful attention in order to learn, but also to respect all the relevant stakeholders. In some cases, it might be advantageous to conduct interviews or a complex survey. In this case however, the relevant group involved were students enrolled in classes using the first edition of the book. Although the authors garnered lively discussion as a group during the class sessions using the first edition, many students seemed unclear as to how they could contribute individually and it not be connected with their course grade; which it could not. The reality of this fact is that students, especially the undergraduate students, are not as familiar with the nuances of empirical research and can become confused or even intimidated if they possibly think that participation in a formal interview or survey connects them officially to anything with a legal connection, such as a published book. In addition, it was difficult for some students to grasp the reality that participation in an interview or survey will not be connected/associated with their course grade. This becomes an especially sensitive reality if the student does not perform well overall in the course and somehow believes their participation, equates to "demonstration" they are a better student than their performance indicates. In other words, the authors considered it unfair to the students to potentially have any student feel pressured or have a false belief about their official participation individually.

Based on this, the authors chose to abandon the attempted administration of a survey of the students, opting to go the less-empirical route of doing what a lot of professors do each semester; make notes on our own observations during the running of the course that semester. Faculty often do this in order to better understand how to adjust/tweak things for the next semester, and such observation is not with respect to any specific individual students, rather it is general in nature. The positive aspect of this methodology is that it allows the professor to understand what "works" or does not for specific chapters or sections of material, or even where adjustment might be needed with respect to the activities students must complete during the semester. In other words, as the professors perform these functions routinely, they are in I fact somewhat proficient in such anecdotal observations with respect to gauging student absorption during the course semesters in which the first edition was used by them (i.e., the authors).

Tracking over time...

With the understanding that survey approach had to be abandoned, the authors chose to refer to the notes made about each semester in which the first edition was used during the semester, and to use this along with the understanding of how the two courses using the book are different in nature and level of student.

Findings

As Table 11.1 indicates, two types of courses regularly used the first edition in them, but in different ways. One course, Crime & Behavior, is a comprehensive course in which theories are presented and then applied to real life via examples from the media

Table 11.1. Implementation process

Course	Level	Offerings since 2011	Module(s) of material	Number of students
Crime & Behavior	*Undergraduate-Level* Upper (theory to practice) with mostly Criminal Justice majors	Spring, Summer, & Fall	Entire course as supplement to a crime theory text book	230 (approximately) per year
Criminal Justice Policy	*Graduate-Level* Policy-based course focusing on all aspects on creation and implementation of specific crime policies	Fall	Entire course as supplement to a criminal justice policy evaluation text book	5–15 per year

and the sources. Importantly, this course is able to show both the professor and the student that learning is happening on current crime societal issues. It is also important in that students begin to realize that the course concepts apply not only to societal issues historically, but in the present as well; in essence giving more value to the material in the eyes of the student. The students in this course used the first edition of Travesty of Justice as a case study on drug crime. It enables the students to apply concepts from their theory book for the course to very specific details when looking at the issue, creation, implementation, negative impact, and eventual modification of the mandatory minimum drug policies dealing with crack cocaine and powder cocaine federally. In other words, the first edition empowered students by helping them go far beyond the news articles on various types of crime issues; it gave them enormous detail, not only about "what" happened on a crime issue, but "how" it happened, as well as "why." The moment that many refer to as the "light bulb" moment of true learning is when students realize that often "when" an issue becomes part of public discussion, it can make a difference in how it is dealt with by politicians and the public.

The second course referred to within Table 1 is a graduate-level course called Criminal Justice Policy. This course is surprisingly the first formal course in public policy that the vast majority of these students actually learn the components of public policy on a societal issue. This is particularly significant in that most of these students occupy roles of either policy formulation or policy implementation (or both), which means that this course must find ways to help students relearn what they have gained via training and to engender appreciation for how complex each policy issue can be. Therefore, the first edition of this book was a tremendous supplement to the other text for that course; a policy evaluation book.

Conclusion

This chapter provided the first ever understanding about how students reacted to learning of the creation of the mandatory minimums federally for crack cocaine and powder cocaine. Moreover, many of the students at the undergraduate level were not born at the time the "ball started rolling" to formulate and adopt these laws. This means that the views of these students in particular are not tainted by any emotion from that original time period; they simply held class discussion based on learning facts. Many students at both the undergraduate and graduate levels made clear during routine class discussions that the best part of the first edition of the book, provided students with two things. First, the first edition provided them with detail directly from verifiable sources and showed the students that this "travesty" was created and implemented in plain sight; people simply needed to look. The second thing students gained from the first edition was that if facts can be laid-out and documented on this social issue, then the same thing can be done on any social issue, and students should consider this power salient to their lives.

As Tables 11.2 and 11.3 denote, there is a clear pattern in the discussion among undergraduates in class versus graduate students in class. Regardless of the level of the student, the authors anecdotally observed that students are not happy with

Table 2. Phase One—Findings after 1-year using the first edition of *Travesty of Justice*

Course	Understanding on creation of mandatory minimum drug laws	Understanding of impact based on the laws	Understanding of efforts to eventually change the laws	Class discussion on resistance for decades to modify the laws	Class discussion on current (Circa 2011) laws at 18:1
Crime and Behavior (upper-level)	High	High	Medium, but students were generally confused in class on what prompted the change in view by politicians after so long	High, students were generally frustrated as to why it is so difficult and why resistance was not highlighted more in the media as oversight/ accountability	High, student conversation was not a debate; it was unanimous (of those who spoke up) that people would rather ignore an issue rather than fixing it, unless they are forced to. Words such as "disgust" were used.
Criminal Justice Policy (graduate-level)	Low, not as vocal as undergraduate students on these laws	Medium, "impact" took on deeper discussion, focusing on "intended" versus "unintended" outcomes of the laws	High, much discussion centered on students connecting lack of proper formulation to lack of effort to modify after the fact	Medium, discussions by students focused on what possible "back stories" exist which resulted in resistance (many of the students work in CJ policy roles during the class)	High, "fairness" is important, and discussion on logistics and resources must accompany additional changes in laws

Table 3. Phase Two—Findings after 2-year using first edition of *Travesty of Justice*

Course	Understanding on creation of mandatory minimum drug laws	Understanding of impact based on the laws	Understanding of efforts to eventually change the laws	Class discussion on resistance for decades to modify the laws	Class discussion on current (Circa 2011) laws at 18:1
Crime and Behavior (upper-level)	High, initially thought there must have been some logic behind formulation of laws, developed outrage	High, attended class concern about Congress' focus on these drugs rather than on more substantive issues	High, students saw frequent stories each week in the news on this topic and wanted to engage in intense discussion	High, students generally commented on Congress as having "bad leadership" on this topic and expressed concern regarding other crime issues and political leadership	High, many students the change was "too little, too late" and debated on how society can focus on addressing crime instead of focusing on looking a certain way to the public and constituents
Criminal Justice Policy (graduate-level)	Same responses for this group as in Table 2	Same responses for this group as in Table 2	Same responses for this group as in Table 2	High, students were surprised that the facts on Len Bias and other significant factors went untapped by the public and by Congress to modify the laws sooner	Same responses for this group as in Table 2

how these laws were created, implemented, and eventually modified. They are equally unimpressed with the reality of resistance for so long on this issue which has had a devastating emotional, physical (to those incarcerated), financial, and moral impact on our nation. Many, not most, students also made the connects during classes that mandatory minimum laws are also connected with other criminal justice issues like community reentry to society for instance. Therefore, the students brought dimensions of larger connections into their discussions, as well as the importance of being more realistic as a society to better address those societal issues. Finally, the authors take away from this chapter that the first edition of the book, along with other important works on injustices, are actually creating a more dedicated cadre of future professionals who have no patience with social issues being addressed in the manner that the mandatory minimum for drugs federally were done. So, our hope in this second edition is to "fuel the fire" of encouragement even more so that similar travesties like this one hopefully do not occur.

Key Terms

ACTIVITY 1
Understanding the Importance
of Learning . . .

Instructions:

In the space above, please provide understanding of what the chapter describes as "anecdotal observation," emphasizing the importance of it for the chapter.

A Chapter 11 Exercise

[Please tear out your completed response so you can turn it in to the instructor]

ACTIVITY 2

Instructions: In the boxes, please provide some understanding of the context in which the following terms were used . . .

Anger

Frustration

Disgust

A Chapter 11 Exercise

ACTIVITY 3

Applying a book concept to a real-life issue...

Phase One-Findings

Phase Two-Findings

Instructions:

Within the two boxes above, please discuss the two phases described in the chapter in how they were informative on student reactions to the actions of Congress . . .

A Chapter 11 Exercise

[Please tear out your completed response so you can turn it in to the instructor]

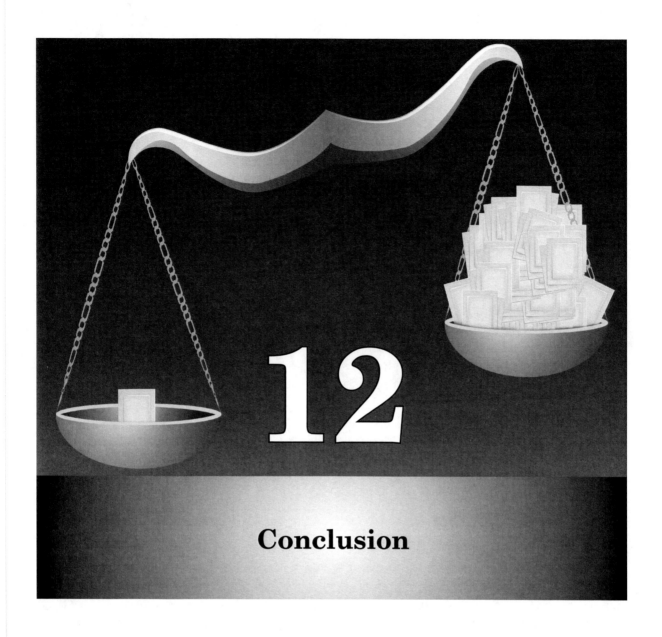

12

Conclusion

Chapter 12 Synopsis: I can accept neither the necessity nor the wisdom of federal mandatory minimum sentences . . . . Our resources are misspent, our punishments too severe, our sentences too long . . . (Supreme Court Justice Anthony Kennedy, August 2003).[1]

ANALYSIS OF THE CBC'S ROLE IN CONGRESS

The Congressional Black Caucus was formed for the purpose of advancing and articulating the interests of African Americans. As such, the CBC sets itself up as an interest group in Congress that represents the whole African American community regardless of constituency differences. As elected representatives, they have concerns about getting reelected, building coalitions with their colleagues in Congress, supporting their political party, and representing constituents within their individual congressional districts. These legislative interests and institutional responsibilities create challenges to the mission of the CBC to act as a collective voice. The unity of the CBC is further challenged when the CBC has as a strategy to operate within the norms of a congressional body, i.e., achieving seniority and advancing to key committee positions. Achieving seniority and advancing to key committees require the support of their non-CBC colleagues. When non-CBC members are in support of tough criminal justice policies that the CBC opposes, it creates a situation in which the CBC as a group must voice opposition to their colleagues' support of such laws or support (indirectly) their colleagues' votes by not creating massive protest against their votes. Further, when the CBC has an interest in its party's maintaining or regaining control of Congress, it may support or at the very least voice little opposition to their colleagues' support of legislation that could harm its national constituency. As legislators in Congress, there are challenges for the CBC to remain united and committed to the interests of its proclaimed national constituency because members must balance their mission with pragmatic politics.

Revisiting the thesis of this Manuscript

African American members of Congress established the CBC as a race-conscious and progressive body with the intent of responding to the needs of the African American community. The CBC was intended/expected to work on behalf of the interests of African Americans. However, as legislators, the CBC must operate within the norms of legislative and party politics, which may conflict with the stated mission of the CBC. This manuscript argues that politically salient issues such as crime and punishment challenge the unity of the CBC. Constituency differences, party politics, and the legislative process result in individual CBC members making compromises, becoming, as a whole, more pragmatic in its goals. The CBC has taken a subordinate role; it has not exhibited the ongoing pressure of its colleagues over mandatory minimum penalties, and is more symbolic in its advocacy of African American issues than substantive. We have presented views of many analysts expressing concern that the CBC would simply be a symbolic group if its members fell into the trappings of power and maintained close ties to one particular party. While acknowledging this, we want to emphasize that many members of the CBC were faced with high crime rates in their respective districts and needed to support legislation that addressed drug violence.

Legislative politics creates a situation where the norm of behavior is compromising one's interest, log-rolling, in order to advance to a key committee seat and reelection. These individualistic norms make it difficult for CBC members to vote as a group, as oppose to as individual members. Further, the CBC member who has seniority is in a key leadership position within the Democratic party. Similarly, a CBC member who has difficulty getting reelected may decide to be supportive of legislation sponsored by his or her party even if it compromises the interest of African Americans. CBC members did not often vote in unison with its leadership and often voted with the leadership of the Democratic party. There were also differences in members' vote choice based on seniority, the percentage of African Americans in their districts, and region. Mandatory minimum laws for crack cocaine have disproportionately impacted the African American community, as every member who was personally interviewed for this study recognized. In spite of this recognition, there has been a reluctance to make this issue a top agenda item.

We argue that the CBC has placed the interests of the Democratic party and individual member needs (that stem from constituency differences, leadership position, etc) above the interests and needs of its national constituency, particularly when mandatory minimums were first passed. African Americans in Congress, as can be demonstrated by the studies presented in this book, are believed to be and are expected to "represent more than their District Constituencies, in a real sense, they represent what Mathew Holden would call the Black Nation."[2] Thus, the CBC is expected to work on behalf of African Americans as a whole, regardless of the political environment and commitment to a party. The political environment in Congress during the 1980s and 1990s when these laws were considered created challenges for the CBC's effort to speak as a collective group. Again, this statement is not an indictment of the CBC, rather acknowledgment that the complexities of issues surrounding African Americans historically make any progressive action of the CBC complex to strategically accomplish. We assert that more effort should be expended to make sure all CBC members and staffers of CBC members are perpetually aware of the nuances of important details associated with these issues. We believe that if such perpetual effort were to be implemented, "institutional memory" on important issues such as drug mandatory minimums would remain a continual focus among all members, those with years of experience and those brand new to understanding Capitol Hill, let alone the CBC.

Mandatory Minimum Penalties for Crack Cocaine

Mandatory minimum penalties for crack cocaine passed at a time when both Democrats and Republicans used the "War on Drugs" to appeal to conservative, White voters. Its initial speedy passage in 1986, coupled with intense media coverage of young African American men engaged in gang activity, contributed to a political environment that focused on law-and-order rhetoric as opposed to crime prevention and rehabilitation. Democrats introduced this legislation and vowed not to let Republicans "out-crime" them. Both Democrats and Republicans felt it was politically expedient to support the Anti-Drug Abuse Act of 1986 and the provision that contained harsh mandatory minimum penalties for crack cocaine that was contained in the legislation. As legislators and as members of the Democratic Party, the CBC had to choose between loyalty to its party and loyalty to the goal of passing and supporting progressive legislation. The CBC's unity was challenged from the beginning of the congressional debate over mandatory minimums for crack cocaine penalties. These penalties have led to widespread incarceration of the group the CBC has as its mission to protect. Yet, over 25 years after passage of the law, the disparity remains in place, although reduced, and it continues to lead to the increased incarceration of both African American men and women for nonviolent crimes.

Chapter 1 of this manuscript began with a quote from 1994 by Supreme Court Justice Anthony Kennedy criticizing mandatory minimum penalties. This chapter begins begins with a quote by the same Supreme Court Justice made in 2003 again expressing criticism of mandatory minimum sentences. Therefore, the continuity of opinion over a decade by a Supreme Court Justice tells us that at the highest level of our court system, there is opposition to these laws passed by Congress. In the statements, Justice Kennedy mentions that the laws are unwise and result in severe punishments and long sentences; nevertheless, the incarceration trend continues.

We have shared the incarceration statistics. They are both disturbing in their impact on the African American community and in the racial bias that exists between the sentencing of African Americans and people of color and Whites, regardless of intent. Do the higher incarceration rates and longer sentences for African Americans reflect a tendency among this population to commit more crimes or is it a result of racial bias in the criminal justice system? The overwhelming evidence is that the latter is the case, and in spite of evidence of such bias, Congress continues to keep mandatory minimum penalties in place. When one considers that drug offenders constitute more than half of the federal prison population and the number of those incarcerated for a drug offense accounts for the largest percentage of the total prison growth in 2003 (48 percent),[3] one can justifiably look at mandatory minimum sentencing laws as a culprit. The laws have a racial bias and have greatly contributed to the incarceration of African Americans since the mid-1980s.

CBC Attitudes Toward Mandatory Minimum Penalties for Crack Cocaine

This manuscript has presented personal interview data of CBC members on their views on CBC unity and on the Democratic use of mandatory minimum penalties for crack legislation in order to win votes. Fifteen of the 38 members of the CBC serving during the 107th Congress were interviewed for this research. The members interviewed consisted of 10 men and five women and represented regional diversity and different levels of seniority. The interviewees were asked a variety of questions to determine their views on the legislative process, crime, the political behavior of Democrats, racial attitudes for mandatory minimums for crack cocaine, and the stated impact the legislation has had on their congressional districts. Each of the members interviewed opposed mandatory minimums in general and mandatory minimums for crack specifically. Further, all believed that the legislation is discriminating against African Americans. However, even with these seemingly united views, the interviewees did show a contrast between those CBC members who have a historic sense of race, the criminal justice system and race in America versus those who believe that users of drugs bring about punitive legislation. In other words, there was a contrast between those who saw racism as playing an underlying role in the increased prison population during the War on Drugs, and those who believed that it was the fault of people who choose to use and abuse drugs.

With regard to attitudes toward the legislative process, there was some disagreement among those with a majority of African Americans in their congressional districts and those with a plurality of African Americans in their districts. However, there was consistency among the CBC members interviewed that the CBC is not a monolithic group. Members of the CBC, in contrast to the mission of the CBC, find it necessary to consider the needs of their own constituents. There are CBC members who oppose the passage of comprehensive bills that negatively impact African Americans, but also support the idea that each CBC member must make decisions on how to vote based on the politics of his or her congressional districts. There are also those CBC members who believe the CBC should oppose the bills regardless of constituency considerations because the African Americans as a whole are disproportionately impacted by them and African Americans do not receive fairness in the criminal justice system. The latter believes that fairness and commitment to the support of progressive legislation should be more important when considering how to vote than the need to maintain unity with the Democratic party and reelection concerns.

CBC Attitudes about Unity with the Democratic Party

The interviews indicate that the CBC does not understand why the Democratic party supported mandatory minimum penalties for crack cocaine in general, and the disparity between the sentencing of crack and powder in particular. Many respondents believed that racism, whether overt or covert, contributed to the passage of the legislation. The majority of the respondents stated that the Democratic party did not consult with the CBC, and some commented that Democrats believed that opposing the legislation would result in a loss of support among their constituents. Thus, the party that the CBC supports engaged in pragmatic politics rather than politics that would help the constituents that the CBC supports. On the issue of the Democratic party's not consulting with the CBC on legislation that would lessen the impact of mandatory minimums on the African American community, one member stated that "even though this was good public policy, members wouldn't vote on the recommendations as they stood because a 30 second commercial would distort their intentions." Along the same lines, a member from the Deep South said that there were many meetings, but the CBC was voted down. He said that Democrats were afraid of the liberal label. Chapter 2 of this study provides greater detail about the CBC attitudes toward their fellow members, the legislative process, mandatory minimum penalties for crack cocaine, and the Democratic party.

Members of the CBC all volunteer to join the organization, thus they themselves, to some extent, lean towards race consciousness and unity. However, there is recognition that the CBC is not a monolithic group. CBC members come from diverse districts, are from different generations, and have diverse ideas about whether one should be pragmatic or maintain progressive ideas. This makes achieving CBC unity difficult.

Further, there is a recognition that the Democratic party should not have used the issue of mandatory minimums for crack cocaine for political reasons, but there is not consistent support among the members interviewed that the Democratic party should overturn the law or at the very least eliminate the disparities between powder and crack cocaine a top priority. Thus, viewing the CBC's position as a caucus, as individual members of Congress, and as members of the Democratic party demonstrates ongoing conflicts within the body.

The CBC and Continued Challenges to its Unity

Chapter 3 of this manuscript focused on the mission and purpose of the CBC. It attempts to examine why the CBC considers itself the voice of African Americans nationwide and how its membership diversity challenges its mission to serve as a collective voice for African Americans. The CBC's relationship with its Democratic colleagues in Congress and with presidents of the United States affected its unity on issues impacting the African American community as measured by roll call votes and personal interviews. The research focuses on one such issue. From its inception, the CBC has struggled with an "identity crisis."[4] The question posed by Champagne and Rieselbach remains valid, "Should CBC members act as a collective body, play a nonpartisan role, representing both inside and outside Congress the interest of the national black population, or should they engage in the fragmented world of pluralistic congressional politics, in which compromise and accommodation of black interests are necessary forms of conduct?"[5] As has been mentioned, with just three exceptions, all members of the CBC who served in the House of Representatives belonged to the Democratic party. As also has been mentioned, the CBC has as its strategy for its members to achieve individuals goals (i.e., committee seats and reelection) in the hopes that these goals would strengthen the CBC. When the Democratic party, where the group is closely aligned, participates in the same types of politics as Republicans rely on in order to get votes, CBC members compromise the values and mission of the group. Can the CBC support the Democratic party while also supporting progressive legislation and its national constituency? This study argues that they cannot, and mandatory minimums, in particular, and crime legislation, in general, have been served to demonstrate the difficulty to be partisan and to be unified as a group.

When mandatory minimum penalties for crack cocaine were first considered, Democrats were attempting to prove that they were tougher on crime than Republicans, as Chapter 4 discussed. Indeed, President Clinton pushed for a crime bill that appealed to moderates. President Clinton's strategy was to move Congress and his presidency toward the center, as opposed to supporting and advocating for progressive legislation that the agenda of the CBC calls for. The Democratic party needs the CBC, and the CBC members feel that they need the Democratic party. Democrats in Congress and in the presidency use CBC members to encourage African Americans to vote in congressional and presidential elections. Democrats also rely on the CBC to support its agenda operating under the belief that much of the agenda is favorable to African Americans. However, as the issue of mandatory minimums indicates, when it comes to African American members of Congress needing the support of Democrats to put on the agenda mandatory minimums, the CBC proved to be ineffective regardless of the party in control of Congress.

The roll-call vote taken on this issue on the floor of the House of Representatives in 1995 was overwhelmingly supported by the CBC, the Civil Rights community, judges, nontraditional civil rights groups, and others, yet Democrats overwhelmingly voted against the USSC's recommendations to eliminate the disparity between crack and powder cocaine and to raise the threshold for which those convicted of crack use and abuse could receive a five-year penalty.[6] The legislation would have also eliminated a mandatory minimum sentence for the mere possession of crack cocaine (a penalty that does not exist for the possession of powder cocaine or any other drug). The last roll call vote was one of the few times the CBC united on the House floor around this issue, yet they could not convince their Democratic colleagues to vote with them nor a Democratic president to veto the legislation. The conservative political environment that Democrats helped to create made it difficult to support this legislation that would have the effect of greatly reducing the number of African Americans serving time in prison for nonviolent drug offenses. We wrote about S. 1789, the Fair Sentencing Act that passed both Houses of Congress in 2010. Unfortunately, S. 1789, which reduced the 100-1 disparity in the treatment of crack v. powder cocaine, did not receive a roll call vote, thus we are unable to see completely which CBC members and which Democrats would have voted for it. If there is a roll call vote on making the S. 1789 (now Public Law 111-220) retroactive, then we will be able to access CBC support and party support of the legislation to bring about more fairness to the criminal justice system.

Concluding Analysis

Twenty-five years is too long for legislation that so many agree is unfair and has a disproportionate impact on the African American community to be in place. Two decades ago, a Supreme Court Justice expressed concern about these laws. It was several years after passage of the 1986 law before Congress held additional hearings on this issue. During the early 1990s, civil rights groups first pleaded with members of Congress to overturn the laws. In 1995, Congress and the president, for the first time, rejected a recommendation by the USSC that would have eliminated the 100-1 disparity and would have likely stopped the flow of first-time nonviolent offenders from entering the prison system. Yet, in the latter part of 2003, the same Supreme Court Justice who criticized the laws nearly 15 years prior expressed the same criticism.

Given the widespread incarceration of African Americans for long periods of time and for nonviolent drug offenses, this is an issue that should be of great concern to African Americans in Congress. Not since slavery has there been such control over a large segment of the African American population. African American representatives in Congress continue to ask their national constituency to support the Democratic party, but, as this research has shown, the party has used the politics of race and crime to support regressive legislation in an effort to win votes. The time is now for the CBC members to end the mass incarceration madness, the time is now for African Americans in Congress to demonstrate true leadership.

We have observed recent efforts to address drug sentencing laws and mass incarceration. Congress may pass the Smarter Sentencing Act of 2013 that we discussed in Chapter 8, and the Obama Administration acted favorable toward addressing mandatory minimum penalties for crack and powder cocaine. Attorney General Eric Holder issued a memorandum to his prosecutors that seeks to provide an "individualized assessment and fairly represent the defendant's criminal conduct."[7] Included in his memorandum:

"It is with full consideration of these factors that we now refine our charging policy regarding mandatory minimums for certain nonviolent, low-level drug offenders. We must ensure that our most severe mandatory minimum penalties are reserved for serious, high-level, or violent drug traffickers. In some cases, mandatory minimum and recidivist enhancement statutes have resulted in unduly harsh sentences and perceived or actual disparities that do not reflect our Principles of Federal Prosecution. Long sentences for low-level, non-violent drug offenses do not promote public safety, deterrence, and rehabilitation. Moreover, rising prison costs have resulted in reduced spending on criminal justice initiatives, including spending on law enforcement agents, prosecutors, and prevention and intervention programs. These reductions in public safety spending require us to make our public safety expenditures smarter and more productive."[8]

Had Holder's directive been in place during the 1990s, the individuals we highlighted in Chapter 10 may have been given a sentence more in line with their involvement in the crimes for which they were accused. President Obama has made efforts to add staff to the Department of Justice's Office of the Pardon Attorney, an office criticized for the way it has handled clemency requests, to help process clemency applications.[9] However, in May 2014, Congress voted in support of a measure introduced by George Holding (R-NC) to block these efforts. According a report by MSNBC, "Holding said he pushed the funding ban because he believes Obama is intent on using his presidential pardon power "solely on behalf of drug offenders."[10]

There has also been a backlash to Holder's directive by prosecutors who want to continue working under the current sentencing laws, arguing that the laws keep the public safe and thus should not be weakened.[11]

There are many voices in Congress, the public, and the Administration with regard to the criminal justice system in general and to these mandatory minimum sentences for crack and powder cocaine in specific. In keeping with the theme of the book, members of the Congressional Black Caucus, as legislators, as members of the Democratic party, and as representatives of their individual constituents, have to navigate the many voices while attempting to pursue the mission of the Caucus. The cases we highlighted provide some insight into why some reforms have been proposed and enacted by Congress, President Obama, the United States Sentencing Commission, and US Attorney General Holder. It is up to the public to continue to engage with their members of Congress so that their input can also be added to the discussion. By going to www.house.gov or www.senate.gov, the public can discover who represents them in Congress. The public can also review legislation that has been proposed and passed by going to the aforementioned web sites. We can avoid travesties of justice when we seek a sound, comprehensive approach to crafting public policy.

What Should be Done?: A Toolkit of Recommendations for the CBC

In order for a relatively small caucus in Congress to influence the larger body, strategies were developed to leverage the power of the CBC. The CBC has largely abandoned its earlier strategies to impact legislation before Congress. A founding member of the CBC, Congressman William Clay, stated that Congressman Mitchell's and Congressman Fauntroy's plans were:

> . . . The most significant strategies . . . and were at the core of whatever caused white members of Congress to redefine their relationship with us. These two mechanisms directly enhanced our influence within the deliberative body.[12]

The CBC should return to those strategies if it wants to return to the original mission of its founding. Based on this, in our final analysis, we recommend the following four-pronged approach in order to provide the appropriate understanding of complex issues associated with the CBC and as a result, increased institutional memory on such issues as drug policy. As mentioned earlier, we assert that by providing greater understanding to all relevant stakeholders, the mission of the CBC might better help not only African Americans, but all Americans as well. Figure 12.1 depicts one way the CBC might choose to implement such a toolkit, and an explanation about the components follows.

First, we recommend that the CBC send out weekly press releases highlighting the disparity in the treatment of the laws and include testimony from those incarcerated. This keeps the attention of the public and their colleagues on this issue. The CBC should stop nothing short of eliminating the disparity in the treatment of crack and powder cocaine and to push for making S. 1789 and other such legislation retroactive.

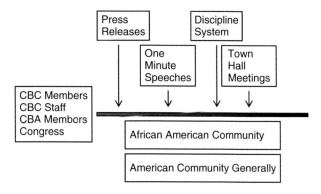

Figure 12.1. Toolkit for the CBC

Those incarcerated, particularly first-time, nonviolent offenders, should not have to remain in prison for what many have acknowledged was an unjust law. Imagine sitting in prison for five, 10, or 15 years for 50 grams of crack, knowing that if you'd have had 300 grams of powder, for example, you would have been out of prison within a couple of years. It should be applauded that mandatory minimums for simple possession of 5 grams of crack were eliminated because no other drug carries this penalty.

Second, during each legislative day, members of Congress are able to speak for one minute about any subject that is of concern to them. We recommend that the CBC attempt to be on the floor of the House of Representatives every day in order to talk about this issue. C-SPAN provides gavel-to-gavel coverage of Congress. This daily attention to the issue by the CBC would help keep the grassroots motivated as well as keeping the attention of their colleagues. When former Congressman Kendrick Meek (D-FL, son of former CBC member Carrie Meek) led the Thirty-Something Working Group, he held a one-hour special order frequently on issues facing the Democratic party and the country. The CBC should do this when issues arise that disproportionately impact the African American community.

Third, we recommend that CBC members hold continuous town hall meetings featuring family members, including children, who are the unintended victims of these laws, scholars, and activists. The meetings could be patterned after a "teach-in."

Finally, because the issue of mass incarceration as a result of draconian drug laws is so serious, the CBC should consider a discipline system for those in the CBC who do not participate in the activities mentioned above. If the CBC is divided on this issue, members will not have clout to persuade their colleagues to address this issue. The CBC should take this issue very seriously as it impacts on so many other issues.

Figure 12-1 depicts how this toolkit could provide direct impact on both the African American community and the American community generally with respect to this drug policy issue and other CBC issues.[13] Going back to our central question for this manuscript, "What should be the role of Black elected functionaries?", our research of the CBC mission and understanding of the historical and current realities of African Americans tells us that Black elected functionaries should consider all people and all angles associated with an issue. More so, we assert that Black elected functionaries should respect all angles as they consider how to strategically use their authority and influence on others toward addressing issues. Most importantly, we assert that Black elected functionaries should "stay the course" toward working as hard as possible toward progression on issues impacting African Americans, while making sure that they are simultaneously working to consider the impact on all Americans. This final statement of Black elected functionary purpose and actions is essential in that it goes back to what we cover in this manuscript as "double-consciousness," meaning that Black elected functionaries (e.g., the CBC) straddle the fence of addressing African American issues in a setting in which they also represent "all-American" issues, which sometimes means that some Americans simply do not understand how African American issues should be a priority. Understanding this difficulty, we ask that the CBC use the toolkit we have suggested to help them gain more understanding and spark more discussion on African American issues in order to reduce the risk of these issues, impacting real people, being marginalized.

Keyterms

Endnotes

1 Rankin, Bill, "Judge Shorten Federal Sentences: Supreme Court Justice Wants Guidelines Revised, Atlanta Journal Constitution, 10 August 2003, sec. A p. 3.

2 Barker, Tate, and Jones, 278

3 Paige Harrison and Allen Beck, "Prisoners in 2002," Bureau of Justice Statistics Bulletin (Washington, DC July 2003. NCJ 200248) p. 1.

4 Champagne and Riselbach, p. 130.

5 Ibid.

6 Note, Congress did not have to vote on the USSC's guidelines of 2007, which allowed some relief for those sentenced for crack offenses (see Chapter 7) because the guidelines go into effect as long as Congress doesn't vote against them. Given that 20 years has passed and that the CBC, Democrats, and even presidential hopefuls in both parties recognized the fallacy of the mandatory minimums for crack cocaine laws, one would have thought that the newly inaugurated Democratic Congress would make a point to support the Sentencing Commission guidelines as the made a point to oppose them in 1995. But, save for speeches, no one called for a vote.

7 "Memorandum to the United States Attorneys and Assistant Attorney General for the Criminal Justice Division," Attorney General Eric Holder, U.S. Department of Justice, August 12, 2013, http://www.justice.gov/oip/docs/ag-memo-department-policypon-charging-mandatory-minimum-sentences-recidivist-enhancements-in-certain-drug-cases.pdf (accessed June 26, 2014).

8 Ibid.

9 "Announcing New Clemency Initiative, Deputy Attorney General James M. Cole Details Broad New Criteria for Applicants," Press Release, April 23, 2014, http://www.justice.gov/opa/pr/2014/April/14-dag-419.html (accessed on April 24, 2014).

10 Melber, Ari, "House Republicans Vote to Black Obama's New Pardon Attorneys," MSNBC, May 30, 2014, http://www.msnbc.com/msnbc/house-gopers-vote-down-new-pardon-attorneys (accessed June 26, 2014).

11 Horwitz, Sari, "Some Prosecutors Fighting Effort to Eliminate Mandatory Minimum Prison Sentencing, " Washington Post, March 13, 2014, http://www.washingtonpost

.com/world/national-security/some-prosecutors-fighting-effort-to-eliminate-mandatory-minimum-prison-sentences/2014/03/13/f5426fc2-a60f-11e3-a5fa-55f0c77bf39c_story.html (accessed June 26, 2014). See also "Holder Urges prosecutors to Back Criminal Justice Changes," Carie Johnson, NPR, May 28, 2014, http://www.npr.org/blogs/thetwo-way/2014/05/28/316846121/holder-urges-prosecutors-to-back-criminal-justice-changes? (accessed June 26, 2014).

12 Clay, p. 269.

13 The text box denoting the relationship between CBC members, CBC staff, CBA members, and Congress, is intended to show that Congress as a whole is the major player in buy-in for the impact of this toolkit and that the other three players (just mentioned) should use their influence toward such buy-in. The CBA is the Congressional Black Associates, which is a membership organization of African Americans who work on Capitol Hill. The CBA is an important player in that the membership includes work for both CBC and non-CBC Members of Congress.

ACTIVITY 1
Summing It Up...

Instructions:

This chapter focuses on the overall points of all the previous chapters. In the space above, explain what the connection between the chapters is (only connect the most obvious things in your response).

A Chapter 12 Exercise

[Please tear out your completed response so you can turn it in to the instructor]

ACTIVITY 2

Instructions: In the box below, describe the realities associated with this "legacy" of having a sentencing disparity between crack cocaine and power cocaine for so many years.

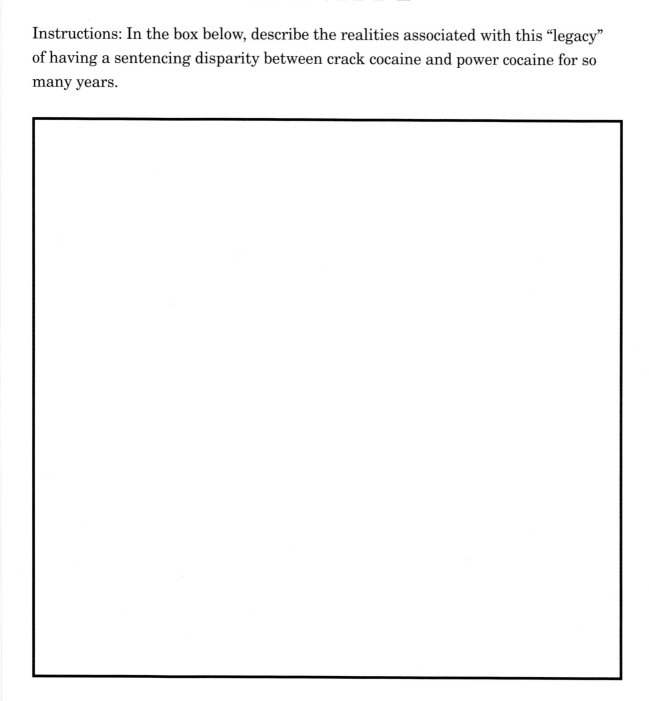

A Chapter 12 Exercise

ACTIVITY 3

Applying a book concept to a real-life issue...

Toolkit of Recommendations for the CBC

Instructions:

Within the Toolkit of Recommendations for the CBC box, please explain how you believe this toolkit could help address issues such the sentencing disparity covered in this book . . .

A Chapter 12 Exercise

List of Acronyms Used

- ACLU—American Civil Liberties Union
- ADA—Americans for Democratic Action
- AIDS—Acquired Immunodeficiency Syndrome
- BOP—Bureau of Prisons
- CBA—Congressional Black Associates
- CBC—Congressional Black Caucus
- D—Democrat
- DEA—Drug Enforcement Administration
- EPA—Environmental Protection Agency
- FAMM—Families Against Mandatory Minimums
- FBI—Federal Bureau of Investigation
- GAO—United States Government Accountability Office
- GOP—Grand Old Party (Republican Party)
- HIV—Human Immunodeficiency Virus
- HR, H.R.—United States House of Representatives
- HSCN, HSCNAC—House Select Committee on Narcotics Abuse and Control
- I—Independent
- LSD—Lysergic acid diethylamide
- NAACP—National Association for the Advancement of Colored People
- NBA—National Basketball Association
- NIST—National Institute of Standards and Technology
- NOBLE—National Organization for Black Law Enforcement Officers
- PCP—Phencyclidine
- PRWORA—Personal Responsibility and Work Opportunity Reconciliation Act of 1996
- R—Republican
- USSC—United States Sentencing Commission

Bibliography

"1986 Major City Survey on Drug Arrests and Seizures: Report of the Select Committee of Narcotics Abuse and Control," One Hundredth Congress, First Session, Washington, DC: United States Government Printing Office, 1987, p. 1.SS

"2008 Leading Presidential Candidate's Platform on Criminal Justice." The *Sentencing Project.* March (2008).

"Attorney General Eric Holder at the Clarence M. Mitchell, Jr. Memorial Lecture Luncheon at the NAACP's Centennial Convention," New York, New York, Monday, July 13, 2000, www.justice.gov/ag/speeches/2009/ag-speech-090713.html, accessed on May 2, 2011.

Angeli, David H. A. "Second Look at Crack Cocaine Sentencing Policies: One More Try for Federal Equal Protection." *American Criminal Law Review 34* (1997).

Barker, Luscious, et al. *African Americans and the American Political System,* 4th edition, Upper Saddle River, NJ: Prentice Hall, 1999,p p. 278–289.

Barnett, Marguerite Ross, and Hefner, James. *Public Policy for the Black Community: Strategies and Perspectives*. Port Washington, NY: Alfred Publishing Company, 1976, p. 9.

Baum, Dan. Book. *Smoke and Mirrors: The War on Drugs and the Politics of Failure,* Chapter 15, entitled "Sarejevo on the Potomac, 1986," Boston, Little, Brown and Company, 1996.

Beck, Katel, et al. "Kicking the Prison Habit: Drug Criminals Fill the Cells: Is there a Better Way?" *Newsweek* (June 14, 1993): 32–33.

Bennett, Jr., Lerone, *Black Power USA: The Human Side of Reconstruction 1867-1877, Johnson Publishing Company, Inc., Ed.1.* 1967, p. 395.

Berke, Richard. "Poll Finds Most in the U.S. Back Bush Strategy on Drugs." *The New York Times* (Tuesday, September 12, 1989).

Berry, Jefferey. *The Interest Group Society*, White Plains, NY, Longman Publishing Group (now combined with Allyn and Bacon), 1997.

Berry, Mary Frances, and John W. Blassingame. *Long Memory: The Black Experience in America* Oxford University Press, 1982, p. x-xi.

Black, Earl and Merle. *The Rise of Southern Republicans,* Cambridge, MA, Belknap Press of Harvard University Press, 2003.

Bositis, David. *The Congressional Black Caucus in the 103ʳᵈ Congress*. Washington, DC: The Joint Center for Political and Economic Studies, 1994, pp. 20–21.

Brown, Peter. *Minority Party: Why Democrats Face Defeat in 1992 and Beyond*. Washington, DC: Regnery Gateway, 1991, p. 103.

Brownstein, Ronald. "Clinton's 'New Democrat' Agenda Reopens Racial Divisions; President's Ideas on Crime and Welfare Don't Sit Well with Blacks in Congress. Liberals' Dissatisfaction May be Rising." Los Angeles Times (Wednesday, February 9, 1994): A5, Column 1.

Canon, David. *Race, Redistricting, and Representation: The Unintended Consequence of Black Majority Districts*. Chicago and London: University of Chicago Press, 1999, pp. 144–145.

Case, Patricia F. "The Relationship of Race and Criminal Behavior: Challenging Cultural Explanations for a Structural Problem." *Critical Sociology, 34*(2) (2008): 213–238.

Champagne, Richard, and Rieselbach, Leroy. "The Evolving Congressional Black Caucus: The Reagan-Bush Years." In Perry, Huey & Parent, Wayne, eds.) *Blacks and the American Political System*, Gainesville, FL, University Press of Florida, 1995, p. 130.

Clay, William. *Just Permanent Interests: Black Americans in Congress, 1870–1991*. New York, NY, Amistad Publishing, 1993.

"Cocaine and Federal Sentencing Policy." Hearing before the Committee on Crime of the Subcommittee of the Judiciary, House of Representatives, One Hundred Fourth Congress, First Session, June 29, 1995, p. 144, 165.

"Commission Votes Unanimously to Apply Amendment Retroactively for Crack Offenses: Effective Date Set for March 3, 2008." Press Release, December 1, 2007, Retrieved May 6, 2008 from www.ussc.gov/press

Confirmation Hearing of Eric H. Holder, Jr. Nominee to be Attorney General of the United States, Thursday, January 15, 2009 (Washington, DC: United States Senate Judiciary Committee) accessed May 3, 2011 http://frwebgate.access.gpo.gov/cgi-bin/getdoc.cgi?dbname=111_senate_hearings&docid=f:56197.pdf.

Congress and the Nation, a division of *Congressional Quarterly,* Washington, DC, (1984, 1985): 698-699.

"Congressional Black Caucus Blasts President's Crack/Powder Cocaine Sentencing Recommendations: CBC Denies 'Consultation' with White House." Press Release, Office of Congresswoman Maxine Waters, July 22, 1998, p. 1.

The Congressional Record, October 2, 1984, p. 28592.

Crack Cocaine Issue for Public Comment (Washington, DC: Families Against Mandatory Minimums), assessed on May 2, 2011, www.famm.org/FederalSentencing/USSentencingGuidelines/USSentencingGuidelinesUpdates/FederalSentencing-Guidelines2011/Crackcocaineissueforcommentonretroactivity.aspx

"Cracks in the System: Twenty Years of the Unjust Federal Crack Cocaine Law." The American Civil Liberties Union, October, 2006.

"CQ House Votes." *Congressional Quarterly* (October 25, 1986): 274–275.

Dawson, Michael C. *Black Visions: The Roots of Contemporary African American Political Ideologies*. Chicago: The University of Chicago Press, 2001.

DeLano, Lynne. "Sexual Assault: Not Part of the Penalty." *Connections*, a bi-annual publication of The Washington Coalition of Sexual Assault Programs, Fall/Winter, 2005.

Derfner, Jeremy. "The New Black Caucus," *The American Prospect* (March 27–April 2000).

"Disapproval of Certain Sentencing Guideline Amendments (House of Representatives-October 18, 1995)" *Congressional Record*, Retrieved May 30, 2003, p. 21-23, 27 of 98.
http://www.gpo.gov/fdsys/pkg/CREC-1995-10-18/pdf/CREC-1995-10-18-pt1-PgH10255-2.pdf#page=1.

Dowdy, Zachery. "Crime and Punishment: How the U.S. Prison System Makes Minority Communities Pay." *The New Crises* (July/August 2002): 34.

Dorsey, Tina L.; and Middleton, Priscilla. *Drugs and Crime Facts - NCJ 165148*. U.S. Department of Justice Office of Justice Programs. Washington, D.C. (Undated), p. 2.

"Drugs and Cities: The Federal Response." House Select Committee on Narcotics Abuse and Control, June 30, 1992, p. 19.

"Drugs and Crime" Public Hearing before the Select Committee on Narcotics Abuse and Control, House of Representatives, One Hundred First Congress, First Session, May 12, 1989.

"Federal Cocaine Sentencing Laws, Reforming the 100-1 Crack Powder Disparity," United States Senate, Subcommittee on Crimes and Drugs, Committee on the Judiciary, Washington, DC (Tuesday, February 12, 2008).

"The Federal Drug Strategy: What Does it Mean for Black America?" House Select Committee on Narcotics Control and Abuse, September 15, 1989, p. 22.

"The Federalization of Criminal Law: Task Force on Federalization of Criminal Law," American Bar Association, Criminal Justice Section, Washington, DC, 1998, pg. 23.

"Federal Legislation Watch: Drug Bills Spark Sentencing Debate." *FAMMGRAM* (Fall 2000), p. 16.

"Federal Mandatory Minimum Sentencing." Hearing before the Subcommittee on Crime and Criminal Justice for the Committee on the Judiciary, House of Representatives, One Hundred and Third Congress, First session, (July 29, 1993): 36-37.

"Federal Prison Population: Present and Future Trends." Hearings before the Subcommittee on Intellectual Property and Judicial Administration of the Committee on the Judiciary in the House of Representatives, One Hundred and Third Congress, First Session, May 12 and July 29, 1993, pp. 28, 223, 242.

Fenno, Richard F. *Going Home: Black Representatives and Their Constituents*. Chicago: The University of Chicago Press, 2003.

Foner, Eric. *Reconstruction in America, 1860-1880,* New York, Harper & Row Publishers, 1988.

Frazier, E. Franklin. *Black Bourgeosie*. New York: Collier Books, 1962, pp. 77–78.

Frymer, Paul. *Uneasy Alliances: Race and Party Competition in America*. Princeton, NJ: Princeton University Press, 1999.

Gerber, Alan. "African Americans' Congressional Careers and the Democratic Delegation." *Journal of Politics*, (August 1996): 841.

Hacker, Andrew. *Two Nations: Black, White, Separate, Hostile, Unequal*. New York: Ballantine, 1992.

Harding, D. J. "Jean Valjean's dilemma: The management of ex-convict identity in the search for employment." *Deviant Behavior, 24*(6) (November-December, 2003): 571-595.

Harris, Darryl. "The Duality Complex: An Unresolved Paradox in American Politics." *Journal of Black Studies* (July 1997): 789.

Harris, Othello, and R. Robin Miller. *Impacts of Incarceration on the African American Family.* Piscataway, New Jersey, Transaction Publishers, 2002.

"Historic Hearing on Mandatory Sentencing: Drug Mandatory Minimums, Are They Working." *Families Against Mandatory Minimums' FAMMGRAM* (Fall 2000): 4–5.

Holmes, Steven A. "Black Lawmakers Criticize Clinton Over Cocaine Sentencing," *The New York Times (National Edition)* (Thursday, July 24, 1997): A15.

House Rpt. 106-878-Part 1- Methamphetamine and Club Drug Anti-Proliferation Act of 2000, from www.thomas.gov (click on committee reports) accessed on May 24, 2008.

House Select Committee on Narcotics, Friday, September 2, 1984, p. 1.

House Select Committee on Narcotics Abuse and Control, July 25, 1991.

House Select Committee of Narcotics Control and Abuse, September 15, 1989, p. 7.

Http://jointcenter.org/DB/table/NOP/NOP_97/politics/policy14.htm

Http://judiciary.senate.gov/member_statement.cfm?id=3089&wit_id=97

Http://www.house.gov/apps/list/hearing/ny15_rangel/cracksentencing121107.html

http://www.justice.gov/opa/pr/2010/July/10-ag-867.html

Http://www.supremecourtus.gov/opinions/07pdf/06-6330.pdf p. 1.

http://webb.senate.gov/issuesandlegislation/criminaljusticeandlawenforcement/ National-Criminal-Justice-Commission-Act-of-2009.cfm.

www.whitehouse.gov/blog/2010/08/03/president-obama-signs-fair-sentencing-act, accessed on April 27, 2011.

http://thomas.loc.gov/cgi-bin/query/D?r110:1:./temp/~r110DtqmVT:

Idelson, Holly. "Democrats' New Proposal Seeks Consensus by Compromise." *Congressional Quarterly* (August 14, 1993): 2228.

"Insights into the Inmate Population," *The Washington Post* (March 21, 2003): A1 .

"Intravenous Drug Use and AIDS: The Impact on the Black Community." House Select Committee on Narcotics Control and Abuse, September 25, 1987, p. 20.

Jackson, Jr., Jesse, with Watkins, Frank E. *A More Perfect Union: Advancing New American Rights,* New York: Welcome Rain Publishers, 2001, p. 206.

Johnston, David. "Bush's Drug Strategy is Criticized as Failing to Seek Views of Cities," *New York Times,* (September 6, 1989): A8.

Johnston, Sara-Michelle, et al. "Methamphetamine and Crack Policies: Different Treatment for Different Drugs?" [Working Paper], 2008.

Jones, Charles. "Testing a Legislative Strategy: The Congressional Black Caucus's Action-Alert Communications Network," *Legislative Studies Quarterly*, XII, 4 (November 1987): 523.

Jones, Charles. "United We Stand, Divided We Fall: Analysis of the CBC's Voting Behavior, 1975-1980." *Phylon*, 98 (1987): 27.

Jones, Stephanie J., ed, "Foreword: The State of Black America, 2007." New York: The Beckham Publications Group, 2007,. pp 9–10.

"The Justice Department's Role in the War on Drugs." House Select Committee on Narcotics Abuse and Control, July 25, 1991, p. 45.

"Justices: Judges Can Slash Crack Sentences." Retrieved May 6, 2008, from /www.cnn.com/2007/US/law/12/10/scotus.crack.cocaine/

Kingdon, John. *Congressman's Voting Decisions*, 3rd edition. Ann Arbor:: The University of Michigan Press, 1989.

Lewinson, Paul. *Race Class and Party: A History of Negro Suffrage and White Politics in the South.* New York: Oxford University, 1932.

Lublin, David. *The Paradox of Representation: Racial Gerrymandering and Minority Interests in Congress.* Princeton, NJ: Princeton University Press, 1997, p. 73.

Lusane, Clarence. *Pipe Dream Blues: Racism & The War on Drugs*, Boston, MA, South End Press, 1991, chapter 2.

McGlone, Tim. "Supreme Court Rules Judges Can Reduce Crack Cocaine Sentences." *The Virginian-Pilot* (December 10, 2007).

Mann, Coramae Richey, et al. Images of Color, Images of Crime. 3rd edition. Cary, NC, Roxbury Press, 2007, p. 243.

Manning Marable. *How Capitalism Underdeveloped Black America,* updated edition. Cambridge, MA: South End Press, 2000, pp. 170–171.

Mathis, Nancy. "Black Caucus, Clinton at Odds Over the Crime Bill." *Houston Chronicle: Washington Bureau* (July 15, 199): A1.

Mauer, Marc. *Race to Incarcerate*. The Sentencing Project. New York: New York Press, 1999, p. 60.

Mauer, Marc, and Meda Chesney-Lind. *Invisible Punishment: The Collateral Consequences of Mass Imprisonment*. New York: W.W. Norton and Company, 2002, p. 51.

"Meet the Attorney General," accessed on May 2, 2011, www.justice.gov/ag/meet-ag. html.

Montague, David R. "Theory to Practice as an Application of Temporal Crime Theory: The 2010 SWACJ Presidential Address." *The Southwest Journal of Criminal Justice,* 7(3) (2010).

Moore, Joan. "Bearing the Burden: How Incarceration Weakens Inner-City Communities." Part of *THE UNINTENDED CONSEQUENCES OF INCARCERATION: Papers from a conference organized by the Vera Institute of Justice.* January, 1996. Retrieved May 18, 2008 from the publications list of www.cejamericas.org, p. 67.

Moore, John W. "Targeting Harlem, Not Hollywood." *The National Journal, The Weekly on Politics and Government* (February 11, 199): 288.

Morris, Lorenzo. Book Chapter. "Race and the Two Party System" in *The Social and Political Implications of the 1984 Jesse Jackson Presidential Campaign*. Santa Barbara, CA, Praegar Pubishers, 1990.

Morris, Lorenzo. Panel Discussion. "Why Americans Don't Vote: Apathy or Alienation." Congressional Black Associates, October 2000.

Myrdal, Gunnar. *An American Dilemma: The Negro Problem in American Democracy.* Transaction Publishers, Piscataway, NJ, 1995.

Nadelmann, Ethan. "Obama Takes a Crack at Drug Reform", *The Nation*, September 3, 2010, accessed on April 27,2011, .www.alternet.org/drugs/148078/obama_takes_a_crack_at_drug_reform?page=1

National Urban League. "The State of Black America: Prescription for Change." Annual Report., Washington, DC: Author, 2005.

"On the Edge of the American Dream: A Social and Economic Profile in 1992." A Report by the Chairman, Select Committee on Narcotics Control and Abuse, One Hundred and Second Congress, Second Session, March 1992.

Obama, Barack. *The Audacity of Hope: Thoughts on Reclaiming the American Dream*, New York: Crown Publishers, 2006, p. 258.

"Obama's Platform on Eliminating Racial Inequality," prepared by Professor Vernellia Randall,http://academic.udayton.edu/race/2008ElectionandRacism/Obama/Obama00.htm#References and Minimal Differences Between Clinton, Obama: Review the NAACP's Questionnaire and a Legal Scholar's Study of Candidates' Campaign Stances, February 6, 2008, accessed on May 3, 2011, from www.blackagendareport.com/index.php?option=com_content&task=view&id=518&Itemid=1

Olsen, Mancus. *The Logic of Collective Action*, Cambridge, MA, Harvard University Press, 1971

Oreskes, Michael. "Party Chief Faults Democrats for Tax Talk in Drug Debate." *The New York Times.* (September 11, 1989): A1.

Orr, Marion. "Congress, Race, and Anti-Crime Policy." In Yvette M. Alex-Assenoh and Lawrence J. Hanks, eds., *Black and Multicultural Politics in America.* New York: New York University Press, 2000, p. 226.

Pefley, Mark, and Jon Hurwitz. *Justice in America: The Separate Realities of Blacks and Whites.* New York: Cambridge University Press, 2010.

Pinney, Neil, and George Serra. "The Congressional Black Caucus and Vote Cohesion: Placing the Caucus Within House Voting Patterns." *Political Science Quarterly, 52*(3) (September 1999): 583–608.

Pinney, Neil,, and George Serra. "A Voice for Black Interests: Congressional Black Caucus Cohesion and Bill Sponsorship." *Congress and the Presidency*, Washington, DC (Spring 2002): 75.

Political Participation in the United States: Report for the United States Commission on Civil Rights, 1968. Washington, DC: United States Government Printing Office, 1968.

"Poll: Blacks Want Stiffer Penalties for Criminals." *Jet Magazine* (June 4, 1984): 4.

"President and Mrs. Reagan on Drug Abuse and Prevention." *Congressional Quarterly* (September 20, 1986): 2227.

Quirk, Paul J., and Sarah Binder, eds. *The Legislative Branch, Institutional of American Democracy.* New York: Oxford University Press, 2005.

Race Class and Party: A History of Negro Suffrage and White Politics in the South. New York: Oxford University Press, 1932.

"Reagan, Senate Republicans Join Drug War." *Congressional Quarterly* (September 20, 1986): 2191.

"Rep. Maxine Waters Unveils Bill to Eliminate Mandatory Sentences for Low-Level Drug Offenders" Press Release, *Families Against Mandatory Minimums*, May 23, 2003.

Report to Congress: Cocaine and Federal Sentencing Policy. Washington, DC: United States Sentencing Commission, May 2002, p. 7, Appendix D-3.

"Restoring Fairness to Federal Sentencing: Addressing the Crack-Powder Disparity," Senate Judiciary Committee, Subcommittee on Crime and Drugs, Senate Hearing 111-559, Wednesday, April 29, 2009, accessed on May 2, 2011, http://frwebgate.access.gpo.gov/cgi-bin/getdoc.cgi?dbname=111_senate_hearings&docid=f:57626.pdf.

Rovner, Julie. "House Passes $6 billion Anti-Drug Package." *Congressional Quarterly* (September 13, 1986): 2125.

"S. 1711, The Drug Sentencing Reform and Cocaine Kingpin Trafficking Act of 2007" (Bill Text, 110th Congress (2007-2008), S. 1711 IS), accessed on April 27, 2011, from http://thomas.loc.gov/cgi-bin/query/D?c110:1:./temp/~c110X4msjY::.

Salisbury, Robert. "An Exchange Theory of Interest Groups," *Midwest Journal of Political Science,* XIII (Feb. 1969).

"Same Drug, Different Penalties." *The Washington Post* (August 4, 1993): A16.

Sampson, Robert J., and Janet L. Lauritsen. "Racial and Ethnic Disparities in Crime and Criminal Justice in the United States." *Crime and Justice, 21*. Ethnicity, Crime and Immigration: Comparative and Cross-National Perspectives (1997): 311–374.

Schattschneider, Elmer E. *The Semi-Sovereign People: A Realist View of Democracy in America*, Florence, KY, Wadsworth Publishing, 1975.

Schneider, Cathy Lisa. "Racism, Drug Policy, and AIDS." *Political Science Quarterly, 113*(3) (Autumn, 1998): 427–446.

Seghetti, Lisa, and Alison Smith. "Federal Sentencing Guidelines: Background, Legal Analysis, and Policy Options" CRS Report for Congress, April 4, 2005, p. 11.

"Sentencing Guidelines." Hearings before the Subcommittee of Criminal Justice of the Committee on the Judiciary, House of Representatives, One Hundredth Congress, first session on Sentencing Guidelines, May-July, 1987.

"Sentencing Revision Act of 1984." Hearings before the House Judiciary Committee, February 22, 1984, pp. 77–80.

Simmons, Evett L. "Women the Target: Children the Victims." *The Impact of the Criminal Justice System on Women & Their Families,* Journal Introduction, Delta Research & Education Foundation (2001): 24.

Singh, Robert. *The Congressional Black Caucus; Racial Politics in the United States Congress*. Thousand Oaks, California: Sage Publications, 1998.

Sirica, Jack. "House Axes Narcotics Committee." *NewsDay*, Long Island, New York. January 27, 1993, p. 28.

Smith, Robert. "Politics Is Not Enough: The Institutionalization of the African American freedom Movement." In Ralph Gomes and Linda Faye Williams, eds., *From Exclusion to Inclusion: The Long Struggle for African American Political Power*. Westport, CT: Praeger, p. 113.

Smith, Robert. *Racism in the Post Civil Rights Era: Now You See it, Now You Don't.* Albany: State University of New York Press, 1995.

Sniderman, Paul; Tetlock, Philip; and Carmines, Edward. *Prejudice, Politics, and the American Dilemma*. Stanford, CA, Stanford University Press, 1993, p. 25.

Special Report to the Congress: Cocaine and Federal Sentencing Policy (as directed by section two of Public Law 104-38), United States Sentencing Commission. Washington, DC: United States Government Printing Office, April 1997, pp. 1–2.

Special Report to Congress: Mandatory Minimum Penalties in the Federal Criminal Justice System. Washington, DC: United States Sentencing Commission, August 1991, p. ii.

St. Clair, Alexander, and Jeffrey St. Clair. *WHITEOUT*. London: Verson, 1998, p. 73.

Staff Reporter. "Retrieving the Jailer's Keys: Attorney General Reno Launches a Review of Mandatory Minimum Sentences." *Time Magazine*, 141(20), May 17, 1993, p. 21.

Stanberry, Artemesia, Pearl K. Ford, and Michelle Adams. "The Georgia Presidential Primaries: A Case Study of the Role of Race and Class in the Selection of a Presidential Nominee." In Pearl K. Ford, ed., *African Americans in Georgia: A Reflection of Politics and Policy in the New South.* Macon, GA: Mercer University Press, 2010, p. 56.

Stengel, Richard. "More Muscle for Crime Fighters: A New Federal Code Tilts Toward the Government." *Time* (October 29, 1984), p. 74.

Sterling, Eric. Personal interview, June 25, 2002.

Sterling, Eric. Personal interview, June 30, 2002.

Sterling, Eric, and Julie Stewart. "Undo This Legacy of Len Bias's Death." *The Washington Post* (June 24, 2006): A21.

Stone, Christopher E. *The State of Black America: 1996*. Washington, DC: The National Urban League, January 1996.

Swain, Carol. *Black Faces, Black Interests: The Representation of African Americans in Congress*. Cambridge, MA: Harvard University Press, 1993.

Taifa, Nkechi. Personal Interview, July 30, 2003 in the offices of the Open Society Institute in Washington, DC.

Tate, Katherine. *Black Faces in the Mirror: African Americans and Their Representatives in Congress*. Princeton, NJ: Princeton University Press, 2003, p. 67.

Thernstrom, Stephan, and Abigail Thernstroml. *America in Black and White: One Nation, Indivisible*. New York: Simon and Shuster, 1997, p. 259.

Tolchin, Martin. "Conferees Agree to Repeal Disputed Medicare Program," *The New York Times* (November 18, 1989).

"Too Little Too Late: President Clinton's Prison Legacy." *Justice Policy Institute,* a project of the Center on Juvenile and Criminal Justice, February, 2001.

Truman, David. *The Governing Process*, New York, Knopf Publishing, 1971.

Ture, Kwame, and Charles Hamilton. *Black Power: the Politics of Liberation*. New York: Vintage Books, 1992, 1967 (reissued in 1992 with a new afterword), p. 4.

"U.S. Prison Population Sets Record for a Year, in Six Months." *The New York Times* (Monday, September 11, 1989).

"United States Sentencing Commission Votes to Amend Guidelines for Terrorism, Sex Offenses, Intellectual Property Offenses, and Crack Cocaine Offenses" Press Release, April 27, 2007 Retrieved May 6, 2008 from www.ussc.gov/press.htm.

"Unity and Struggle: The Political Behavior of African American Members of Congress." *The Black Scholar, San Francisco, 24*(4) (Fall 1994): 16–28.

Unnamed inmate. Quote. *Community Reentry to Society Program at the Wrightsville Prison Unit.* Wrightsville, AR (March 2009).

Wallison, Ethan. "Black Caucus faces a Changing of the Guard: Group Becomes More Mainstream on Several Fronts, Which Brings Its Trade-Offs," *Roll Call* (Monday, September 9, 2002).

Walters, Ron. "Targeting Resources to Central Cities: A Strategy for Redeveloping the Black Community." *The Black Scholar: The Urban Crisis* (1993): 3.

Walters, Ronald. *White Nationalism Black Interests: Conservative Public Policy and the Black Community.* Detroit, MI: Wayne State University Press, 2003.

Walters, Ronald, and Robert C. Smith. *African American Leadership.* Albany: State University of New York, 1999.

Walton, Jr., Hanes. "Public Responses to the Million Man March." *The Black Scholar* (Fall 1995).

Weatherspoon, Floyd D. *African American Males and the Law: Cases and Materials.* Lanham, MD: University Press of America, 1998, p. 4.

Weisskopf, Michael. "Eric Holder: The Prosecutor," *Time Magazine*(February 5, 2009), accessed May 2, 2011, www.time.com/time/magazine/article/0,9171,1877386-2,00. html.

Williams, Art S. "The Psychosocial Plight of the African American Male." *Fulfilling Our Dreams by Bringing All Cultures Together: 2007 Monograph Series.* National Association of African American Studies & Affiliates, Scarborough, ME, 2007, p. 296.

Williams, Juan. "From Caucus to Coalition: Can the Black Freshman Class in Congress Shape the Clinton Program," *The Washington Post* (Sunday, January 10, 1993): C2.

King, Jr., Martin Luther. *Why We Can't Wait.* New York: Harper and Row Publishers, 1963.

"Women in Prison: Issues and Challenges Confronting the US Correctional Systems." GAO Report to the Honorable Eleanor Holmes Norton, Washington, DC, December 1999. Retrieved at www.gao.gov/archive/2000/gg00022.pdf.

Wren, Christopher. "Reno and Top Drug Official Urge Smaller Gap in Cocaine Sentences." *The New York Times*, (July 22, 1997), p. 1.

www.famm.org, accessed on April 27, 2011 and Artemesia Stanberry, "Mandatory Minimums for Crack Cocaine: A Change Has Got to Come, May 23, 2010, http://politicsroundtable.blogspot.com/2010/05/mandatory-minimums-for-crack-cocaine.html.

www.thomas.loc.gov (107th Congress).

Zucchino, David. *Myth of the Welfare Queen: A Pulitzer Prize-Winning Journalist's Portrait of Women on the Line.* New York: Touchstone Book/Simon & Schuster, 1999.

Appendix 1:
Judge's Criticism of the Media for Portraying Negative Images of African American Males.

This is a direct quote from Floyd Weatherspoon's book entitled *African-American Males and the Law: Cases and Material.* In U.S. v. Clary, 846 F. Supp. 768 (1994), the court cited how the media projected negative images of African American males, which led to the enactment of the crack statute:

Crack cocaine eased into the mainstream of the drug culture about 1984 and immediately absorbed the media's attention. Between 1985 and 1986, over 400 reports had been broadcast by the networks. Media accounts of crack-user horror stories appeared daily on every major channel and in every major newspaper. Many of the stories were racist. Despite the statistical data that whites were prevalent among crack users, rare was the interview with a young black person who had avoided drugs and the drug culture, and even rarer was any media association with whites and crack. Images of young black men daily saturated the screens of our televisions. These distorted images branded onto the public mind and the minds of legislators that young black men were solely responsible for the drug crisis in America. The media created a stereotype of a crack dealer as a young black male, unemployed, gang affiliated, gun toting, and a menace to society. These stereotypical descriptions of drug dealers may be accurate, but not all young black men are drug dealers. The broad brush of uninformed public opinion paints them all as the same. These stereotypical images undoubtedly served as the touchstone that influenced racial perceptions held by legislators and the public as related to the "crack epidemic." The fear of increased crime as a result of crack cocaine played into white society's fear of the black male as a crack user and as a source of social disruption. The prospect of black crack migrating to the white suburbs led to legislators to reflexively punish crack violators more harshly than their white, suburban, powder cocaine dealing counterparts. The ultimate outcome resulted in legislators drafting the crack statute with its Draconian punishment. The media reports associating blacks with the horrors of crack cocaine caused the Congress to react irrationally and arbitrarily. The evolution of the 100 to 1 crack to powder ratio mandatory minimum sentence was moved to action based upon an unconscious racial animus. The "frenzied"' state of Congress led members to depart from normal and substantive procedures that are routinely considered a part of the legislative process. What cannot be clearly gleaned from the transcripts of floor discussions among congressional members may well be inferred from the exhibits that were introduced in the record. Legions of newspaper and magazine articles regarding the crack cocaine epidemic depicted racial imagery of heavy involvement by blacks in crack cocaine. Practically every newspaper account featured a black male either using crack, selling crack, involved in police contact due to crack, or behind bars because of crack (See chapter 1).

Appendix 2:
Press Release issued by
Congresswoman Waters

FOR IMMEDIATE RELEASE July 22, 1998

CONGRESSIONAL BLACK CAUCUS BLASTS PRESIDENT'S CRACK/POWDER COCAINE SENTENCING RECOMMENDATIONS CBC DENIES "CONSULTATION" WITH WHITE HOUSE

Today, Congresswoman Maxine Waters (D-CA), Chair of the Congressional Black Caucus, sent a letter to President Bill Clinton on behalf of the CBC, expressing their disappointment at the new sentencing recommendations on crack and powder cocaine and their concern at White House claims that they consulted with the Congressional Black Caucus (CBC).

"We have fought very hard to make people understand the disproportionate impact of these disparities on African-American and Hispanic communities. These impacts have been cited by the U.S. Sentencing Commission, General McCaffrey and even the President. Yet, these new recommendations call for continuing disparities, rather than eliminating them as they should be.

"While the recommendations are an improvement," added Waters, "they are far from fair."

The current recommendations call for a five-year mandatory minimum threshold for crack at 25 grams and a corresponding threshold for powder set at 250 grams, a 10-1 ratio. This is a change from the current 100-1 ratio. Clinton has accepted the new recommendations and instructed the Justice Department to move forward with bringing them to Congress.

"If the White House had consulted us, as they claim, considered our views and then rejected them, that would be one thing," added Waters. "We wouldn't be happy with their conclusions, but we could live with that. But to claim consultation when there was none, is unacceptable."

(See chapter 5).

Appendix 3: Congressman Gray (D-PA) and Congressman Rangel's (D-NY) response to Ron Brown, Chairman of the Democratic Party.

"Each Democrat has a right to his own opinion," Representative William H. Gray 3rd of Pennsylvania, the House majority whip, said in an interview, "and I suppose the party Chairman will come to know that."

It was not the leadership. But other Democrats who called for new taxes to fight drugs.

. . . . . One Democrat who did speak out for new taxes last week was Representative Charles Rangel of Manhattan, who said today, "I apologize to any I have offended for looking at this problem in an honest way." He added, "Anyone who looks at the drug crises and says, 'no new revenues are needed,' is not being honest with the American people" (See chapter 5).

Appendix 4:
Opening Statement of Randolph Stone at the House Select Committee on Narcotics Abuse and Control Hearing on the Federal Drug Strategy.

Randolph N. Stone, a Public Defender in Cook County, IL, did mention in his opening statement that the jails were filling up in Chicago not because of increased drug use, but because of mandatory penalties. His opening statement is entitled: "The war on Drugs: The Wrong Enemy and the Wrong Battlefield." He states:

I am here to say that the ever-increasing arrests and building more courtrooms and jails will not resolve the problem. The United States already incarcerates more people per capita than any other democratic nation in the world. Since 1970, we have tripled the number of people locked up in our prison system in this country. In 19 years, we have tripled that number. We now have more than 600,000 people locked up in prisons in the United States. In the next year or two, with the next policies, we'll have more than a million people locked up. Approximately 50 percent of those will be black males. It is expected that in a year or two we will have more young black men in jails and prisons in this country than we have in colleges and professional schools. Our criminal system every day is looking more and more like South Africa's criminal justice system (See chapter 5).

Appendix 5:
Exchange between Congressman Kweise Mfume and Attorney General Dick Thornburgh during a House Select Committee on Narcotics Control and Abuse, July 25, 1991.

During this same hearing, Congressman Mfume asked a question that specifically dealt with mandatory minimum sentences. His question is as follows:

I've got two questions, the first of which deals with section 202 of the President's crime package. That deals specifically with proposing adult prosecution for juveniles who are charged with possession of 5 grams of crack. A couple of questions. Number one, I notice that marijuana and PCP and heroin were not on the list, and I think they are just as serious offenses, and want to know your opinion on that, and to ask you also, do you think it might be more beneficial in the short run and even perhaps in the long run, to attempt to channel those juvenile users into treatment and rehabilitation programs rather than sending them to prison as adults? And in Baltimore at least—I can't speak for the rest of the country—but our prison system has been under a court order to cease the overcrowding—three or four to a cell. We reduce that, and then we're back up again, and we reduce it, and we're back up again. It seems to me if we adopt section 602—no matter how well intentioned it might be, that perhaps we are exacerbating the problem of prison overcrowding in certain areas and some cities around the Nation, and does the Federal prison system have the resources to incarcerate and to then rehabilitate that many juvenile offenders?

Thornburgh's response was as follows:

I think your point is well taken with regard to juvenile users of drugs. The cutoff point of 5 grams of crack really is based on a perception that that is not a personal use quantity, that this is a person who is engaged in trafficking in the crack, and deserves the kind of sanction that is provided for, and all substances are covered for distribution under drug laws...I think when you talk about the crack offense, that for the first time in 1988, the Congress singled out crack as a particularly destructive substance that should be dealt with in a particularly harsh manner, a tough manner, so that when you mention the differentiation made between crack and marijuana and heroin and cocaine and other drugs, that's a judgment that's within the ability of the Congress to effect (See Chapter 5).

Appendix 6:
Schumer's Statement at a 1993 Congressional Hearing on Federal Mandatory Minimum Sentences

When judges and defense lawyers came into my office, I would ask them to give me examples of egregious sentences. My view then was that if the law was resulting in egregious sentences, we would have a hearing, we would expose these egregious cases, and the public and the Congress would see that the law had to be changed. We made a diligent effort....My staff—and I want to commend them—diligently reached out to defense lawyers, to judges, and to others, asking them to bring to us the most egregious cases. The cases that really pluck at people's heartstrings. What we found was that, when it came time for hard facts and examples, there weren't huge numbers of cases. We had to sort of pull teeth to get many of the cases that were truly egregious. Now there are some egregious cases, and we will hear about those today. I think we should do something about them. But the idea that there are thousands and thousands of people in the Federal prison system who had a small amount of marijuana in their pocket and were sitting in jail for 5 or 10 years is just not supportable (See Chapter 5).

Index